GREAT ANSWERS

TO

TOUGH
CAREER
DILEMMAS

WITHDRAWN

Funded by
MISSION COLLEGE
Carl D. Perkins Vocational and Technical Education Act Grant

GREAT
ANSWERS

TO

TOUGH
CAREER
DILEMMAS

**Test your aptitude, be inspired
and discover your ideal career**

MIKE BRYON

KoganPage

LONDON PHILADELPHIA NEW DELHI

First published in Great Britain and the United States in 2011 by Kogan Page Limited

120 Pentonville Road	1518 Walnut Street, Suite 1100	4737/23 Ansari Road
London N1 9JN	Philadelphia PA 19102	Daryaganj
United Kingdom	USA	New Delhi 110002
www.koganpage.com		India

© Mike Bryon, 2011

The right of Mike Bryon to be identified as the author of this work has been asserted by him in accordance with the Copyright, Designs and Patents Act 1988.

ISBN   978 0 7494 5413 5
E-ISBN 978 0 7494 5926 0

British Library Cataloguing-in-Publication Data

A CIP record for this book is available from the British Library.

Library of Congress Cataloging-in-Publication Data

Bryon, Mike.
  Great answers to tough career dilemmas : test your aptitude, be inspired and discover your ideal career / Mike Bryon.
     p. cm.
   ISBN 978-0-7494-5413-5 – ISBN 978-0-7494-5926-0   1. Career development.
2. Vocational interests–Testing.   3. Occupational aptitude tests.   I. Title.
   HF5381.B6785 2011
   650.14–dc22

                                                                                2011010658

Typeset by Graphicraft Limited, Hong Kong
Printed and bound in India by Replika Press Pvt Ltd

CONTENTS

USE THIS BOOK TO ANSWER THE QUESTION 'WHAT SHALL I DO?'

Countless people have found a career they love. You could too if you settle on what career you want. If you are one of the many who find it impossible to decide, if you ask yourself over and over 'what shall I do?' then this book is for you. Find the answer by completing the questionnaire in Chapter 3. Score it and find out your motivations, interests and personality traits. Browse hundreds of careers ideally suited to your personality and interests. In all you will find 1,000 career ideas, along with inspirational case studies and an account of the countless opportunities available in today's exciting new world of work. Finally make your dream a reality by following the clearly explained steps.

TO GAIN MOST FROM THIS BOOK

First, obtain from Chapter 1, insight into the major themes shaping the world of work and the countless new opportunities. Next, see from the case studies in Chapter 2 that many people who love their work did not find their dream career immediately and for some the path to their true vocation was long. Others found that things had changed, and indeed they themselves changed. Now, suspend any disbelief and complete the battery of questionnaires as truthfully as possible; that way you will obtain a more objective assessment of your motivations and interests and are more likely to identify your perfect career. Score your answers to the questionnaires, complete the matrix in Chapter 4 and read the descriptions of your personality traits. Look up the listings of jobs in Chapter 5 that are linked to the three traits in which you scored highest and study the careers linked to them. When you read the suggestions, don't immediately dismiss the unexpected and do risk a smile at some of the suggestions as they are intended to be thought provoking as well as fitting and current careers ideas. If you are hungry for still more ideas feel free to browse the remainder of the list of careers. Once you have found what you are looking for, all that will be left to do is to set out to make your new career a reality by following the guidance in Chapter 6.

When you have discovered the career of your dreams, check out *Great Answers to Tough CV Problems* and *Great Answers to Tough Interview Questions* (also published by Kogan Page) for CV and interview help and advice.

HOT TOPICS IN THE NEW WORLD OF WORK
and the career opportunities they create

These days it is rare to spend 40 years working for the same organization. It is also increasingly unusual for people to stay in the same discipline. It is likely that you will have three or even four careers in your working life. And, for a great many reasons, your first career is unlikely to be the one in which you find most happiness. What people once enjoyed doing may no longer please them. Workers today are more courageous, and because there are now far more opportunities people are less inclined to remain unhappy in work. Instead, they will choose to embrace change and embark on a programme of retraining and a new career.

The world of work has changed

You owe it to yourself to take a new look. Change brings challenges but it also brings opportunities. In the last 10 years the world of work has changed beyond recognition and mostly for the better. In fact, the world of work is in a constant state of change. Some traditional occupations have faded away. It was not long ago, for example, that people trained and worked as typists, telephonists, assemblers, machine minders and setters. These occupations and many others have all but vanished with the advent of computers or they have been exported. A great deal of manufacturing has moved from Europe and the United States to China, and the jobs with it. Many service industry jobs in the English-speaking world are moving to locations such as India. Some careers, such as bank managers, publicans, travel agents and milk-round operative, are in seemingly terminal decline. Other careers flourish today that only a few years ago did not exist: energy conservation workers, police community support officers, teaching assistants, recycling operatives, web page designers, technicians for home entertainment systems and carbon credit consultants, for example. Careers too change, some so dramatically that they hardly resemble what they once were. A nurse who specializes in care for people with mental health problems will now provide care in the community rather than on a hospital ward. A firefighter will work as much on initiatives to prevent fires as on putting them out, and an ambulance driver is now a highly skilled paramedic. Some occupations have seen the full circle of decline and then resurgence. Tattoo artists, internal auditors and educational administrators are examples of careers that for a host of reasons are currently enjoying a revival after a period of decline. Below are reviewed seven of the newest developments and some of the careers opportunities that they have given rise to.

Hot topics in the changing world of work

The emergent class of the super-rich

Twenty-five years ago there were fewer than 20 billionaires in the United States. Today there are more than a thousand, not to mention the hundreds of thousands of multi-millionaires. This is a phenomenon repeated around the world. More people are making fortunes and they are making them faster than ever before. The wealth of the super-rich has come from advances in technology and the quantum growth in global trade. To join the club of the super-rich, consider the following hot favourite routes. Vast sums have been made by:

- **Fund managers**. This role involves the management of shares, bonds, investments and assets. The fund manager directs how the fund is invested and the amount of risk taken to serve the fund owners' objectives.

- **Private equity partners**. A private equity partner is a firm or individual that invests in companies to fund management buy-outs, buy-ins, acquisitions and expansion in return for a stake in that company.

- **Entrepreneurs**. Ben & Jerry and Bill Gates are famous entrepreneurs. Ice cream and operating systems have nothing in common, but an entrepreneur has an idea and starts an enterprise to fulfil it and assumes responsibility for the risks and the gains. For inspiration see, for example, www.entrepreneur.com

- **Electronic engineers** design and test consumer electronics, and electronic equipment for every area of industry, including the financial industry, aviation and telecommunications. Design the next thing after the iPod and who knows how wealthy you might become.

- **Applied mathematicians** who bring their training to the worlds of insurance and finance can earn big salaries as, for example, actuaries or business analysts, and they might just spot a gap in the market or develop the system to beat the casino that makes them a fortune.

- **Bio-engineers** are searching for the clean fuel to replace our dependence on petroleum products. The researchers and engineers who hold the rights to this technology are going to be very rich indeed. How good would it be if you could save the world from carbon pollution and make yourself a personal fortune?

- **Computer engineers** have in some cases already made fortunes, and the opportunity to join those who have made them remains.

- **Physicists** who move into software development or systems engineering are sought after. They are able to bring their training to problems and just might suggest a novel solution that revolutionizes a process. In any event they are soon earning a six-figure dollar salary.

- **Chemists** might discover a new substance, or with a **Chemical Engineer** develop the next big product. The chemical industry is huge and includes pharmaceuticals, cosmetics, fabrics and building materials. Even if they don't make the breakthrough to the next big thing, by the time they reach senior positions they can earn in excess of $100,000 per annum. It won't make you super-rich but it's a good salary by any standard.

If you can't join them consider working for them

The super-rich enjoy a luxurious lifestyle that the vast majority of us can't begin to imagine. But they have a problem that a lot of us would love to share. Their fortunes are growing at such a rate that they just can't spend it fast enough. So they employ armies to spend it for them. Their agents buy estates of land, fine and decorative art, private jets and super-yachts. The super-rich obviously live in opulent homes, but not just one; they all own many and each requires interior designers, domestic staff, drivers, gardeners and a maintenance manager. They employ gamekeepers, machinery operatives to manicure their estates, pilots, ground staff and hostesses for their private jets, and a captain, first mate, deckhands, cooks and engineers for their super-yacht. Their professional advisors manage the staff, keep count of the fortune and catalogue the ever-growing list of possessions. They employ nannies for their children, take their families' personal security and privacy seriously and employ teams of the best people to oversee it all.

Many of their staff get to work in some of the most beautiful locations in the world. They may fly ahead to prepare things the way the family likes them, to buy provisions and, for example, make sure the in-house cinema complex or karaoke machine is fully operational. Or move the super-yacht to meet the owner who flies in.

The super-rich can only be in one place at a time and they own so many homes they can only be in each a few weeks or months of the year. When the owner is at home or on board the staff work really hard to ensure everything is perfect, but the rest of the time they simply keep things ready for the next visit. Workers are usually accommodated in a nearby hotel or staff housing. They are well paid and sometimes their earnings are paid tax-free.

There are some fantastic career opportunities in the service of the very wealthy. Here are a few that might just make you take the opportunity seriously:

- **Super-yacht captain**. Someone has to be in charge and why not you? You can get started in this career at a number of sea schools around the world. See for example www.UKSA.org, which has a career service for its graduates and a series of open days where you can find out more about a career in yachting.

- **Private security**. The head of security might be a former Israeli special forces' soldier or a retired Scotland Yard police inspector, but the team will comprise people from a wide variety of walks of life.

- **Computer geeks** ensure that communications remain private.

- **Electronic technicians** manage sophisticated alarm systems.

- **Lighting engineers** hamper the best efforts of the Pavarotti.

- **Interior designers** help the super-rich to lavish money on their homes and make them truly beautiful. As an interior designer you have to stick to the brief, so most of the time it's certainly not to your own taste, but you get to do things that you like from time to time.

- **Super-yacht valet**. Would you like to hang out in Antibes or Palma, Majorca? Do you own an immaculate white T shirt, shorts and trainers? If so then find your way there and first thing in the morning get yourself along to the super-yacht dock and inquire about a morning's work. You will spend it polishing the topsides of the ship and earn €100 cash. Then it's off to the beach for the rest of the day.

The third age

We used to have to work until we dropped, but these days when career ambition is no longer a prime motive you enter a period of transition that starts at the peak of your career and ends in retirement – it's called the third age. You might have just got on with your first career. You might have embarked on it without much understanding of what it involved. When launching a career in the third age people go in fully aware and far better prepared. What they lack in ambition they make up for with motivation because they have chosen the career and made sure it fits with their interests. They have a lot to offer and it's a different offer from that of younger employees.

Employers find that third-age staff settle and train younger staff, and are also appreciated by customers. This means that the third-age candidate does not have to compete with younger applicants. Many employers seek them out to ensure a better balance of their workforce and to ensure that their workforce reflects the profile of their customers.

Many more people are choosing to delay retirement. Laws in the UK, for example, on age discrimination and retirement mean that workers no longer have to retire before receiving their pensions. A tenth of all people over retirement age are now working. In the UK a number of national companies pioneered programmes to encourage and retain the employment of older workers. American companies have been at it for years. Most celebrated in the UK is the DIY chain B&Q. Over a fifth of their staff are aged over 50. Another is the supermarket chain Asda, which offers its 'Asda Goldies' programme that includes flexible working and a week's unpaid leave on the birth of a grandchild. Most third-age workers declare themselves more satisfied when they work part time. Many retrain before embarking on their new career and some choose to invest funds in low-risk ventures.

Ideal careers for the third age include:

- **Airport baggage, passenger and hand-luggage screener**. International terrorism makes daily headlines, and fear of financial insecurity is matched only by concern for our physical safety. A mature, dependable approach and the skills to handle situations delicately are highly rated in the security industry.

- **Parenting coach**. Parents with grown-up children, especially those with experience in social work, might be interested in becoming a coach for families.

- **Government inspectors**. Workers can sometimes capitalize on their experience in an industry by moving into a regulatory job.

- **Dog walker**. Why not keep fit and at the same time supplement your income?

- **Running a bed-and-breakfast establishment**. If your children have left home and the house is feeling empty, and if you like meeting people, then offering bed-and-breakfast accommodation is something you might enjoy. Your home does not need to be by the sea or a national park, though this might help. You can advertise on sites such as www.ownersdirect.com or www.tripadvisor.com.

- **Freelance work**. Third-age people offer their skills for hire in every imaginable area from babysitting and completing tax returns to advice on employment law, copywriting and illustrations. The big challenge is finding the clients. One way is to join outsourcing sites. Companies post a job and freelancers bid for it. The company that outsourced the job then reviews the bids, awards the work and pays the freelancer. See for example www.peopleperhour.com.

The fact that we are living longer, sometimes with health conditions, and are richer means that careers in the healthcare industry have a very rosy outlook. There are opportunities for both healthcare professionals and support staff such as secretaries, accountants and administrators. Some of the new careers in this sector include:

- **Pharmacy technician**. If you have a scientific background, then this career might be for you. Pharmacy technicians work with licensed pharmacists to fill prescriptions, assist customers and stock the shelves of pharmacies.

- **Counsellors** work with individuals, families and groups in a great many fields; one of the fastest growing is mental health. Counsellors use a variety of therapeutic techniques to address problems, including depression, anxiety, addiction or stress.

- **Electronic medical records and health information administrators**. These jobs demand attention to detail and tact, and third-age applicants are preferred, especially if they have had a previous career in nursing.

Opportunities in the participatory media revolution

The printed word, the radio and television used to be the only sources of information available to a mass audience. Journalists and radio and television presenters were household names, they decided what we heard and saw, and their opinions carried great authority. But people no longer passively consume media content. And they are beginning to value their own opinions and offer them alongside those of the supposed experts. They post online ratings for the restaurants they visit, they share their homemade podcasts and videologs, they contribute entries to collaborative sites offering advice or answers to questions posed on every imaginable subject. They are quickly realizing that the experts and authorities have feet of clay and that only too often a rank amateur offers a more profound contribution to the debate. It is the beginning of an expressive revolution that has only recently become possible and will embrace most people in the future.

The revolution is creating considerable pessimism amongst the employees of the traditional media corporations as they realize how gravely the business model to which they have become accustomed is threatened. They can barely believe that users might put as much, or more, onto the network as they download. They had seen the internet as simply another outlet for their products. How wrong they turned out to be. There are challenges too for the owners of the sites that people are posting on. The challenge is not how to attract users but how to make money. In particular they must work out how to generate income while reconciling the interests of the users, who expect the service to be free and expect their privacy to be maintained. Advertisers are willing to pay in order to market to the millions of users, but the business model has yet to fully emerge.

There are many opportunities to work in this fast-changing new industry. Consider for example:

- **Moderators**. It's all very well to have people uploading content but the site owners are legally responsible for what appears on their sites and they employ moderators to remove material that is for example offensive, libellous or illegal.

- **Virtual sales, administration and order fulfilment**. We have just begun to use the internet as an entertainment medium in publishing; music and film consumers are increasingly feeling more comfortable in buying products through the internet. And online shops need virtual assistants to process purchases, maintain security, respond to queries, post details of new stock and prices, and fulfil orders.

- **Virtual-market traders**. Online auctions are the new street markets and a throng of people sell goods on the many online auction sites. Some operate to the extent that they have a significant second income; others have taken the step to operating a full-time business selling anything from car parts to vintage postcards.

- **Webmaster** is the title for the person who manages a website. They ensure the operation of the server and software, they will know scripting language such as Java and commission illustrations, applications or write the copy, and are responsible for the site's architecture, marketing, the collation and analysis of statistics, and the security of the site (to ensure for example that the site is not used to generate spam or spread viruses).

- **Self-publisher**. It has never been harder for new authors to find a traditional publisher. If that is the bad news, the good is that with the advent of e-books, on-demand printing and internet sales, self-publishing and marketing is fast coming of age. Think carefully before you part with your money and be sure to explore all the pros and cons. For a frank discussion of the issues, review threads on, for example, the forums at: www.absolutewrite.com.

- **Online artist and photographer**. It has never been easier to promote your work to buyers in the advertising, publishing and corporate sectors. All you need to do is subscribe to and upload your images to any number of rights-managing sites that showcase artists' work and, for a commission on sales, protect it against unauthorized copying and handle payments. See for example www.photolibrary.com.

- **Graphic designer, writer and translator**. While much content is uploaded, there remains a considerable amount that the site provides and this requires graphic designers, writers and the translation of the site into other languages.

Jobs that make a difference

We now have much more choice as to the career we follow, and consequently a lot of people are choosing a career that will help make the world a better place. Making a difference can range from washing the kit of the local weekend soccer team to the global health programme of the Bill and Melinda Gates Foundation. The charity or voluntary sector, sometimes called the third sector, is most closely associated with these good works. It has grown in importance to the point where it is now responsible for spending many tens of billions, of which about a third comes from government. You can work on the front line delivering services, on managing, co-ordinating or administering services, as a part of campaign, communication, research or fundraising teams, or you can give your time as a volunteer.

The activities of the third sector cover every sphere of human activity and condition. As well as health and sport, there are organizations active in poverty relief, education, housing, unemployment, substance dependency, victims of crime and the rehabilitation of criminals, governance and citizenship, environmentalism and global ethics, social exclusion and family planning, to name but a few. The focus of these initiatives is both national and international. In a significant minority of cases they are faith based.

- **If you are the sporty type**. Millions of people each week give time to help organize or coach sporting events. Even the Olympics relies on volunteers. Many thousands are also employed working for sports governing bodies, at public venues, as coaches and managers.

- **Sharing skills internationally**. Organizations such as VSO UK manage overseas placements for volunteers with skills in fields such as building, education, health or administration. They aim to make the world a fairer place and work extensively in Africa and far-flung locations such as Papua New Guinea. They even have placements for volunteer couples.

- **Faith-based programmes**. A large part of the third sector is provided by faith-based organizations. These are drawn from every religion and their services are offered to clients irrespective of whether or not that person has faith or shares the same faith as the organization. Leading international examples include the Red Crescent and Red Cross.

Frontline careers that make a difference include **special-needs teachers** who teach pupils with emotional, physical or cognitive disabilities. The work involves the assessment of needs, the identification of appropriate educational milestones for the individual and the delivery of a programme of teaching that will result in the achievement of those milestones. Special needs teachers must qualify as teachers and then obtain further qualifications if, for example, they want to teach pupils with sensory impairment. Courses are available for qualified teachers to train to teach pupils with special educational needs or specific conditions such as dyslexia.

- **Nurses** who work in hospitals, health centres and in the community help evaluate and care for patients. To become a nurse you must first qualify by completing an approved nursing diploma or degree course.

- **Mental health counsellors** work with individuals, families and groups to help alleviate the effects of, for example, depression, anxiety, addiction or stress. Obtaining a professional qualification as a mental health counsellor takes two or three years and includes supervised clinical experience.

- **Probation officers** supervise offenders serving non-custodial sentences in the community or after their release from prison on licence. They work to prevent re-offending and encourage the safe rehabilitation of the criminal into society. They help solve challenges their clients may face such as homelessness and unemployment that would otherwise increase the risk of re-offending. Currently the minimum qualification for a probation officer remains at honours degree level. However proposals exist to introduce an NVQ level 3 minimum qualification and also to introduce a foundation degree.

Vocations that do NOT need a degree

The graduate category comprises traditional graduate jobs – doctors, lawyers, engineers, teachers and technical occupations. Changes in the world of work mean that a 'graduate job' now also encompasses a great variety of other jobs. For example, many managerial positions and high-skilled sales positions stipulate that non-graduates need not apply.

For a while it seemed as if you had to have a university degree before you could apply for the vast majority of worthwhile jobs. But things have changed. Above all else employers are looking for committed and conscientious staff with common sense and the hunger to succeed. Candidates who show these qualities will create opportunities for themselves irrespective of whether they have a degree. Graduating does not guarantee that you have these qualities and this is one of the reasons, perhaps, why in some subjects up to a quarter of the graduates who have successfully completed their studies work in non-graduate jobs stacking shelves or answering phones in call centres.

There are plenty of worthwhile careers that do not need a university degree and a close look at the qualifications and experiences required for most high-level careers reveals that while they require a high level of education, experience and training, it is not necessary for this to be gained at a university or to be a degree. In law enforcement, insurance, sport, administration, catering, retail, construction and transport, there are many highly paid careers to be had without the requirement of going to university. Take **airline pilots** for example: no degree is necessary for this job and most are on salaries of over $100K. **Air traffic controllers** and insurance **underwriters** are other examples. Many people achieve qualifications equally valued by employers through night school or college for a fraction of the cost of a university degree. Examples include:

- **Recruitment consultant**. In this role you fill vacancies for client companies by advertising or networking to attract candidates that match the position. The posts may be temporary or permanent, entry or high level.

- **Junior and middle-rank Civil Servants**. Applicants to the position of administrative assistants, administrative officer and executive officers in the UK Civil Service do not need to be graduates. Most vacancies will be advertised through government websites, local papers and job centres. Executive officer positions may be advertised on the public service days in the national press, for example the *Guardian* on Wednesdays.

- **Sales representative**. The primary duties in this role are to generate interest in your company's goods or services, explain or demonstrate products, respond to questions or expressions of interest, and realize sales. Some positions involve a great deal of travel to visit prospective clients or represent your company at business fairs.

- **Casino floor managers**. These workers oversee the gaming floor and the staff working there. The hours are unsocial in that the work is mainly from the evening until the early hours, the dress code formal and the demeanour very professional.

- **Desalination plant operatives**. These workers operate and maintain machinery to produce fresh water from seawater. The plant may be large scale, in which case you work as a part of a team, or an auxiliary plant at a hotel, in which case the operator may work alone.

Livelihoods delivered from a spare room or an island paradise

Warning: don't hand your money over to websites promising to make you rich with some fantastic work-at-home idea. They are bogus.

If you look back into history most trades were practised from home, but then someone realized they could make more money if they locked us up in factories, de-skilled us with their machines and became middlemen selling what we produced at a fat profit. Many self-employed workers still work from home. Carpenters, bookkeepers, chimney sweeps – you name them. It is a perfect way to keep down costs and keep other people's fingers out of your pockets! However, if you are unable to leave the home because of, for example, care commitments and you are not self-employed, then home working used to mean very low-paid manual work: envelope stuffing, needlework and hand-finishing of novelty products, for example.

Now things have changed for the better because home working has been transformed. Lots of workers now work some of their week from home and an increasing number work solely from there. Never has there been more opportunity to earn a good living and enjoy a rewarding career without crossing your doorstep. Consider the following examples:

- **Home based agents**. A home-based agent is someone who works from home gathering, entering and confirming customer information, answering customer questions, resolving issues, providing customer care, engaging in live chat, responding to e-mails and handling sales calls with customers.

- **Paid surveyor**. Paid surveys are online surveys where you receive a payment for each response to survey questions.

- **Online tutors**. These professionals work for internet-based educational companies that offer study within a huge variety of subject areas to students of all ages.

- **Virtual assistant**. These home workers provide administrative, secretarial and clerical support, as well as creative and technical services.

Now allow your imagination to run for a moment. Have you ever dreamed of living on a tropical island, somewhere where there is a bit more space, a less hectic pace of life or in a favourite city? If you have, then take your dream seriously because it is a real possibility these days. Computers and the internet have transformed the way we work but they have also transformed the locations from which we can work. Employers are becoming more open minded to such suggestions; after all what difference does it make to them where you live so long as you provide a first-class service?

Why shouldn't an online tutor, virtual assistant or for that matter corporate PR specialist, commodities trader, telecommunications executive, publisher or insurance underwriter work from home? And, why shouldn't that home be somewhere where they would like to live rather than somewhere near to where they work? Some very big and very successful companies employ home workers, including Google, Dell, American Express and Nationwide Insurance to name but a few. Some will be perfectly happy if that home happens to be a long way away because video conferencing, twittering and the odd trip back to base ensure sufficient face-to-face contact to get the job done and maintain working relationships. In some cases home working from another part of the world is positively encouraged. Take, for example, work such as the checking of legal documents, the proofing of consultancy reports, data processing and analysis. Much of this work has to be done overnight so that it is available for the start of the next working day. Time zones mean that it can be undertaken on the other side of the world during normal working hours and so avoids the extra social and financial cost of night shifts. In some cases home working from another part of the world is an essential part of the job. A great deal of manufacturing has been moved overseas and the outsourcing company needs trusted local representatives to oversee quality. Businesses keen to win a share of overseas markets need local sales representatives but do not want to risk the cost of opening an office, so many of these representatives are based at home.

If this possibility catches your imagination, if you are tied to working from home and want a rewarding career, then start by browsing these suggestions and seek out sources of further information. You will be surprised how real a possibility it has become.

Ok so not everything has changed

It is true to say that some things never change. If it is security you are seeking, if you want to be in a career that will still employ you when everything else looks like going to the wall, then avoid careers linked to things that people can choose not to do or buy. When times are hard people don't buy new cars. They don't go to the hairdresser and dentist as often. Long-weekend vacations are out and holidays are skipped. Restaurants are empty so even if you can afford to go it's no pleasure sitting alone in a dining hall.

Think of essentials, the things we can't do without. We will always need sewage and water treatment. Funeral directors will always have jobs. Unfortunately, chronic illness will always strike so health professionals and support staff will remain in business. Pets are a part of the family so veterinarians and veterinary technicians will always have work. Demand for ATM and office machine repairs may reduce but will always remain. Crime never goes away so law enforcement and security remain as steadfast a career as ever. Education and training become even more of a priority as people strive to remain competitive and invest in their own or their children's future.

People have to eat, and when money is tight they turn more to staples and seek out value for money. This means that jobs connected to the food industry are safer than most jobs; they include:

- **Local agent for a vegetable box scheme**. Growers or a co-operative of growers may operate a scheme to deliver their produce directly to local consumers. Some schemes are run on a regional basis; see for example www.riverford.co.uk. Many employ a network of local agents who take delivery of the produce; subscribers to the scheme call round to collect their purchase or the agents deliver the boxes of vegetables or fruit to their homes.

- **Supervisor in a food hall**. Indoor food markets and halls operate at many locations, including the prestigious such as Selfridges and borough markets as well as countless one-day-a-week locations up and down the country. In many cases the owner of the venue receives a rent from each retailer and employs a supervisor who ensures the event runs smoothly, that the retailers adhere to the regulations and that the venue is cleaned and garbage removed at the end of the day.

- **Departmental manager in a supermarket**. The meat, bakery, fish and pharmacy departments of large supermarkets have departmental managers who are responsible for directing and managing department members. They order products and oversee hygiene and safety policies and procedures.

- **Order fulfiller for online grocery orders**. Online supermarkets offer a huge choice of groceries and products for home delivery. Customers submit their orders and a team of fulfillers make

the orders up, selecting substitutions if necessary.
See for example www.sainsburys.co.uk.

● **Cashier at a company like the New Covent Garden Market**.
New Covent Garden is the largest fruit, vegetable and flower
market in the UK. It is located in the heart of the capital and
supplies many leading chefs, florists, restaurants, hotels,
schools and hospitals. There are over 240 wholesalers on
the site and each employs a cashier to take payment for
purchases. The work begins early and the pace is fast.
Visit their website at www.newcoventgardenmarket.com.

Think too of the people that government can't do without: tax
inspectors, border customs and immigration officers, welfare officials
and members of the armed services and environment inspectors.
Local government will always need refuse collectors, school and health
inspectors, teachers, civil engineers and town planners, and administrators to keep the bureaucratic machinery running.

If you find embracing change too stressful, if you have been
through the pain of losing your job and want to minimize the chance
of it happening again, then careers linked to these areas are the
ones that you should explore.

HOW PEOPLE REALIZE THEIR DREAM CAREER

This book is about finding the pull to a new career and this chapter explores how some people have taken the plunge and navigated towards one. You will find below 16 case studies of individuals who have successfully changed career. Some of the case studies are detailed and go into the push and pull of it, describing how the person successfully took the plunge. Others are short and simple outlining a move from one career to another and a few pointers the individual considered most relevant. All of them are true. You will see that for many the career they settle in is not their first or sometimes even their second occupation.

They say it takes three miles for a supertanker to change course. We build our lives into something approaching supertankers. All the possessions we have, our ties to a location, schools, clubs, friends, our skills, qualifications and experience all point in one direction. We run our lives at full speed, so no wonder people find the challenge of changing careers/direction difficult. First we must slow down; that takes time. Then we can start our turn and take the first few tentative steps towards our new career. It is a major undertaking. It often means retraining, going back to the lecture room, laboratory or workshop. It can mean a considerable loss of earnings that can only be accommodated if sacrifices are made. It may require the investment of savings to pay for tuition fees, tools for the new trade or to cashflow the new venture. Most of all it requires a considerable investment of time and energy. All the same it can and, if you are to be true to your dreams, must be done.

Change is easiest when there's both a push for it, because someone is not content in what they do, and a clear pull to something they believe will be more fulfilling. These forces don't have to be in equal balance but both are needed if the person is most likely to take the plunge. Change gets hard, impossible even, when you have no clear idea of where you are going. Things get difficult when there is lots of push, when you really want to do something else, but no clear pull, when you have no idea of what to do next.

There are a number of common themes to be drawn from the examples. One, we have already covered, is the fact that like Earl (Case Study 13) you must not give up on your dream if it doesn't happen overnight. Putting others first is another common theme and commendable; it may mean like Jeremy (Case Study 5) that for many years you choose to live with the status quo because of family, financial or other commitments. You may already have put off change, in some cases for decades. You may have convinced yourself that your happiness is less important than the happiness of others, and sometimes is it. However, you owe it to yourself and the ones you love to find your fulfilment. Like Glen (Case Study 9), don't underestimate the effect of your unhappiness on others around you. Change brings inconvenience. It usually generates heat in the form of conflict and tension. It does not happen unless you decide it must. Realize like Mark (Case Study 6) that rarely is the moment perfect. In truth there are many moments that can serve as the right moment. Almost any is better than none. Like Tony (Case Study 3), realize that things don't always go to plan. Sometimes life can seem like trying to walk through treacle. Be courageous like Jan (Case Study 7) because you may well have to face the unexpected. And, if for some reason your preferred course is impossible, as it was for Westley (Case Study 12), be prepared to find a different path.

Another common theme – best described by Cliff (Case Study 10) – is that you should go with your passions and interests. Like Carole and Clare (Case Study 4), be prepared to modify your plan. Think laterally and around something that you did not foresee. You may end up doing things quite differently from the way you had at first imagined.

By being pragmatic regarding the means, you are far more likely to achieve the desired end.

Finally, know that it is going to work because it's what you really want. Once you have made a decision, chew it over for a while. Look at it from a number of different angles, then commit and within reason push doubts aside. Remain loyal to your dreams, take advice on how to achieve them but, like Gwenda (Case Study 11), politely ignore advice suggesting that you abandon them all together.

CASE STUDY 1

A STEP BACK TO TAKE A LEAP FORWARD

LIZ CLEERE

Location India
Relevant qualification/profession
BA (Hons) in librarianship and English

I'd spent four years as firstly assistant librarian, then librarian. It was a two-person research, or 'special' library, for a large firm of consulting engineers. By year four I started to take my career seriously; I wanted to enjoy what I was doing in the day, not simply live for evenings and weekends. And as a research librarian I had no concept of job satisfaction. I realized I needed a career change and a plan.

To start the process I made lists. A list of all the things I liked doing and a list of all the things that interested me. These lists contained things like going to the pub, buying clothes, art, holidays, spending time with friends, skiing, music, dancing, writing, reading, singing, watching films, living in London, mountains, the countryside. I realized that I was attracted to the pleasure-seeking and artistic side of life.

The world of fashion seemed to tick all the boxes. I'd been bonkers about clothes and style since I could walk. The most attractive job for me was fashion design, but I knew that unless I went back to university to get a fashion degree I would not be taken seriously. I felt at the time that I was too old at 26, but with hindsight I don't agree.

I chose the next best thing, fashion buyer. I now had a goal and set about finding the fastest way of achieving it.

I wrote to all the big London stores and the Dickens and Jones personnel officer took a chance on me. She offered me a position as sales assistant with a guarantee that I would be promoted to supervisor after my six-month probationary period. I accepted the offer.

Within four years I climbed the slippery pole to assistant buyer and then departmental sales manager (equivalent to buyer). I changed jobs several times, each time gaining good managerial and product experience and taking something from even the most unrewarding posts.

I worked across the industry, first in retail, then in wholesale, and at one point I moved out of 'clothes' altogether and became show organizer for a well-known fashion trade event. I travelled frequently, much to my initial pleasure. My final job with the largest silk supplier in China saw me working with the top retailers in the UK at director level and using all the skills and techniques that I had acquired along the way.

In my mid-forties I moved to my next adventure: selling up, downsizing and moving to live on a sailing yacht. Once again I have the freedom of limitless possibilities.

Find out more at **www.followtheboat.com**.

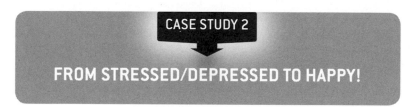

CASE STUDY 2

FROM STRESSED/DEPRESSED TO HAPPY!

ROS

Location UK

I used to be a teacher. I now work as a counsellor in the NHS. I moved from stressed and depressed as a teacher to happy and contented as a counsellor. The two roles have a lot in common and you might expect someone unhappy in one to be unhappy in both. But this was certainly not true for me. The emphasis in counselling on one-to-one work and small groups was the key to my happiness. I realized from my experience that seemingly minor distinctions can make a huge difference to one's sense of job satisfaction. If like me you find yourself stressed/depressed at work, then set out to change things; the change may not need to be as drastic as you fear.

A LIFE I COULD NEVER EVEN IMAGINE WHEN I LEFT SCHOOL

TONY

Location Middle East

I was working as a general builder after failing A levels at 18 in 1981. I had intended to go to university and study mechanical engineering. When I failed in this ambition my self-esteem was low and the sense of failure stuck with me. I needed a job and I would have taken any that came along; it just happened that it was in construction. It took a full 10 years before I felt able to try education again and by then I had come to love construction. I began an HND in building and construction and then a degree in quantity surveying in 1995. Since then nothing has stopped me and I have passed a law degree and a master's in construction law, and I should finish an MBA this year.

Having worked overseas on some of the biggest oil and gas projects since 1998 and just moved to the UAE as operations director for a UK consultancy company, I have a life I could never have even imagined when I left school under the shadow of failure.

IF YOU CAN'T FIND YOUR DREAM CAREER, THEN CREATE IT

CAROLE SLEIGHT and CLARE BURGESS

Location Europe

I [Carole] worked for 10 years at the BBC.

My last staff job as *Video Nation* editor was transferred from London to Birmingham and as the commute was not feasible I had no alternative but to leave the post. I did a few freelance media jobs after that, but found that the job was hard to mix with childcare requirements. I also wanted a new challenge that meant I could have a flexible job and work within an area that enthused and excited me.

So I became the co-founder of the company and website called 'Let them eat Cake'. My colleague Clare and I make and sell vintage mis-matched cake stands. It is a completely new area of work for both of us and draws upon a lot of the skills we have amassed. For Clare it draws upon her previous accounting experience and her continued artistic talents in creating visual displays, photography, and writing product and production ideas. For me it draws upon my web and writing experience, my enthusiasm for press and product placement.

For both of us it has been the first time we have 'created' our own product. Whilst we do not make the plates for our cake stands, we use a lot of creative talent in sourcing our plates and putting them together to create one-off beautiful objects.

Along the way we have had many unexpected challenges; sourcing the china has been far more time-consuming than we anticipated. The storage and creation of the cake stands has been a major challenge, with Clare and her family taking the brunt of this initial production work. We also set up the 'Let them eat Cake' website at the same time, which has required us to learn new skills on how to run it and more time than we currently have to keep the blog element alive. In addition to this we have had to navigate our way through various financial hurdles of PayPal accounting, posting abroad, insurance, wholesale costing, business spreadsheets etc. The most unexpected hurdle has been just how much time is needed to run a business, how you get from it being a lifestyle business to providing an income, and most importantly how you maintain your friendship throughout the whole process.

www.letthemeatcake.co.uk

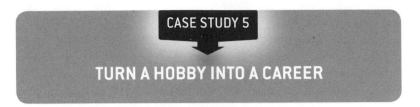

CASE STUDY 5

TURN A HOBBY INTO A CAREER

JEREMY

Location UK

I recently changed career from an IT project manager to a professional photographer. I only felt able to do this when my children had grown up and left home. Only then after decades of project management did I feel able to take the risk and do something for myself. Photography was my lifelong hobby and now it is my dream career.

CASE STUDY 6

BE COURAGEOUS

MARK

Location Australia

Music was my first love and my mother tells me that as a child I would not leave the piano. A career in music was not considered in my best interest and I was given a series of well-meaning pushes towards something thought of as more respectable. I ended up as a lawyer. Throughout university and when practising law I still played. I was doing three or four gigs a week in jazz clubs and was in one band or another.

If I was not advising clients on contracts, I was playing in clubs or learning new songs. What little time was left saw me socializing with my musician friends, only I had more money than they did! The music commitments grew and I found it harder and harder to maintain the two careers. One was going to have to go and it was not going to be my music. The trouble was there never seemed the right moment to take the plunge and play full time. I delayed the move for a number of years and ended up very tired. Eventually I simply went in to work and resigned. Now I sometimes do law-related things to supplement my playing.

CASE STUDY 7

YOU ALWAYS HAVE OTHER OPTIONS

JAN MORGAN KAUFMAN

Location UK

After university I drifted into employment in local authority housing. I married, had my first child and for the first 18 months of his life was a full-time mum. Shortly after having my second child I needed to return to employment as we were facing financial difficulties. I decided that I didn't enjoy housing as a career so I applied to go on the temporary employment register at the local university, which happened to be the Open University. I was offered a three-month temporary contract in the Business School to manage its collaborative partnerships in Central and Eastern Europe.

The three months turned into several years and during my time the partnerships expanded to six countries across Central and Eastern Europe, with 17,000 students studying OUBS courses at a distance and in translation. I obtained significant funding from the Foreign Office and met regularly with senior staff and ministers both in the UK and internationally. Our team even won the Queen's Award for Export in 1997. Not bad for a single parent mother of three.

I loved working at the OU. It was a huge decision to leave but I did and spent the next four years as a freelance consultant. However, I needed greater stability of income and so I submitted my CV to a number of recruitment consultants. One day I received a telephone call from one of the Big Four inviting me to an interview. I had been headhunted!

I started work as an education consultant. I worked on many projects, mostly for central government departments. Some work I led or acted on as project manager, whilst on others I was a team member or had discrete tasks. The variety gave me a buzz. Never knowing what work you will have or where you will be from one week to the next was exhilarating. Certainly boredom never came into it.

The negatives included the travel — and not to exotic locations, but a lot of time on trains and in hotel rooms. You didn't have a desk or a permanent base; everything was 'hot-desking', which meant that your office was your laptop backpack... the concept of 9–5 didn't exist.

Although I had joined the Big Four, the section I joined felt small, welcoming and friendly. However, it was part of the bigger organization and after a few months I began to understand what that meant. It became apparent that true equality and diversity did not exist. There was also age discrimination, and being in my late 40s I chose to leave.

I set up my own consulting company and I have just celebrated my first year of business.

This too has had its ups and downs. The lack of a regular salary has been the biggest adjustment. There have been times when I have had no money; literally no money. My coping strategies have been tested to their absolute limit. However, the advantages have more than outweighed the disadvantages. For example I have just collected my youngest child from school and we walked through the park eating ice creams. I have made an effort to set aside one day a week to do all the things I have wanted to do, but never had the time. I still work as a consultant and still work long hours, including weekends, but this time the deadlines are ones that I have agreed and not ones that have been imposed onto me. There is no 'corporate politics'.

www.mgnk.co.uk

CASE STUDY 8

EVEN UNWELCOME CHANGE CAN BE OVERCOME

ROBERTO

Location all over the world

Straight from school I went to work for my father's construction company and everyone assumed I would one day run it. Unfortunately the business went into receivership after more than 60 years of trading. It was a really tough time. I was angry and the events that led to the business failure haunted me. Eventually I realized my anger was making things worse and I knew I needed a complete change. I emigrated and started working as a kitchen assistant in my new country. One thing led to another and I now work as the personal assistant to a rich family. I manage their staff and properties. I get to travel all over the world and I really enjoy my work.

GLEN

Location Mexico

I worked for my older brother building stone walls for holiday villas. He was a sub-contractor working for one of two construction companies in our town. I didn't mind the fact that it was hard work but I could not abide the working culture. Supervisors would swear, and at times were intimidating. My relationship with my brother suffered.

I had always like fishing and the coast of Mexico is blessed, so I started working as a fisherman, catching spiny lobster. The whole family, including my wife, was against me leaving but I knew I had to. Eventually they came around to the fact that I couldn't work for my brother and that I wanted to be a fisherman. It took a long time, but I made the right decision. I couldn't be happier.

CLIFF HUGHES

Location Liverpool, UK

I can count on one hand (just about) my previous careers: community artist, youth and community worker, art lecturer, film and TV design work, and in recent years marketing executive. If I'm honest I would say that each job presented me with new challenges, excitement, variety and a good living.

I have been working towards my most recent career change for a while, possibly all my life. The push/trigger was heralded by redundancy – thank you credit crunch – I find myself at a crossroads!

My newest career move will be successful. How do I know? Because it is shaped and formed by the things I love. In my spare time (and there hasn't been much) I have trained in a number of holistic therapies and Oriental exercise systems: reflexology, Shiatsu, Reiki, sports massage, Swedish body massage, holistic facial, Indian head massage, Hopi ear candling, aromatherapy, Tai Chi and finally Qi Gong and Do-in. They seem disparate but they have the common thread of treating the individual not the ailment. Increasingly I am becoming aware that it's all about working with energy. I have also found I am increasingly directed towards traditional Chinese medicine.

The systems and techniques I have studied and practised so far have been acquired while holding down a demanding full-time job. While I place high value on them all, they are also stepping stones to gain experience and supply an income toward my main goal.

The next step is the scariest; I have chosen to enter a three-year BA (Hons) course in acupuncture. I am 48, a lone parent with four kids still at home — almost grown up it has to be said, but nevertheless I still need to keep a roof over everyone's head and put bread on the table. It's a scary step but the time is ripe. I have postponed long enough. So I have embarked on a career as a holistic therapist augmented by teaching holism, Oriental exercise and art.

So what's it all about? It's about taking the jump and doing something you love. It's about the key to a happy and successful working life, and that is to concentrate on what you love. It's also about quality of life.

Cliff.hughes@talktalk.net

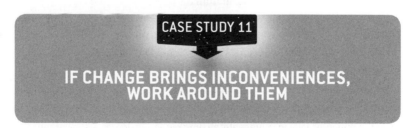

CASE STUDY 11

IF CHANGE BRINGS INCONVENIENCES, WORK AROUND THEM

GWENDA

Location USA

I went from homemaker to accountant. I married my childhood sweetheart when we were both young and kids soon arrived. I spent 11 years as a full-time homemaker and mother and I can look back and say they were very happy, satisfying years. I wanted to remain a homemaker but I also wanted to help support the family financially; I knew the kids would not always be there. I decided to follow a correspondence course in bookkeeping and asked my parents and my husband's if they would help with the cost of the study fees. My husband's parents agreed but mine were set against it. They believed that going out to work would mean I would fail in my responsibilities to my children and my husband. Their view took me rather by surprise but I decided they were wrong and I went ahead without their support or encouragement. In all it took me four years of part-time study to complete all the components and by the time both children were in high school and sufficiently independent I was working part-time in a local practice. As the children got older I took on more hours and larger clients. By the time they had all left home I was a full-time accountant.

CASE STUDY 12

COME TO TERMS WITH DISAPPOINTMENT AND PURSUE THE NEXT BEST THING

WESTLEY

Location USA

I had dreamed of a career in medicine and with the encouragement of our family doctor I tried for medical school. I worked as an intern in his office most school holidays and he wrote a glowing reference in support of my application. The interview with the medical schools went well and I was all set to go. The only hurdle that remained was my grades and they simply weren't good enough. Nowadays I would have the option of joining a graduate programme in nursing or a specialization in genetic science, but back in the mid-1980s these options were not around. I turned to my second choice — architecture — and with time I came to terms with my disappointment. I am now a tenured professor in the architecture department of a US university but I couldn't stay away from medicine altogether and I have trained in first aid.

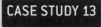

CASE STUDY 13

BE PREPARED TO MODIFY YOUR PLAN

EARL

Location UK

Ever since I can remember I have wanted to be a firefighter. The trouble is, and you may not know this, that an awful lot of people want to become firefighters and the competition is really tough. The first time I tried I failed miserably. On the advice of my girlfriend I telephoned the recruitment team of the service and asked why I had failed. Their advice was hard to take but very helpful and I realized that I was going to have to improve my reading and arithmetic, something I had never really faced up to before. I signed up for some literacy and numeracy classes at my local college and after six months of part-time study, with high expectations I applied to the fire authority once more. Unfortunately I was unsuccessful again and this time the disappointment really affected me. I decided to do something drastic in the hope that the experience would bring me the skills and experience I needed to succeed in my ambition. I joined the army and completed five years' service. I decided on the army because I had read that many firefighters had previously been in the forces. I also reckoned that fighting fires must be a lot like fighting a battle. One of the many things the army taught me was how to drive trucks, and after leaving I worked as a truck driver while I applied once more to the fire service. On my fourth attempt I passed the assessments and realized my lifelong dream. I don't think I could have done it without my spell in the armed services.

CASE STUDY 14

CONSIDER A MID-TO-LATE-CAREER CHANGE

PATRICK

Location UK

I gave up a financial job in a city of London firm to teach in secondary school. After four years teaching I applied for and won a place on a 'future leaders' course in school leadership. I am now a head teacher in what is termed a 'challenging urban school'.

How did I do it? It was easier than you might think. There is loads of information about switching from industry to a career in teaching and I simply applied to complete a postgraduate certificate in education at my local university. On qualifying I applied for jobs at local schools, which were really interested in employing me because of my 'real life experience'. I would never have won a place on the 'future leaders' course without my City of London experience. Part of the selection procedure involved sitting a battery of psychometric tests, which I did well in because my city firm was forever putting us through such assessments.

If you are a graduate and considering a mid-to-late-career change to teaching, then sign up at **www.tda.gov.uk** to find out all about it. Register at the site and call the teaching information line if you would like to talk to a teacher or visit a school.

CASE STUDY 15

REMAIN LOYAL TO YOUR DREAMS

LOTI MARTENS

Location the Caribbean

I started my career teaching Italian abroad as I've always been truly happy when travelling and seeing the world. I moved back to London in my late 20s to start a family.

On a cold, wet January day in 2009 I was placing an advert for a client and I saw a job offer as a villa manager in the Caribbean. How could I resist that? After a night dreaming of lush palms on white sandy beaches I quickly updated my CV and sent it off with a smile on my face. The position was offered with live-in accommodation for a single woman. I had to convince my potential boss that I was the ideal candidate for her, and that she wanted to move me with my family. It took a few conversations but eventually she came around to my way of thinking and invited me for a week's induction in the Caribbean. Whilst there she offered me a position more related to my skills and experience. I now live and work in a truly gorgeous island in the Caribbean, working as the PA to the general manager of an international construction company. Every lunch break I go swimming, and my dream has come true.

CASE STUDY 16

CHANGE CAREER TO A VOCATION THAT HELPS OTHERS

MARGARET

Location London, UK

I worked as a manager in a very successful chain of department stores. I wanted a change but I did not want to walk away from my years of experience in retail. I discovered a company that trains unemployed adults in retail skills and I landed a job there as a trainer. I had to take quite a cut in salary but I enjoy helping others and watching students grow in confidence. I am still in touch with many of my students and my contacts in the retail industry have proved really valuable in gaining employment for many of them.

3

THE QUESTIONNAIRE

This chapter comprises a questionnaire made up of 108 statements. The questionnaire is divided into 18 sets and each set comprises six questions. Your task is to agree, disagree or in some instance neither agree nor disagree with each statement. Only offer one of the suggested responses to each statement, and try not to sit too much on the fence by answering 'Neither agree nor disagree' too often.

Within reason, the longer you take over the questionnaire the better. This is because you will obtain a more objective set of results by reflecting carefully before deciding your responses.

Be sure to complete the questionnaire before reading Chapter 4. Avoid trying to work out what is behind the questions and sets. Approach them by suspending any disbelief you may have as to the likely value of the process, and be sure to complete the questionnaire as objectively and truthfully as possible. Do this and you will obtain the best possible assessment of your motivations and interests and are more likely to identify your perfect career. Also put aside any competitive feelings or efforts to get a high score because they too can skew the results.

You will find instructions on how to score the questionnaire in Chapter 4, along with an interpretation of your personality traits, motivations and interests. Once you know your score, look up the listings of jobs in Chapter 5 that are linked to your personality traits.

The questionnaire

Set 1

Q1   It has not always been the case but for one reason or another I now find my energy drained.
　　　2 I agree
　　　3 I neither agree nor disagree
　　　3 I disagree

Q2   I don't want to continue doing what I am doing now.
　　　2 I agree
　　　3 I neither agree nor disagree
　　　3 I disagree

Q3   I am willing to study or retrain and develop my skills in order to find a new direction in my life.
　　　2 I agree
　　　3 I neither agree nor disagree
　　　3 I disagree

Q4   Possessions that once gave me pleasure now seem part of the problem.
　　　2 I agree
　　　3 I neither agree nor disagree
　　　3 I disagree

Q5   I wake up more days than not really looking forward to what I have planned for the day.
　　　3 I agree
　　　2 I neither agree nor disagree
　　　2 I disagree

Q6   I don't feel sufficiently well qualified to do very much.
　　　2 I agree
　　　3 I neither agree nor disagree
　　　3 I disagree

Set 2

Q1 I am able to express my observations concisely and prefer to express them in a businesslike style rather than adopt a scientific approach.

   2 I agree

   3 I neither agree nor disagree

   3 I disagree

Q2 Others would describe me as unassuming.

   2 I agree

   3 I neither agree nor disagree

   3 I disagree

Q3 If a colleague was performing below par I would think very carefully before I criticized him, and even then I would feel uncomfortable about voicing that criticism.

   2 I agree

   3 I neither agree nor disagree

   3 I disagree

Q4 I find the subjects of economics and IT more interesting than physics and biology.

   2 I agree

   3 I neither agree nor disagree

   3 I disagree

Q5 I would rather work behind the scenes than assume a high-profile public or lead role.

   2 I agree

   3 I neither agree nor disagree

   3 I disagree

Q6 I prefer to be left alone to get the job done and find multitasking stressful.

   2 I agree

   3 I neither agree nor disagree

   3 I disagree

Set 3

Q1 I like to keep up to date with developments, especially in technology.

⟦2⟧ I agree

⟦3⟧ I neither agree nor disagree

⟦3⟧ I disagree

Q2 I like all things digital.

⟦2⟧ I agree

⟦3⟧ I disagree

Q3 I have always prided myself on being able to think laterally and outside the box.

⟦2⟧ I agree

⟦3⟧ I neither agree nor disagree

⟦3⟧ I disagree

Q4 I believe that every business must have some written procedures but too many will hold back development.

⟦2⟧ I agree

⟦3⟧ I neither agree nor disagree

⟦3⟧ I disagree

Q5 No matter how gloomy the news I can't help but expect the future to be brighter.

⟦2⟧ I agree

⟦3⟧ I neither agree nor disagree

⟦3⟧ I disagree

Q6 If you must change direction or tactics it is best not to do so while busy with something tricky.

⟦3⟧ I agree

⟦2⟧ I disagree

Set 4

Q1 I am prepared to risk some of my own money on the things I want to do.

2 I agree

3 I neither agree nor disagree

3 I disagree

Q2 I feel resentment if my work impinges on my private life.

3 I agree

2 I neither agree nor disagree

2 I disagree

Q3 I will turn my hand to most things and I am good at one or a few things in particular.

2 I agree

3 I neither agree nor disagree

3 I disagree

Q4 I like to get on with something challenging.

2 I agree

3 I neither agree nor disagree

3 I disagree

Q5 I am looking for something that I can call my own

2 I agree

3 I neither agree nor disagree

3 I disagree

Q6 I tend to get stressed if things don't go to plan.

3 I agree

3 I neither agree nor disagree

2 I disagree

Set 5

Q1   I could be described as being too philosophical and I am prone to observe everyday life as a photographer does his or her subject.

2 I agree

3 I neither agree nor disagree

3 I disagree

Q2   I believe that relying on a partial understanding of a subject will lead to problems.

2 I agree

3 I neither agree nor disagree

3 I disagree

Q3   I prefer a style of teamworking where results are shared rather than a competitive, individualistic style of working.

2 I agree

3 I neither agree nor disagree

3 I disagree

Q4   I criticize my own work too much and I would try to improve on something that is working.

3 I agree

2 I neither agree nor disagree

2 I disagree

Q5   I see nothing strange about browsing definitions in a dictionary or counting the number of frogs in a pond.

2 I agree

3 I neither agree nor disagree

3 I disagree

Q6   I would describe my numerical skills as an area of personal weakness.

3 I agree

3 I neither agree nor disagree

2 I disagree

Set 6

Q1 I am open to new suggestions and if there is a subject in which I have an interest then I am readily drawn into discussion.
2 I agree
3 I neither agree nor disagree
3 I disagree

Q2 I believe that we should all look after our own interests first.
3 I agree
? I neither agree nor disagree
2 I disagree

Q3 I can tough my way through difficult times and can afford to work without pay for a cause I believe in.
2 I agree
3 I neither agree nor disagree
3 I disagree

Q4 I am prepared to bring about change by working from within the current system.
2 I agree
3 I neither agree nor disagree
3 I disagree

Q5 I am willing to work for a cause, whether I get paid or not, that champions the disadvantaged and seeks to make a difference.
2 I agree
3 I disagree

Q6 I can take time out and put something back into society.
2 I agree
3 I disagree

Set 7

Q1 I often feel that situations are made more complex than is necessary and feel far more at ease with the normal and straightforward.

2 I agree

3 I disagree

Q2 I believe that if a job is worth doing it is worth doing well.

2 I agree

3 I neither agree nor disagree

3 I disagree

Q3 I have a strong sense of beauty of both human-made and natural things.

2 I agree

3 I neither agree nor disagree

3 I disagree

Q4 I would rather replace something with the latest model than have it repaired.

3 I agree

3 I neither agree nor disagree

2 I disagree

Q5 I feel more comfortable dealing with something abstract than with something solid.

3 I agree

2 I neither agree nor disagree

2 I disagree

Q6 I believe that I must first serve my time in order to reach my full potential.

2 I agree

3 I neither agree nor disagree

3 I disagree

Set 8

Q1   My social life is busy.
    ☐2 I agree
    ☐3 I disagree

Q2   It is not important to me that I stand out as an individual.
    ☐3 I agree
    ☐2 I neither agree nor disagree
    ☐2 I disagree

Q3   I often suspect that people are talking about me behind my back.
    ☐3 I agree
    ☐3 I neither agree nor disagree
    ☐2 I disagree

Q4   I am sometimes a bit one-track-minded and can be very determined.
    ☐2 I agree
    ☐3 I neither agree nor disagree
    ☐3 I disagree

Q5   I love to feel appreciated.
    ☐2 I agree
    ☐3 I neither agree nor disagree
    ☐3 I disagree

Q6   I have found that being personable helps avoid many potential pitfalls.
    ☐2 I agree
    ☐3 I neither agree nor disagree
    ☐3 I disagree

Set 9

Q1 I want to see incredible earning power from day one and am prepared to work hard for it.

2 I agree

3 I neither agree nor disagree

3 I disagree

Q2 More than anything I want a role where I help make the world a better place.

3 I agree

2 I neither agree nor disagree

2 I disagree

Q3 There are many things I want to do in my life and when I am on holiday I want to enjoy a few luxuries.

2 I agree

3 I neither agree nor disagree

3 I disagree

Q4 I prefer work that is familiar and routine because it helps with my confidence.

3 I agree

2 I neither agree nor disagree

2 I disagree

Q5 My motivation to work to a high standard might suffer if I were in a role that involved delivering the same procedure over and over again.

3 I agree

3 I neither agree nor disagree

2 I disagree

Q6 Others can claim the fame so long as they leave me the fortune.

2 I agree

3 I neither agree nor disagree

3 I disagree

Set 10

Q1 At this point in my life I have more to lose than win.
- 2 I agree
- 3 I neither agree nor disagree
- 3 I disagree

Q2 Within reason it is right to plan for the worst even it is unlikely to happen.
- 2 I agree
- 3 I neither agree nor disagree
- 3 I disagree

Q3 I suspect it is usually better to rebuild a ship plank by plank while remaining afloat than borrow money to commission a new one.
- 2 I agree
- 3 I disagree

Q4 Prudence is undervalued in a lot of businesses.
- 2 I agree
- 3 I neither agree nor disagree
- 3 I disagree

Q5 A consistent correct approach is far better than an equally correct one that relies on inspired bursts of energy.
- 2 I agree
- 3 I neither agree nor disagree
- 3 I disagree

Q6 I have taken risks with my career but now I feel I should play it safe.
- 2 I agree
- 3 I neither agree nor disagree
- 3 I disagree

Set 11

Q1   I feel trapped in my current job because of commitments to, for example, my family or a mortgage.

2️⃣ I agree

3️⃣ I disagree

Q2   I am by nature cautious and will think something through before embarking on it.

2️⃣ I agree

3️⃣ I neither agree nor disagree

3️⃣ I disagree

Q3   I sometimes wish I showed a bit more courage and enterprise.

2️⃣ I agree

3️⃣ I neither agree nor disagree

3️⃣ I disagree

Q4   I would not turn my hobby into my job.

3️⃣ I agree

2️⃣ I neither agree nor disagree

2️⃣ I disagree

Q5   One day when circumstances are favourable I plan to do more of what I love most.

2️⃣ I agree

3️⃣ I neither agree nor disagree

3️⃣ I disagree

Q6   I have a leisure interest that I really enjoy and have followed for years.

2️⃣ I agree

3️⃣ I neither agree nor disagree

3️⃣ I disagree

Set 12

Q1   I have lived by the maxim that when the going gets tough the tough get going.

2 I agree

3 I neither agree nor disagree

3 I disagree

Q2   People without an underlying health condition who are physically unfit can only hold themselves responsible.

2 I agree

3 I neither agree nor disagree

3 I disagree

Q3   I might feel inhibited in some situations but I would describe myself as optimistic.

2 I agree

3 I neither agree nor disagree

3 I disagree

Q4   Winning is not important to me.

3 I agree

2 I neither agree nor disagree

2 I disagree

Q5   I would rather stay at home and read a book than meet some friends to play sport.

3 I agree

3 I neither agree nor disagree

2 I disagree

Q6   I know from personal experience that in order to perfect a skill I have to repeat it over and over.

2 I agree

3 I neither agree nor disagree

3 I disagree

Set 13

Q1   Irrespective of my age I have a broad life experience.
   [2] I agree
   [3] I neither agree nor disagree
   [3] I disagree

Q2   I have an infectious sense of adventure.
   [2] I agree
   [3] I neither agree nor disagree
   [3] I disagree

Q3   I am charmed by one continent in particular and keep travelling there.
   [2] I agree
   [2] I neither agree nor disagree
   [3] I disagree

Q4   My friends would describe me as independent, responsible and resourceful.
   [2] I agree
   [3] I disagree

Q5   Despite what others may say I suspect that running away some-times does help.
   [2] I agree
   [2] I neither agree nor disagree
   [3] I disagree

Q6   I have an infatuation for travel.
   [2] I agree
   [3] I neither agree nor disagree
   [3] I disagree

Set 14

Q1 Others would describe me as passionate for life.
2 I agree
3 I disagree

Q2 I believe that impressive things can be created quickly but complex things cannot.
2 I agree
3 I disagree

Q3 I get enthuslastic about lots of things that I do or read about.
2 I agree
3 I neither agree nor disagree
3 I disagree

Q4 I would rather be a fox than a butterfly.
3 I agree
2 I disagree

Q5 I am ruled more by my heart than my head.
2 I agree
2 I neither agree nor disagree
3 I disagree

Q6 I have never quite understood why I can't have my cake and eat it.
2 I agree
3 I neither agree nor disagree
3 I disagree

Set 15

Q1   I would prefer to write something than help make something.

☐3 I agree

☐2 I neither agree nor disagree

☐2 I disagree

Q2   On a rainy day I would feel much more comfortable in a field than a crowd.

☐2 I agree

☐3 I disagree

Q3   I would rather a job that allowed me to walk to work than one that involved me catching a plane.

☐3 I agree

☐2 I disagree

Q4   I would rather work as a scientist stationed at the South Pole for a few years than spend the time as a director of human resources in downtown New York.

☐2 I agree

☐2 I neither agree nor disagree

☐3 I disagree

Q5   I would prefer to fix something outside rather than attend a meeting to discuss who will fix it.

☐3 I agree

☐3 I neither agree nor disagree

☐2 I disagree

Q6   I would prefer to live in a city rather than halfway up a mountain.

☐3 I agree

☐2 I neither agree nor disagree

☐2 I disagree

Set 16

Q1 I would rather read an article on current social trends than one on home finance.

2 I agree

3 I neither agree nor disagree

3 I disagree

Q2 I find people more interesting if their views are different from mine.

2 I agree

3 I neither agree nor disagree

3 I disagree

Q3 I would get tongue-tied if I tried to speak in front of a large group of people.

3 I agree

2 I neither agree nor disagree

2 I disagree

Q4 I enjoy spending time with friends where the conversation is free ranging.

2 I agree

3 I neither agree nor disagree

3 I disagree

Q5 I am capable of hard work and people would describe me as accomplished.

2 I agree

2 I neither agree nor disagree

3 I disagree

Q6 I would complain if I received bad service in a smart restaurant.

2 I agree

3 I disagree

Set 17

Q1   I don't find the explanations of mainstream science entirely pertinent to the things that interest me.

2 I agree

3 I neither agree nor disagree

3 I disagree

Q2   I am open-minded when it comes to therapies that are based on holistic and mind–body approaches or folk knowledge.

2 I agree

3 I neither agree nor disagree

3 I disagree

Q3   I am comfortable in providing a justification for the conclusions I have reached.

2 I agree

3 I neither agree nor disagree

3 I disagree

Q4   I would find it slightly frustrating to listen to someone who spoke slowly.

3 I agree

3 I neither agree nor disagree

2 I disagree

Q5   I am more compassionate than passionate.

2 I agree

3 I disagree

Q6   To be non-judgemental is to be without an ethical code.

3 I agree

3 I neither agree nor disagree

2 I disagree

Set 18

Q1 I prefer a role in which I enjoy a high degree of autonomy.
2 I agree
3 I disagree

Q2 I believe that integrity should not be compromised.
2 I agree
3 I neither agree nor disagree
3 I disagree

Q3 I like to work in a discipline in which I am qualified.
2 I agree
3 I disagree

Q4 I can commit to working in the same sphere and with similar people for decades.
2 I agree
3 I neither agree nor disagree
3 I disagree

Q5 I am prepared to spend years qualifying and then establishing myself professionally.
2 I agree
3 I neither agree nor disagree
3 I disagree

Q6 The views of those who are qualified in a field should count more than the views of those who are not.
2 I agree
3 I disagree

End of questionnaire.

4

YOUR SCORE AND WHAT IT MEANS

For each question you would have marked an answer notated with either a number two or a three. To identify the sets in which you score highest simply add up the twos.

To score the questionnaire you calculate a total mark for each set. Each set contains six questions. Treat the twos as positive and the threes as negative. So for each set add together the twos (if there are any) and then subtract any threes. For example, if you answered Set 1 with three responses that scored two and three responses that scored three, then you have obtained for that set a score of 6 − 9 = -3. If on the other hand all your answers scored three, then your score would be −18. A set of responses that all scored two would give a score of 12.

Now record your score in each set on the matrix over the page. Ring or highlight your score on the row that corresponds to each of the 18 sets. The possible score range of each set is −18 through to 12. A negative or zero score suggests that you are not interested in careers associated with the set. A positive score suggests you have a preference for work in the area, and the stronger the positive score the stronger your likely preference.

Set 1

-18	-17	-16	-15	-14	-13	-12	-11	-10	-9	-8	-7	-6	-5	-4	-3	-2	-1	0	1	2	3	4	5	6	7	8	9	10	11	12

Set 2

-18	-17	-16	-15	-14	-13	-12	-11	-10	-9	-8	-7	-6	-5	-4	-3	-2	-1	0	1	2	3	4	5	6	7	8	9	10	11	12

Set 3

-18	-17	-16	-15	-14	-13	-12	-11	-10	-9	-8	-7	-6	-5	-4	-3	-2	-1	0	1	2	3	4	5	6	7	8	9	10	11	12

Set 4

-18	-17	-16	-15	-14	-13	-12	-11	-10	-9	-8	-7	-6	-5	-4	-3	-2	-1	0	1	2	3	4	5	6	7	8	9	10	11	12

Set 5

-18	-17	-16	-15	-14	-13	-12	-11	-10	-9	-8	-7	-6	-5	-4	-3	-2	-1	0	1	2	3	4	5	6	7	8	9	10	11	12

Set 6

-18	-17	-16	-15	-14	-13	-12	-11	-10	-9	-8	-7	-6	-5	-4	-3	-2	-1	0	1	2	3	4	5	6	7	8	9	10	11	12

Set 7

-18	-17	-16	-15	-14	-13	-12	-11	-10	-9	-8	-7	-6	-5	-4	-3	-2	-1	0	1	2	3	4	5	6	7	8	9	10	11	12

Set 8

-18	-17	-16	-15	-14	-13	-12	-11	-10	-9	-8	-7	-6	-5	-4	-3	-2	-1	0	1	2	3	4	5	6	7	8	9	10	11	12

Set 9

-18	-17	-16	-15	-14	-13	-12	-11	-10	-9	-8	-7	-6	-5	-4	-3	-2	-1	0	1	2	3	4	5	6	7	8	9	10	11	12

Set 10

-18	-17	-16	-15	-14	-13	-12	-11	-10	-9	-8	-7	-6	-5	-4	-3	-2	-1	0	1	2	3	4	5	6	7	8	9	10	11	12

Set 11

-18	-17	-16	-15	-14	-13	-12	-11	-10	-9	-8	-7	-6	-5	-4	-3	-2	-1	0	1	2	3	4	5	6	7	8	9	10	11	12

Set 12

-18	-17	-16	-15	-14	-13	-12	-11	-10	-9	-8	-7	-6	-5	-4	-3	-2	-1	0	1	2	3	4	5	6	7	8	9	10	11	12

Set 13

-18	-17	-16	-15	-14	-13	-12	-11	-10	-9	-8	-7	-6	-5	-4	-3	-2	-1	0	1	2	3	4	5	6	7	8	9	10	11	12

Set 14

-18	-17	-16	-15	-14	-13	-12	-11	-10	-9	-8	-7	-6	-5	-4	-3	-2	-1	0	1	2	3	4	5	6	7	8	9	10	11	12

Set 15

-18	-17	-16	-15	-14	-13	-12	-11	-10	-9	-8	-7	-6	-5	-4	-3	-2	-1	0	1	2	3	4	5	6	7	8	9	10	11	12

Set 16

-18	-17	-16	-15	-14	-13	-12	-11	-10	-9	-8	-7	-6	-5	-4	-3	-2	-1	0	1	2	3	4	5	6	7	8	9	10	11	12

Set 17

-18	-17	-16	-15	-14	-13	-12	-11	-10	-9	-8	-7	-6	-5	-4	-3	-2	-1	0	1	2	3	4	5	6	7	8	9	10	11	12

Set 18

-18	-17	-16	-15	-14	-13	-12	-11	-10	-9	-8	-7	-6	-5	-4	-3	-2	-1	0	1	2	3	4	5	6	7	8	9	10	11	12

Record the set numbers below in which you scored highest

First

Second

Third

Now review the interpretations of your score in each of these sets and review the careers associated with these sets in Chapter 5.

Case study Roberto scored highest in Sets 6, 10 and 15. He scored +7 in all three sets (his next highest score was +4). He found the interpretation and careers linked to Set 15 ('the outdoor type', discussed later in this chapter) most relevant, especially the sentiment that he 'would rather come back later than queue at the post office, and window shopping on a busy high street is really not his thing'. He has recently started work as a horticultural assistant.

Case study Jo scored +12 (the maximum) in two categories and +2 in five other categories. All her other scores were negative. Of the five +2 categories, she thought two were totally off the mark. Once she had dismissed these, she found the analysis insightful.

What if I obtain my highest score in more than three sets?

Some people are harder to read than others. If your questionnaire does not reveal a strong preference but instead indicates a preference for a good few areas but no outright winners, then first recalculate your scores to make sure you have not made an error in marking the questionnaire. If this does not change things, then review the questions that comprise those sets in the questionnaire in which you obtained your highest scores and change any that on reflection you would answer differently, and re-score your questionnaire. If you still face a top score in more than three sets, then read the interpretations of the sets below and decide on three that you find most pertinent to you. The feedback below, while hopefully you find it to be true of you, may be in some respects exaggerated.

What your score means

Your motivations and interests as identified in the questionnaire provide insights into the sort of person you are and the sort of work that you would enjoy.

Set 1

You have increasingly felt dissatisfied with your current situation. You accept it as what you have to do to survive but increasingly you feel frustrated by it and you know that in the long run you will need to start afresh.

You have not always cared for the trappings of modern life but you have nevertheless collected a good many and now they hang heavy around your neck. You find the impulse to get out and go somewhere, anywhere, almost irresistible. You know that the day approaches when you will need to cut yourself free and go and do something completely different. The good news is that, while you may not know what you want to do, you are willing to study or retrain and develop your skills further and this will help identify a pathway to your next adventure.

Set 2

You work best undisturbed and unknown, a safe distance from the public eye. You have the potential to be or are already accomplished in what you do. You are happiest when you can be a master of your trade but prefer not to take up the role of the person in charge or the name on the cover. You take quiet pleasure from a reported compliment and are able to learn from informed criticism but may feel uncomfortable if you come face to face with either praise or complaint.

You know what is best and what could be better. You are pragmatic and difficult to fool. You make your words count and have little time for vague hypotheses or sweeping generalizations. You like to establish the facts of the matter and would make a good scientist but you prefer commerce over science.

You would describe reading as a means to an end and you find facts much more interesting than fiction. You have a number of interests that you pursue in your leisure time. You are IT literate, a good communicator and can rely on your own initiative. You possess good problem-solving skills and have excellent planning and organization abilities.

Set 3

You have optimistic expectations for the future and are a fan of change; you are careful to stay up to date in your outlook and do not find it at all difficult to break with the past or tradition. In the spheres in which you work or study you may be considered ahead of your time and therefore you sometimes feel misunderstood. You are dynamic and feel frustration at the slow pace at which some colleagues adopt new working practices. You feel that too many regulations stifle progress.

Set 4

It is time you gave serious consideration to working for yourself or starting a business. You are a pragmatist and more interested in results than the means by which the results are obtained, but this does not mean that you lack integrity. You have an infectious enthusiasm and a strong drive to succeed. You believe luck is something people make rather than find. You rarely cave in to outside pressures. You may not enjoy it but you know that you can perform well, even shine, when stressed and you know that it pays to minimize disagreements because they are bad for business. You have the passion and the obsession to be an entrepreneur.

Set 5

You value a logical and scientific approach and prefer something to be substantiated before you rely on it. Collaboration and teamwork are your preferred ways of working. You have a commitment to lifelong learning and are attracted to the idea of full-time guiding learning in a new discipline. You have a good eye for detail. Compromise is not something you find easy or even something you much respect. You are idealistic, loyal and honest, if inclined towards a philosophical detachment that means you sometimes feel the need to withdraw or stand back. Simplicity is in your eyes a great quality. It sometimes comes as a surprise that not everyone agrees with you.

Ideas, abstract concepts and plans may consume you to the point where others find it difficult to get close to you. You see little point in compromise and would prefer to see an idea through to its logical conclusion. On occasions you may have to force yourself to pay suitable attention to the world of daily life and appointments. You are not afraid to revise your views and embark on a radical overhaul of your assumptions and conclusions. You are capable of originality. When wrapped up in your thoughts you are prone to forgetfulness.

Set 6

You are interested in society. Up to a point you are happy to go with the flow but you have clear ideas on a wide range of subjects and an unwavering view of what is right and wrong. In a quiet, unassuming way you will serve a cause. You believe that everyone should be given an equal chance and that we need to find a more sustainable way to live. You are interested in developing new skills. You feel a strong bond with the environment and humanity. But you are more a reformer than a revolutionary.

You are inclusive by nature but frustrated by time wasters. You are open to the need to keep your skills up to date through further training when necessary. You may want to rebuild your own confidence and definitely want to put something back.

You enjoy listening to the current affairs programmes on the radio. When excited about a subject you will discuss it and reflect on it long after the interest of others has waned. You are not over concerned with money or material possessions, needing only enough to be comfortable.

Set 7

You ultimately have a very straightforward approach to life. You are creative and intelligent, but express your thoughts and creativity through tangible things. You see the past as at least as good as the present and you mistrust industrial processes that alienate and de-skill. You are socially aware and find the process of production as interesting as the product itself, and you most certainly don't believe in change for its own sake. You have a strong sense of tradition.

Necessity has shown that you can turn your hand to most things. But your thoroughness means that you yearn to truly master one thing. You take pleasure from the achievement of something that might appear to others as routine but that you see as something approaching perfection. You will not easily give up once you have embarked on a project or course of action. And you will work at something until it meets with your own meticulous standards.

Set 8

You are thrilled when others are attracted to you. You are at your best when the attraction is mutual, and then almost anything seems possible and sometimes it is.

You are goal oriented. You like to finish a job and find it difficult to ask others for assistance. Friends and family turn to you and have usually taken your advice. People would describe you as possessing charm and persuasiveness.

You are never short of something to say and find it entirely natural to strike up a conversation with a complete stranger. You have a wide circle of friends and love a party. You are extremely aware of how you appear to others and are happy to look, dress and act the part.

Set 9

After a hard day's work you don't expect to have to visit the value range of foods at your local supermarket; you like to be able to spoil yourself with some choice items from the deli counter, or to hail a taxi without worrying unduly about the cost. You know that having no money at all is extremely difficult and is something to be avoided. It might seem shallow to some, but you don't have much problem with the fact that earning good money is a sign that you are respected and valued. You would always choose more cash over fringe benefits such as a company car, subsidized canteen and medical insurance.

Putting money first does not mean that you have few interests. The truth is quite the opposite as there are lots of things you like to do. It's just that you expect your work to fund these things and it all comes down to money.

Set 10

From your perspective, preserving and protecting what has already been achieved is the logical first priority. You nurture things if necessary for months and years and are capable of demonstrating great dedication to a task. You are not opposed to change or new developments but see the day-to-day job of getting something done as equal to, or more important than, the implementing of radical change. You see risk as a necessary evil to be taken only when circumstances demand, and only then when careful safeguards have first been put in place. You can stay calm in a difficult situation and, no matter your age, would agree that you have a mature attitude. You now want to take profit from the rewards of the past and place those gains out of harm's way.

Set 11

You believe in being fully prepared before you get on with something worthwhile. You are capable of holding down an ordinary job while in the evenings and weekends you pursue your true interest. You may not consciously realize it but in this way you have put yourself through years of quiet training. When you are ready you must take the step to present the fruits of your labour to an audience wider than friends and family. At some stage you must give up the day job and spend the greater part of your time doing what you love most. When the right moment arrives, be sure you are ready and go for it.

Set 12

You have the courage and daring to try to win. Your willingness 'to go one step further than others' is born of a quiet optimism. You are naturally competitive even against yourself. You know how to make sure that people function well as a part of a team but you find it difficult to be anywhere but in the driving seat. Like a caged animal you pace when constrained and feel intense frustration if denied the opportunity to keep up your exercise regime. Your physical appearance is an important aspect of your self-esteem and you judge yourself and others harshly if they let themselves go. You would agree that much of life is a competition.

Set 13

Free you must be. You have itchy feet and often find yourself absorbed in dreams about faraway places. You pursue those dreams at every opportunity. You are counting the days to your next trip. Your favourite television is travel shows and you are an avid reader of travel books and magazines. If only you could travel more, or better still be paid to travel. Sooner or later you must follow your heart and make travel your career. All that is left to decide is whether you are a travel geek or a wannabe beach bum.

Set 14

You sparkle and are fun-loving and expressive, and people love you for it. There is hardly a dull moment in your life. Your passion brings such energy and commitment, but alone it will not carry you further than a year or two into a project and you risk once more finding yourself tired and looking for something new. You must find a role that daily, even hourly, highlights the reason for your early excitement. This will help sustain you and the role will continue to be enriched by your flair and creative endeavour.

Set 15

You are meant to live and work where you have space to breath. This might well be in the wilderness but in the right role it could also be in an urban setting. You would rather come back later than queue at the post office, and window shopping on a busy high street is really not your thing. The idea of being tied to an office is for you as attractive as serving a prison sentence. You are more impressed by action than talk. You may or may not be physically large but you have a physical presence that means you are noticed. You may not have a great deal to say but you are insightful and have a talent at bringing a conversation to the main point.

Set 16

You value the art of conversation and debate, and are adept in it. You find quickness of thought, wit, charm and humour attractive. An exchange of views is your oxygen and, while you try not to show it, you enjoy an audience. You will not submit to what you perceive as

injustice and when necessary can be combative. While not deliber-
ately setting out to do so, you often find that you have made yourself
indispensable.

Set 17

Your own and others' well-being and inner health are things you are
interested in and you nurture them. You are emotionally open, sensi-
tive to the feelings of others, receptive to possibilities and a seeker
of truth. You are fascinated by the ways of nature and the power of
healing, and are curious to understand better things that as far as you
are concerned are currently not fully explained. You value non-verbal
communication as much as or more than verbal. You appreciate the
importance of touch and know the power of silence and listening.

Set 18

Your good name is more important to you than money. You have a
highly developed sense of integrity and independence and are
capable of sustained hard work. You will not rest until you have estab-
lished yourself and won the respect of others. You are prepared, if not
always happy, to continue in a chosen activity for the duration of your
working life. You recognize the need to maintain and nurture working
relationships and get the job done to your own exacting standards.
You feel a need for or have an in-depth knowledge of a subject, are
able to administrate your own affairs and work under pressure.

5

BANG-UP-TO-DATE CAREER IDEAS

This chapter describes 900 career ideas. They are organized into groups of 50 or more and listed under 18 sets of interests and motivations. The only exception is Set 4, 'Impatient for some venture', which has a listing of 25 suggestions.

To make best use of this chapter, start with the jobs listed under the three sets in which you obtained the highest scores. These will be the jobs that are best suited for someone with your interests, aptitude and inclinations. Review the lists and descriptions. Don't worry at this stage if the ideas seem too ambitious or just not realistic. Suspend your disbelief and push aside any practical objections until later.

Sources of further information are provided for all ideas. In some cases these sources will apply to many of the suggested career ideas, so do investigate them even if that particular example is not the one that most catches your interest. The descriptions are intended to provide sufficient information for you to make a decision to include them or rule them out. They have succeeded in this objective if you are able to decide that they warrant further investigation or that you know enough to reject them as not for you.

You will of course immediately know that some of the suggestions are not what you are looking for, but try not to reject too many of the suggestions out of hand. Sleep on it so that your subconscious has a chance to work. Go over the three sets again after a few days to see if on reflection there is merit to an idea that you missed on the first read. Allow yourself the luxury of giving consideration to something you have not considered before.

The three sets of ideas will total between 125 to 170 suggestions, depending on the mix of sets. These jobs represent a (long) shortlist from the 900 ideas, and once you have allowed yourself some time to mull over them all you should begin to shorten the list with the aim of producing your own dream list of career ideas. Start by selecting at least one, two or three suggestions from each set and add them to a list of possible dream careers. By all means select more. It may be that a good few similar careers interest you, and if that is the case then your dream list may number tens of ideas. Now widen your search and browse the entire list of 900 suggestions, adding further careers to your dream list as you go. No one can say how many dream careers you should have. And for the time being, the more the better. Later you can try and prioritize them in terms of your favourites.

If you suffer a disability and if your ability to undertake a job could be adversely affected, then speak to an employer in the area that interests you at an early stage and seek their advice as to whether or not it is possible to organize things in that occupation in a way to accommodate your needs.

Create your own shortlist of dream careers by placing a tick in the box alongside the ideas that really appeal.

Set 1: Something completely different

It's time for something completely different, so reflect on the following 56 career ideas, and the courses and training pathways that lead to them.

1   Agriculture. If you like the idea of growing food, flowers or biofuels, then give farming a look. There are many courses of study to follow in farm management, livestock and crop growing. These days farming demands skills such as the operating of large machinery, managing gangs at harvest time, completing paperwork for subsidies and keeping accounts. See the *Farmers' Weekly* website at www.fwi.co.uk.

2 Tourism and travel. There are a great many specializations in tourism and travel. You can study to obtain qualifications in air fairs and ticketing, children's holidays rep work, worldwide travel destinations, or work as a resort rep, tour guide and in management. It really helps if you can speak a foreign language or two and specialize in a continent or a type of holiday such as skiing and snow-boarding, cruises or eco holidays to name but a few. You will find lots of information on careers in tourism and travel at, for example, www.travelweekly.co.uk, www.visitbritain.org and www.ttglive.com.

3 Jazz band musician. Learn to blow your own trumpet or trombone, tuba, French horn or for that matter any musical instrument. Further information is available for every local college of further education that will offer classes in most instruments. Many musicians offer private lessons to supplement their earnings.

Further information: why not train for and take part in the London New Year's Day parade, which is televised and watched by tens of thousands of spectators lining the streets. Find out more at www.londonparade.co.uk and click on the 'how to be in it' button.

4 Storyteller. Have you ever seen a group of children captivated by a good storyteller? It's a lost form of art and one that can provide a livelihood reading or telling stories at libraries, community centres and children's parties. It might be just what you are looking for if you like myth, folklore and the dramatic arts. For further information check out your local college as many offer courses on myths of the British Isles, magic, witchcraft and classical mythology. Why not get along to one of the many storyteller festivals. You can find details at, for example, www.festivalattheedge.org, www.weststoryfest.co.uk, www.beyondtheborder.com or www.scottishstorytellingcentre.co.uk.

5 Digital animation. Cartooning for profit might well interest you if you are artistic and computer literate. Digital animations are used widely by the health and safety industry and on public transport as well as in advertising and entertainment. There are one-day animation seminars, introductions to clay modelling for animation, cartoonists' workshops and full-time two- or four-year professional courses. For further information contact, for example, The Camberwell College of Art.

6 Homemaker. Some people are trying to get away from home, others are trying to escape work. If you are in the second category then why not consider making a career as a homemaker. It's a role that is increasingly undertaken by men as well as women. It's without a doubt a full-time job and brings many rewards. A recommended read is *The Art of Homemaking for Today* by Daryl Hoole.

7 Ranger. Rangers manage common land, national parks or sites of special scientific interest. They patrol, help maintain fencing, remove invasive foreign species and keep a log of visitors and other records. For further information courses exist for ranger skills certificates and ranger supervisors. See, for example, Capel Manor College: www.capel.ac.uk.

8 Run away and join the circus. Why not learn a circus art such as juggling, fire eating or clowning. There are open days, youth programmes, adult evening classes and degree courses available. For further information visit, for example, www.circusspace.co.uk (London) or www.circuscentre.org (San Francisco).

9 Classic vehicle repair and restoration. There isn't a form of transport that doesn't have an enthusiastic following; car maintenance classes are available almost everywhere and courses in classic car maintenance and repair, body repair and restoration are also widely available. There are classes too in motorcycle and heavy vehicle repair offered at most colleges of further education. For inspiration visit www.classicautorepairandrestoration.com.

10 Sports training and management. Courses for aerobic instructors, circuit training, body conditioning, pilates, weights workout, personal trainers and fitness instructors ranging through to training for professional and managerial qualifications are offered all over the country. Delivering classes will not make you rich financially but you sure will be fit. Sports management involves the running of a sports facility or centre. See, for example, the University of Kent's site, www.kent.ac.uk/careers/workin/sport.htm.

11 Help industry go green. Waste management, recycling, energy awareness, energy conservation, environmental policy and action planning, environmental impact assessments and cleaning science are just a few of the disciplines that you can study and apply professionally. You can undertake a BSc in environmental geology, or a cleaning operative proficiency certificate or one of the many applied environmental science courses that equip you with the skills needed by industry. Find out more at www.greenjobs.co.uk and www.environmentjob.co.uk.

12 Soft furnishings and upholstery. Soft furnishing includes curtain and blind making, chair caning and rush work, loose covers, patchwork and quilting. Retraining in upholstery is available for beginners through to advanced levels. See the Association of Master Upholsterers and Soft Furnishers at www.upholsterers.co.uk.

13 Civil engineering and ground work. This is hot, hard, really satisfying work. Moving mountains, shifting roads, clearing vegetation and top soil, excavating hills, backfilling to make level, and landscaping and replanting the site are some of the tasks undertaken. See the Institution of Civil Engineers at www.ice.org.uk/.

14 Recording and production of music. There are 10-day introductions to the audio industry and 10-week evening courses on making and recording music digitally, as well as one-year HND courses in music production. For further information check with your local college of further education.

15 Community worker. Community and youth workers promote the social inclusion and development of young adults and individuals drawn from disadvantaged communities. You can obtain professional qualifications at degree or postgraduate level or specialize in a great many activities such as child protection, managing challenging behaviour and being a community warden. You will find jobs as a community worker listed at www.opportunities.co.uk.

16 A hair professional. Why not create looks and wow factor as a stylist or hairdresser. Top stylists can earn very good money and choose between job offers. Once you are qualified and experienced, there is nothing stopping you becoming self-employed and working from home, running your own salon, working on a cruise ship or at a hotel in some exotic location. For further information google 'hair stylist careers' and you will find loads of information and suggestions.

17 Complementary therapies. You can take up the study of anatomy and physiology to lay the foundations for your study of complementary therapies, or get started straight away by joining a class in acupressure, Chinese herbal medicine, Reiki healing or music therapy, to name but a few of the options available. You can also study complementary health science, on courses ranging from a few days introduction to a three-year full-time degree course or postgraduate MPhil. Find out more by browsing www.chisuk.org.uk and www.ctha.com.

18 Forklift truck or excavator operator. If you like to drive or play computer games, then consider a career as a heavy plant or forklift truck operative. There are always unfilled vacancies in this important skill area, and with enough practice you can become really good at it. For training, see the Association of Truck Trainers at www.itssar.org.uk and for information see www.logisticshandling.com.

19 E-commerce. Find out how to set up an e-shop or make the most of eBay and online selling and marketing. Further information: there are courses from two weeks' duration to one-year part-time or evening training in e-commerce. Start your research by reading www.websitemagazine.com or www.internetretailing.net.

20 Welding and light metalwork. Fabricating bespoke items from wrought iron and mild steel for the home or garden can make a satisfying, varied, small business activity. There are introductory and competency classes in metal arc gas welding and fabrication lasting from a few weeks to a year. Longer classes lead to craft qualifications. See for example www.hgt.gwynedd.gov.uk/emta/weldingasacareer.htm.

21 Cook or chef. French, Italian, Japanese, Asian, Chinese and Arab cookery classes are available at evenings and weekends. Making ice cream, baking bread, preparing soups, sauces, sandwiches and cakes are offered as specialist subject classes too. There are certificated courses from a few days in length leading to a health and hygiene certificate through to professional cookery scholarships that last two years full-time. Find out more at www.caterer.com and www.chefsearch.co.uk.

22 Pest controller. When animals like rats, mice, roaches, wasps, bees and pigeons pose a risk to public health, they get labelled vermin and it is the responsibility of a pest controller to remove them. Controllers do this by using physical barriers, poisons and traps. Qualifications and courses are available. For further information search The British Pest Control Association's site at www.bpca.org.uk/.

23 Floristry. Flower-arranging classes are hugely popular and florists use their strong sense of colour, form and artistic sense to create displays and sell flowers. You can work as an assistant florist while you train. You will find lots of useful information at, for example, www.fusionflowers.com and www.britishfloristassociation.org.

24 Inshore fisherman/woman. While the opportunities on the larger fishing fleets are in decline because of overfishing and quotas you can still earn a living through sustainable inshore fishing for shellfish and white fish especially if you sell directly to the public through farmers' markets or from your boat. For further information visit www.seafish.org.

25 A trade in the construction industry. Or for that matter any of the building trades from painter and decorator or carpenter to heating and ventilation installer. If you enjoy DIY then there are dozens of vocational courses and taster courses on offer for people like you who want to find out if they would like to join one of the trades. There are even courses that offer additional encouragement to women to take up one of the trades. For further information and advice on courses and training in the construction industry, see www.cskills.org.

26 Recycling officer. Recycling officers work for local authorities and help residents recycle a larger portion of their waste. They plan, help form policy and set targets for recycling, and get involved in the detail of where to place recycle bins, how to communicate the value of recycling, and educate the public. Successful candidates are likely to hold qualifications in environmental science or environmental management and to have been active in related voluntary projects. Google 'Recycling officer' and you will find loads of job descriptions and some job leads.

27 Childcare. Vocations involving the care and development of pre-school children account for the majority of work in this important area. You can provide childcare in your own home,

at a nursery school or in a crèche at a public place, or run
a playgroup at a holiday resort or on a cruise ship.
You can specialize in the care of bilingual children or those
who speak English as a second language (ESL) and children
with special or additional needs. For older children you can
train in supporting children in the classroom who have
difficulty reading or who are dyslexic, or provide care after
school or during school holidays. Useful sites include
www.professionalchildcare.co.uk and
www.nurseryworld.co.uk.

28 Costume designer. If you have always been dazzled by
glamour and glitz and have sewing skills, then get yourself
along to the Venice or Rio Carnival for inspiration and join a
course in design and textiles. For further information you will
find short and taster courses offered by the London College
of Fashion and Saint Martins College of Art and Design.

29 Beauty and makeup. Makeup for photography, the catwalk,
the theatre, film and TV are some of the specialist training
courses available. There are also classes on natural
treatments, body art, and products such as Henna and
age-defying makeup as well as subjects such as Spa
management and nail art. For inspiration visit, for example,
www.beauty-school.co.uk.

30 Gardening and garden crafts. There are many careers to enjoy
if you have a passion for gardening and there are a great many
courses to consider. Amenity (public) gardens, allotments and
organic gardens, urban and small gardens, ponds and water
features, hanging baskets, hard landscaping and weed and
pest control are a small sample of the subjects covered.
There are also courses on the operation of equipment such
as chainsaws and brushwood clippers, and courses on garden
design and planting design. For inspiration see Waterperry
Gardens (Gardening Courses, Arts Courses and Craft) at
www.waterperrygardens.co.uk.

31 Counselling. If supporting individuals, couples and families
interests you then browse the host of training courses
available in counselling. You can specialize in a variety of
techniques and train to help with, for example, eating
disorders, parents, adolescents, substance dependency,
mental illness, domestic violence, sexuality, bereavement

and anger. For more information go to www.bacp.co.uk; for jobs see www.nhscareers.nhs.uk.

32 Sugar craft. This work includes, for example, exotic floral creations, novelty figures and models as well as cake decorating. There's always a market for cakes for children's birthdays, weddings, anniversaries and Christmas. There are many courses available at every level from beginners to advanced in sugar craft and cake decorating. For inspiration see www.sugarcraft.com.

33 Animal care. A love of animals can make a rewarding vocation, and training in the discipline is an excellent way to make it a career. There are courses in pet store management, veterinary nursing, animal technology and livestock health as well as introductory and hobby courses in dog training, grooming, pet first aid, even yoga for pets. See for example www.rspca.org.uk/in-action/aboutus/careers.

34 Forensic science. You can work as a crime scene investigator, collecting evidence and preventing its contamination, or as a forensic scientist. There are many access-to-science courses available and these would serve well as a feeder to both occupations. To become a forensic scientist, taking one of the forensic biology, forensic science or investigative analysis courses at the BSc level would be a good next step. It might help to gain a postgraduate qualification and extensive laboratory experience on the way. For further information google 'crime scene investigator' or 'crime scene officer'.

35 Interior design. If you love home-makeover programmes and have turned your own space into something rather special, then investigate a career in interior design.

Further information: The Chelsea College of Art and Design and lots of other colleges have a wide range of courses. And many other institutions offer short, weekend and longer programmes for the beginner right through to the professional. Get yourself along to www.interiorsbirmingham.com. And view www.100percentdesign.co.uk.

36 Photography. The art of photography and photographic processes has expanded and diversified since it went digital. There are introductory and highly specialist courses that last just a day through to full-time three-year programmes of guided learning. For further information see for example www.blake.ac.uk.

37 Journalism. News for the papers, television, radio and internet is written by either highly specialist freelancers or salaried generalists. Freelance journalists will specialize in science, medicine, engineering – in fact every profession – or any of a huge number of special interests from parenting to computer gaming. The emergence of the internet has greatly increased the opportunities for a career in this once cut-throat business. There are many courses to follow, from speechwriting, writing a press release, journalism for broadcasting or magazines, sub-editing, editing or proof-reading. For further information see www.nuj.org, the site of the National Union of Journalists.

38 Calligraphy and sign writing. Beautiful lettering produced by traditional methods is highly valued. Restaurants, hotels and antique shops for example prefer handmade signs. Calligraphic gifts and Chinese calligraphy are popular.

For further information there is a wide range of classes from one-day introductions to 36-week part-time courses in lettering, calligraphy and sign writing. For inspiration see, for example, http://ozichalkart.com/services.html.

39 Housing. A great number of people and specializations are employed in housing and its related occupations. Planning, the provision of social housing, sustainable communities, city regeneration, real estate management and sales, lettings, the inclusion of tenants in the planning process, surveying, valuation and conveyancing are but a small sample of these roles. Training and professional qualifications in housing are widely available. For further information, see www.cih.org (Charted Institute of Housing).

40 Retail. Whether you sell on eBay or manage a supermarket with a multi-million pound turnover every week, you are in the retail business. Retail obviously involves selling but it also involves warehousing, management, finance, marketing, buying, stock control, record keeping and administration. There are short courses in customer care, sales techniques and range-building, and full-time year-long programmes in for example retail management and specialist retail areas such as fashion. If you are interested in a career in retail, then visit www.inretail.co.uk and www.retailcareers.co.uk.

41 Care. The care of adolescents, adults and older people involves a great many specializations. You can concentrate on helping older people improve their memory or care for those suffering from dementia, you can help support vulnerable people or people in secure settings, you can offer palliative care or help people realize new horizons, you can help teenagers and adolescents make the transition to adult life. Find jobs in senior care at, for example, www.workhound.co.uk/jobs and www.indeed.co.uk.

42 Physiotherapy and massage. Sports injury therapy, rehabilitation therapy, remedial massage, Shiatsu, deep tissue massage, aromatherapy and anatomy are some of the subjects you can study to prepare you for practice as a physiotherapist or masseur. For further information, visit the www.londoncollegeofmassage.co.uk.

43 Marketing. If you have a background in either sales or the collection and analysis of data, then marketing might be for you. In some roles you will need to have people skills; in others data analysis and data building experience will be essential. There are many courses in both the analysis and evaluation of data and communications. There are specialist programmes of learning in sectors such as marketing for the travel industry and luxury brands, as well as academic courses in social research and professional courses leading to membership of the Chartered Institute of Marketing. See for example the Marketing Society's website at www.marketing-society.org.uk, the Chartered Institute of Marketing at www.cim.co.uk and the Direct Marketing Association at www.dma.org.uk.

44 Law. Don't just think barristers and solicitors when it comes to law. There are also clerks, paralegals, court staff, representatives and certified conveyancers, to name but a few of the legal occupations. There are a huge number of specialist areas, including for example employment law, medical and media law, international, European and human rights law, intellectual property law, maritime law and Islamic law. For further information visit www.lawsociety.org.

45 Join the Faststream. The UK Civil Service's accelerated promotion scheme is called the Faststream. Competition is so strong that it's a job in itself to get on the programme. But if you are up for a challenge and fancy getting involved in some of the more interesting projects in government, then visit www.faststream.gov.uk.

46 Become a firefighter. Firefighters save people and property from the dangers of fire, road accidents and flood. They also work in their local community to help prevent fires and accidents. For every vacancy there are around 40 applicants, so you will have to train yourself to pass the recruitment process that examines your physical fitness, personality and aptitude for the role. Each fire authority has its own recruitment team but follows national standards. Search, for example, www.London-fire.gov.uk.

47 Tailoring. Caps, berets, bags, purses, hats, scarves, African and Asian clothes, bridal wear, drapery, millinery and couture garments are but a few of the specialist courses available to the budding or advanced tailor. For further information there are a huge variety of courses from taster to advanced at community colleges and prestigious establishments such as the London College of Fashion.

48 Jewellery, ceramics and glass. Allow your artistic/craft side to flourish by training in bead making, enamelling, silverwork, throwing on the wheel, mosaics, glass art or stained glass. There are classes ranging from the beginner to advanced levels. Once you are ready, book a table at a local craft fair and offer your work for sale. You never know where it might lead. You can find out more about the jewellery industry at, for example, www.bja.org.uk and www.jewellerylondon.com.

49 Community liaison officer. If you have experience of working with community groups in your area and have great communications skills, then community liaison might interest you. All sorts of employers recruit them, including police authorities, embassies and airports. Get yourself trained for such a position by undertaking voluntary work, learning a minority language and attending training in equality and diversity. A great source of job leads in local authority and the public sector is found at www.opportunities.co.uk.

50 Nutrition and food science. There are many openings in these fields, including detoxification, dieting and healthy eating advice, food hygiene, food safety, clinical nutrition and food technology. A food hygiene certificate qualifies you to prepare food in a sandwich bar for example. A year-long course in diet and nutrition will allow complementary therapists to offer advice on healthier foods and special diets. A degree or Higher National Diploma in food technology will qualify you to start work in the food industry in the development and production of processed foods. See for example the University of Nottingham's BSc degree at www.nottingham.ac.uk/biosciences/prospectivestudents/undergraduate/courses/bscnutritionandfoodscience.

51 Hospitality management. Managers in the hospitality industry run hotels or restaurants – anything from fast-food outlets to five-star establishments. It's multi-skilled and if you want to work internationally, then study languages as well as international hospitality management. There are apprenticeships, short courses such as the Welcome Host certificate operated by the UK tourist board, or training in silver service and courses for supervisors as well as managerial roles. Begin your research at, for example, www.enjoyengland.com, www.visitlondon.com and www.visitbritain.org.

52 Key skills trainer. Trainers in key skills deliver training for life and employment to adults. They will teach for example literacy, numeracy, IT, job-search skills and pathways to work. There are many courses offering training for trainers in, for example, life coaching, skills for working life and citizenship. For information visit www.keyskills4u.com/KS/whatareKS.

53 Charity shop volunteer and manager. The volunteers are unpaid but the manager usually has a salary. Many of the organizations that raise funds through the shops provide training for both their volunteers and managers. Courses for charity shop volunteers are also offered by a few colleges. See, for example, www.redcross.org.uk/, www.supportus.cancerresearchuk.org and www.charityshops.org.uk/links.html.

54 Digital hardware maintenance and repair. If you are fed up with the 'it's broken let's buy a new one' culture or simply would love to know how things work, then consider one of the many courses available on hardware maintenance. There are courses available on the maintenance and repair of digital cameras, mobile phones and computers to name but a few. For a host of companies offering computer repair and maintenance visit www.computerrepaircompanies.co.uk.

Visit the website of a distributor of repair products at www.uk.farnell.com. For training, see what this organization is doing: www.digital-links.org.

55 The French Foreign Legion. If things are really bad you might consider the Legion. They don't recruit criminals any more (and they only take men), all recruits must assume a new name on joining and they can expect a hard time.

56 Jobs in space. Imagine helping to build satellites for weather forecasting or observations. EUMETSAT, based in Darmstadt, Germany, does just that and if you are a citizen of one the many countries that contribute to this European organization's work then you can apply for work there. Visit www.eumetsat.int.

Set 2: Away from the full glare of publicity

You prefer to be a step away from the limelight so a back-of-house, back-room or behind-the-scenes role might be just right for you. There are hundreds of them. Review the 50 suggested below and see if any catch your imagination.

1 Secret shopper. Pose as a customer and gather information on the service you receive and get paid to do it. Secret shoppers are quite widely used in retail and restaurant chains and hotel and holiday resort groups. Secret shoppers are market researchers by training. To find out about careers in market research and training that can lead to a career as a secret shopper, visit www.mrs.org.uk, the site of the Market Research Society.

2 Proof readers and copy editors review manuscripts, website copy, publicity material reports, in fact virtually anything written that needs to be without errors. Proof readers make sure the work is consistent with the house style, that references are complete and the grammar is correct. Further information can be found at www.sfep.org.uk.

3 Statisticians generate, prepare, analyse and categorize statistical data. They amass the data and prepare it for release in the form of statistical reports used in forecasts and decision making. To see careers in many of the areas where statisticians work, visit the Royal Statistical Society's website at www.rss.org.uk/careers.

4   Cargo tracker. This role involves following the progress of valuable or important cargoes. The consignment might be cigarettes on the back of a lorry, works of art for an exhibition, a container full of silicon chips on a shipment or diamonds being flown into Amsterdam. The career is an expanding area and draws from logistics, security and the insurance industry. For careers and vacancies, visit for example www.fedex.com.

5   Auditor. Auditors analyse and test financial information to verify its accuracy. They usually work internally if employed by a company, or externally if, for example, they work for government. For a career in auditing, visit www.kpmgcareers.com.

6   Access officer. Local authorities employ access officers to inspect access arrangements for people with restricted mobility or sight to public buildings, including businesses and restaurants. They also advise on arrangements for new buildings and restorations. For vacancies, visit www.opportunities.co.uk.

7   Systems analyst. If you would like to develop solutions to business problems then this role might interest you. They decide how information is collected, processed and shared, and what software and computer hardware is the most appropriate for the job, and customize the systems so that the job is done well. For information on both business and systems analysts, visit the business analyst forum at www.modernanalyst.com.

8   Database administrator. These workers are responsible for the performance, security and recoverability of a database. They will assist in the system's design or development, and nowadays may work remotely from the server. See, for example, jobs at *Computer Weekly* at www.computerweekly.com.

9   Accounting technician. In this role you support professional accountants in the preparation of accounts, the submission of a company's returns and the computation of tax.

For further information, visit www.aat.org.uk, the official website of the Association of Accounting Technicians.

10 Network engineer. Network engineers install, support and maintain computer-based networks. For example they block access to certain sites, register and deregister users, administer passwords and troubleshoot. For information on this career and thousands of others, visit www.prospects.ac.uk.

11 Paralegal. Paralegals support lawyers in their day-to-day work. They specialize in particular areas of law and help with the research and drafting of advice and the completion, serving and submission of documents to respondents and courts. Recruitment expert Hays have an extensive database of positions for paralegals across the UK. Visit their site at www.hays.com and www.hays.co.uk.

12 Investment analyst. This occupation involves providing fund managers with research findings on the performance of companies and sectors of industry. Its members analyse, for example, companies' accounts and reports in specialist publications and produce summaries and updates on developments. For jobs view www.ft.com.

13 Economic and social policy specialist. If you would like to work with governments and departments as a special advisor and help formulate and implement social and economic policies, then look further into this role. To succeed you will need to be excellent at summarizing academic research findings and preparing policy briefing documents. For further information visit www.economist.com.

14 Advanced computing systems administrator. These workers install, configure and maintain large-scale data-management computer systems and support their users. To browse a leading technology publication, visit www.physorg.tradepub.com.

15 Research assistant. In this role you would provide research support and project management assistance; such workers have excellent communication skills, and experience in data analysis and project management. Find research assistant jobs and thousands of others on the Monster job-search site: www.monster.com.

16 Wholesaler. Wholesalers resell goods to retailers and large buyers and are often also importers or exporters. Wholesale has changed and grown with the advent of e-commerce, and wholesalers are now likely to be based near the manufacturer in, for example, China and export directly to retailers all over the world. Find out more at www.thewholesaler.co.uk and www.thetrader.co.uk.

17 Quality analyst. Maintaining the quality of service is a top priority for business; quality analysts design reporting systems, collate and monitor the output data and report their findings to management. If it is data quality analysis work that you are looking for, then visit www.microsoft-careers.com/job.

18 Industry analysts. They work in, for example, intelligence units and help provide authoritative reports on developments in their specialist industrial sector. They nearly always have experience of working in the sector or have covered it through journalism or work in government. They have exemplary research and writing skills and have a network of contacts that help keep them up to date. For news and views see, for example, www.petroleum-economist.com. For jobs, see www.economist.com.

19 Country or continent risk analysis. Risk analysts report on, for example, the political and security risks of a region, country or continent. The information they provide is purchased by subscribing organizations who operate in those areas. Analysts have local contacts and detailed knowledge of their area of specialization, are proficient in local languages and often have a background in journalism. You will find jobs listed in the jobs section of www.ft.com.

20 Equipment leasing. Leasing is used by both large and small businesses and even governments to spread the cost of high-value items evenly over the term of the lease. The list of equipment that can be leased rather than purchased is extensive. Vehicle leasing is perhaps the most common example but you can lease almost any capital item, including for example office equipment, medical equipment, even software. In some instances the manufacturer leases the equipment it makes. Leasing is a form of financing so for a career in leasing look at any of the large finance houses, for example www.lloydstsb.com/careers.

21 Procurement investigators. Procurement officers police and control an organization's procurement activities to prevent and, should it occur, discover fraud, corruption, misappropriation or mismanagement. Procurement is very big business and investigators are drawn from a number of professions, disciplines and backgrounds, including finance, management, procurement and accountancy.
For more information visit www.tendersdirect.co.uk and www.scribd.com.

22 Forensic accounting. This involves investigating crimes such as fraud, money laundering and embezzlement, and for example bankruptcies on behalf of creditors to establish if all their money has in fact been lost. Google 'forensic accounting' for lots more information and job leads.
For information about one of the major players in the field visit www.ey.com.

23 Stage manager. If you like the theatre but do not want to be in the show, then why not instruct the technical crews, including lighting, sound and scenery? Stage managers get involved in anything that affects the flow of the rehearsal or production, including wardrobe or makeup for example. They oversee the timely entrance of actors on stage. They have usually worked their way to the position first as production assistants, perhaps through amateur productions or through productions at drama school or university. Be inspired by browsing www.carolinemeer.co.uk.

24 Administrator in the arts. All galleries, museums and dance companies employ administrators to undertake all aspects of management, including finance, banking, insurance, maintenance of the building and arranging tours. Competition is fierce for these positions so obtain professional training in administration or work experience as an administrator generally, and undertake voluntary work in the arts if you want to stand out from the crowd of other applicants. Start your research and catch up on essential background reading at www.fineart.co.uk and www.antiquestradegazette.com.

25 A librarian in a research institute. Librarians undertake research, classify information and help users find what they need. The role has changed from one of primarily dealing with paper records to digital resources and the internet.

A librarian in a research institute or consultancy is likely to be professionally qualified to postgraduate level.

For a librarian in a school or community setting, skills in outreach and community involvement will be preferred over academic training. For information, visit the site of the Chartered Institute of Library and Information Professionals at www.cilip.org.uk.

26 Research computing officer. These workers provide IT, research and administrative support to colleagues in academic or commercial settings. Find jobs listed at the jobs pages of www.newscientist.com.

27 Claims administrator. The role involves tasks such as filing and reviewing documents and responding to correspondence relating to claims against insurance policies. Claims administrators check documents, invoices and policies, and make decisions as to whether a claim is valid or not. Find out more by visiting the career pages of www.aviva.co.uk and www.axa.co.uk.

28 Compliance auditor. This role requires the post holder to undertake accident and incident investigations to establish any procedural failings or compliance issues that contributed to the event. For information on how to develop a career path in corporate compliance or governance, visit www.barclaysimpson.com.

29 Administrative assistant. This position is often the starting point in a career in administration. Admin assistants undertake basic but key clerical duties such as responding to straightforward correspondence, answering telephone enquiries and obtaining information. Find a listing of public sector vacancies at www.direct.gov.uk.

30 Broadcasting researcher. Broadcasting researchers gather and authenticate information for documentaries, quiz shows, music programmes and chat shows. See, for example, the BBC Academy at www.bbctraining.com.

31 Purchasing officer. These people are professional shoppers. They compare suppliers, selecting the best ones, and negotiate the prices and terms and conditions of the agreement with the supplier. Google 'purchasing officer' for loads of leads.

32 Personal assistant. This work involves providing one-to-one secretarial and administrative support to managers. Assistants prioritize the work of the manager and act as gatekeepers. They need to know the organization and the key players well and must show discretion. You will find vacancies listed at www.indeed.co.uk and www.totaljobs.com.

33 Advisor. Advisors counsel managers and executives on strategy, service issues, making decisions and solving challenges. They are experienced professionals in their fields and play a key backstage role in determining priorities, policy and strategy, and ultimately success. Information and advisor positions with the employment service are listed at www.jobseekers.direct.gov.uk.

34 Assistant archivist. This job is about establishing and maintaining historic records. Assistant archivists work with paper, film, and electronic records that are identified, preserved, and made accessible for research. Further information can be obtained from the Society of Archivists at www.archives.org.uk.

35 Legal officer. Legal officers are employed by large corporations to provide advice and sound judgement internally. They will draw up legal documents, undertake legal research, brief external lawyers and specialize in the aspects of law most relevant to the activities of the organization. For more information visit, for example, www.civilservice.gov.uk/jobs.

36 International freight logistics. The global distribution of goods by the most cost-effective, secure and prompt means is big business, and it is growing fast with the development of internet shopping. When goods move from the seller to the buyer across national boundaries, then consideration must be given to any duty payable on imports and legal restrictions on the export of some goods. For further information google some of the big names such as FedEx careers or TNT careers and check out the opportunities.

37 Equal opportunities advisor. Equal opportunities is a part of human resources, and inequality is bad for business and is sometimes illegal. Every large business has an equality policy and employs equality specialists to draft or update policies and promote equality of opportunity within the organization. Further information visit www.cipd.co.uk, the site of the Charted Institute of Personnel and Development.

38 Activities tracking officer. Very large organizations, especially international ones, need to track the great number of projects and activities they are involved in and the funds spent on them. Responsibility for keeping track of activities and mapping the flow of resources against those activities is undertaken by activity tracking and resource flow officers. Find vacancies listed at, for example, www.jobs.guardian.co.uk/job or www.simplyhired.com.

39 Meetings technician. These workers are responsible for the setting of rooms for meetings and events at conference centres or conventions. They organize refreshments, ensure furniture is arranged according to the client's requirements and that audio and visual equipment is provided and functioning. Openings in these and many other positions can be found at for example www.hiltonworldwide.com careers.

40 Executive officer. In the UK Civil Service executive officers are managers. They manage small teams of administrative assistants and officers and supervise the spend of moderately sized budgets. They are appointed either through promotion or direct entry with qualifications equal to A level or above. For further information see the Kogan Page title *How to Pass the Civil Service Qualifying Tests.*

41 Information manager. This role involves the effective retrieval and analysis of records. A major area of employment for information managers is in healthcare, where they manage patient records. For further information visit www.ihrim.co.uk, the site of the Institute of Health Records.

42 Hospitality revenue managers. These specialists are responsible for maintaining and improving reservations in hotels. They summarize financial and technical data for reporting to colleagues and work with the general manager and marketing manager to offer promotions and offers at low occupancy times. You can find out more at, for example, www.hilton.com and www.travelodge.co.uk.

43 Computer and information systems managers. These workers seek to achieve an organization's business goals by planning and directing computer-related activities. For information take a look at the BSc business information systems management degree at www.mdx.ac.uk.

44 Surveillance agents. The hotel industry, among others, employs surveillance agents to monitor common areas and points of access. They oversee vehicle movements and the start and finish times of staff. They carry out searches and check that doors and entrances are secure. See for example the careers section at www.raffles.com.

45 Efficiencies officer. This role involves working as a part of a team within very large corporations, assessing value for money and efficiency and identifying duplication. Their findings are reported to senior managers or executives who will reply on the findings to inform the management and administration of the business. In government, see for example www.civilservice.gov.uk/jobs. In local government, search www.opportunities.co.uk.

46 Health and safety officer. They create, maintain and improve our working environment to ensure it is healthy and safe. Health and safety officers carry out inspections to identify potential hazards, assess risks and formulate safe operational procedures. You can study health and safety management up to degree level. For further information visit the official site of the Institute of Occupational Safety and Health at www.iosh.co.uk.

47 Archaeological scientist. This work involves analysing archaeological finds to reveal further details; for example, the analysis of a tooth from a skeleton can reveal the area in which a person grew up and whether their diet was that of a peasant or aristocrat. Browse the Archaeology master's degree course at www.ucl.ac.uk; for careers in archaeological science, visit www.jobs.ac.uk.

48 Trainee air traffic controller. If you have exceptional spatial awareness and mental agility then this role might suit you very well. For information on becoming a trainee air traffic controller, visit www.natscareers.co.uk.

49 Specialist technical author. This work involves producing or amending manuals and working procedures. You may work on anything from the manual for electronic equipment or instructions for home-assembled furniture to the employment manual for a large organization. You will find loads of information about starting a career in writing at www.absolutewrite.com.

50 Helpline co-ordinator. Some charities and government departments maintain banks of volunteers or workers taking calls from the general public. The helpline co-ordinator supports the volunteers and ensures a consistent high-quality service. Many charities and local government departments recruit helpline co-ordinators; for an example of the kind of organization see the Stroke Association, www.stroke.org.uk.

Set 3: Fascination with the latest technologies and know-how

There is a career for everyone who like you has an interest in innovation and new technologies. Below are 50 suggestions, any of which may make a rewarding career. Some but by no means all require an IT, science or engineering background.

1 Digital rights assistant. Holders of intellectual property employ people to check that their copyrighted material is not being illegally 'shared', pirated or sold. These assistants search blog sites and file-sharing sites for example, and if they find pirated material instruct lawyers to issue injunctions. It's a constant game of cat and mouse trying to find the latest sites frequented by the pirates. See for example the website of the UK Performing Rights Society for Composers, Songwriters and Music Publishers at www.prsformusic.com, the Copyright Registration Office for Songs and Lyrics at www.songrite.com and the UK Copyright Service, whose site provides useful information on intellectual property protection at www.copyrightservice.co.uk.

2 Innovations specialist. Innovations specialists highlight technological developments and innovations in processes and systems that are relevant to the work of the organization or corporation for which they work. They report to senior management, who decide whether the innovation should be adopted. Find out what's new at, for example, www.mitpressjournals.org and www.technologyreview.com.

3   Purchasing officer. Many large organizations have central purchasing departments through which all procurement takes place. Purchasing officers must keep up to date with products and research to find the item that represents best value and offers most features. You will find useful information at the American Institute for Supply Management's site, www.ism.ws/careercenter/careersinpurchasing.cfm, and UK jobs listed at, for example, www.reed.co.uk/purchasing.

4   Front-end web designer with a love of everything digital. E-retailers of digital equipment must constantly update their websites and so need people who understand the products and enjoy keeping up with the latest advances. Get the latest news on the web design and development industry at www.websitemagazine.com and www.allgraphicdesign.com/magazines. And for video, view www.mcvuk.com.

5   Telecommunications technician. We take our mobile phones totally for granted but we would not be able to use them without the technicians maintaining the cell equipment that connects us to the network. For further information and jobs, see www.computerweekly.com and the Institute of Engineering and Technology, whose site is found at www.theiet.org.

6   Telecommunications help desk technician. These workers help customers by answering queries and solving problems over the phone or by e-mail. Find out more at, for example, the BT career centre at www.btplc.com/careercentre.

7   Customer contact assistant for satellite broadcaster. You are technology literate, so why not help others get the best from their purchase of a media and communications package. You would work at a call centre and handle calls from customers with queries about the system or problems with the setup. Find out more at www.sky.com.

8   Telecom security analyst. This role involves monitoring telecom systems for threats and logging incidents. Analysts use security tools to discover threats and vulnerabilities and respond to events, threats and incidents encountered. You can discover graduate development programmes at Vodafone UK: www.careers.vodafone.co.uk/

student-and-graduate. Learn about careers generally at www.careers.vodafone.co.uk/application-process and www.vodafone.com/start/careers.

9 Video communications technicians. In this profession you install and operate multimedia and IT-based video communications systems. These technicians have an in-depth and up-to-date knowledge of audio visual and videoconferencing systems and give advice and support to users of these systems. For information on the sort of company you might work for, see www.videohighway.co.uk.

10 Telecom account executives. In this position you would design, propose and sell integrated voice, data and internet packages to businesses. Browse all the career opportunities at T-Mobile at www.t-mobilecareers.co.uk.

11 Wireless network engineers. Wireless engineers install equipment and software, connect peripherals and configure systems and software for business. For further information see for example www.e-skills.com, and for advice on wireless network engineering and thousands of other roles, see www.careersadvice.direct.gov.

12 Telecommunications software testers. People employed in this role review and evaluate software products and systems to ensure that they are suitable for the proposed task and adhere to company and customer quality standards. You can find out about vacancies at Nokia: www.nokia.com/careers.

13 Telecom cell site installers. They are responsible for setting up new cell sites or expanding the capacity of existing ones. Cell site installers have to have a head for heights and work well as part of a team in some out-of-the-way or hard-to-reach locations. The listing of vacancies at O2 is found at www.o2careers.co.uk.

14 Telecommunications engineers. These engineers install, test and repair networking and communications equipment at exchanges and hubs in large businesses or local sub-stations. You can join apprenticeships or study at university to get qualified in this field. For further information google 'telecommunications technicians' for loads of leads. For further information browse www.bt.com.

15 New product trainer. New lines in photography, computing and audio are being introduced all the time, and retailers rely on store managers or trainers to ensure that front-of-store staff know the benefits the latest laptop or digital zoom camera has to offer. In the finance section see, for example, www.lloydstsbjobs.com.

16 Chief technology officer. In this work you are tasked with evaluating the newest and most innovative technological advances to determine whether they can assist your organization's objectives. Find these jobs at www.ft.com/jobsclassified.

17 Technology retail apprenticeship. In this position you would work at one of a number of retail outlets that sell digital technology or services, and at the same time work towards a national qualification in retail. For further information visit, for example, virginmedia.com and see their retail apprenticeship scheme. For training opportunities see, for example, www.hotcourses.com/uk.

18 Home digital technicians. These are technicians who install and repair household equipment for telecommunications, internet and digital TV in people's homes. They need to understand all things digital and be presentable and tidy workers. The Dixons group for example have technicians who install digital equipment. You can see the current vacancies at www.dsgiplc.com.

19 Media coverage assistant. Organizations want to know what people are saying about them, their products and services. To this end they employ assistants to find and collate reviews, forum or blog discussions, articles, complaints – in fact anything said about them. This coverage is organized and published for internal circulation. Find out more at, for example, www.mediauk.com or www.jobs.guardian.co.uk.

20 Field support technician. The services of a field support technician are offered by many technology retail chains. When someone buys a flat-screen TV or a home entertainment centre, the customer may opt for a technician to attend their home to install and configure the equipment and interface it with existing hardware. For information on apprenticeships in this role and many more, visit www.apprenticeships.org.uk.

21 Operations and business processes consultants. These specialists constantly keep their fingers on the pulse of change so that they can inform their clients of the latest developments in key sectors such as pharmaceuticals, aerospace, telecommunications, biotechnology and electronics. You will need to be considered a specialist in your field and have a network of contacts. If this is the case, then start your search at the website of the Management Consultancy Association at www.mca.org.uk.

22 Returns quality inspector. This work involves inspecting items returned as faulty and establishing the nature of the fault and the best remedy. They log all faults and provide management with reports that form the basis of negotiations with suppliers and manufacturers. To find hundreds of job leads in the quality inspection sector, simply google 'quality inspector'.

23 Particle accelerator engineer. If you are mad about theoretical physics then you will have read everything about the Large Hadron Collider at CERN. Accelerators are used in the treatment of cancers too, and you can train in accelerator science at for example the Cockcroft Institute. For information visit www.cockcroft.ac.uk.

24 Financial advisor. If you are interested in the world of investments and pensions, then consider becoming a financial advisor selling pensions, life insurance and services in trading and investments. It's a fast-changing environment. You will have to become licensed before you can practise and you must keep up with the latest products and legislation. For further information visit www.fsa.gov.uk and www.aifa.net.

25 Customer-service advisor. These workers take calls from customers and provide advice on the right product, resolve queries and problems. Very often the call is from someone who has further questions or issues once they have left a store or viewed a product online. For examples of the kinds of businesses that rely extensively on customer-service advisors, visit www.vodafone.co.uk, www.ticketmaster.co.uk/h/customer and www.business.hsbc.co.uk, to mention just a few.

26 Automotive engineering. If motorsports is your thing, then consider studying automotive engineering or motorsport vehicle dynamics. There are a number of courses in engineering faculties at UK universities. For example, visit www.engineering.kingston.ac.uk.

27 Online distribution operative. This work involves fulfilling online orders for, for example, home electronics. These operatives work from large warehouses and compile, package and dispatch orders. For example, in the business of distributing books see www.thebookservice.co.uk and www.lbsltd.co.uk.

28 Returns administrator. The post holder handles digital equipment that has gone wrong and is returned by the customer. They keep in touch with the customer on the progress of the repair or replacement of the item and liaise with colleagues to ensure that inconvenience is kept to a minimum. See opportunities at, for example, www.littlewoods.com.

29 Repair technician. These technicians mend and refurbish faulty goods such as mobile phones, digital cameras, TVs, computers and audio equipment. The major retailers of home electronics employ teams of technicians at centralized workshops/laboratories. For further information see, for example, www.careersatcarphone.com.

30 Computer game testers. New and updated games need testing at a series of points in their development, and testers need to know something of all the components that make a good game. Qualifications range from short intensive courses in gaming up to four-year BSc courses in gaming technology. For further information see, for example, www.gamescareerguide.com.

31 Warranty support advisor. In this role you would handle claims from customers regarding equipment still under warranty or covered by extended warranties. You will handle claim paperwork and validate claims. Find all sorts of jobs, including warranty and after-sales support advisors, at for example www.jlpjobs.com/jobs.

32 Graduate courses in engineering. There is a shortage of engineering graduates in the UK, which means there are careers in engineering waiting to be filled. Courses are available in manufacturing systems, data communication, sustainable energy and building services engineering, to name but a few. Find out more using the course search facility at www.ucas.ac.uk, and find out about engineering careers at the site of the Institution of Engineering and Technology at www.theiet.org.

33 Technical copy writer. Every catalogue and website that describes the latest electronic gadget has been written by a technical copy writer. If you have a love of all things digital and the ability to make the complex sound simple, then this might be the opportunity for you. For everything to do with the business of writing, visit for example www.absolutewrite.com.

34 Technology and gadget freelance journalist. A wide number of newspapers and magazines carry regular articles on the latest electronic gadgets, Christmas present ideas and reviews. For information on how to get started and find out more, visit www.journalism.co.uk and www.freelanceuk.com.

35 Website tester. These specialists have programming or scripting experience and understand how both the front and back ends of websites tick. They work with developers and users to establish test requirements and then run tests to find glitches and snags in the product, from an early stage in the project's development through to it going live. For further information visit, for example, www.websiteoptimization.com, www.browsershots.org or www.usertesting.com.

36 Installing and servicing video and television systems. CCTV systems and video-display monitors are so prevalent these days that a career in their installation and servicing has become possible. You would work for a local authority or transport authority, ensuring maintenance of the surveillance and information systems. For further information about this career visit, for example, www.e-repair.co.uk and www.tvrs-uk.com.

37 Installing and servicing domestic aerial systems. This work involves the installation of aerials to maximize signal reception for digital or satellite broadcast reception. You will need to have a head for heights and be comfortable working in confined spaces. To join an apprenticeship in this trade, start with a search at www.apprenticeships.org.uk. An employer in the industry is found at www.hotfroguk.co.uk.

38 Installing and servicing video and audio equipment. You may work for a high street retailer and provide the after-sales support for customers who purchase, for example, home entertainment systems. You can find out about an apprenticeship in the field at www.apprenticeships.org.uk.

39 Instrumentation electrician. This is an advanced profession and involves the installation and maintenance of complex equipment in, for example, hospitals, laboratories and industry. For a listing of companies, see the Electrical Contractors Association at www.eca.co.uk.

40 Installation electrician. This role involves installing new electrical systems – anything from rewiring a residential property or a tower block to the many different and complex systems in an airport terminal. Electricians are responsible for the installation of all electrical systems, including power, lighting, surveillance, closed communication systems and security. Find electrician jobs listed at, for example, www.simplyhired.co.uk.

41 Refrigeration and air-conditioning technician. Refrigeration and air conditioning are used in a great many situations and are relied on extensively in, for example, the food, distribution and health industries. A technician in this field would install new systems or repair and service existing installations. Find out more at www.careersadvice.direct.gov.uk.

42 Highway systems electrician. Keeping the traffic moving has become a science and uses the very latest technologies. Advance hazard-warning systems, speed management, automatic tolls and number-plate recognition are just some of the recent innovations. For training opportunities see, for example, www.notgoingtouni.co.uk and www.jtltraining.com.

43 Maintenance electrician. These craftpeople service, repair and maintain equipment on production lines, in factories, workshops, power plants, hospitals and depots, for example. You can find jobs at either www.indeed.co.uk/Maintenance-Electrician or www.jobsearch.monster.com.

44 Auto mechanic. Cars now come with computers, GPS navigation and electronics that control almost every system. Hybrid engines and vehicles powered by green fuels are increasingly common. As a result, service mechanics with an interest in electronics, computers and the next generation of engines running on alternative fuels will be at a considerable advantage over their colleagues. To find a job or training as an auto mechanic and thousands of other jobs and training opportunities, visit www.jobseekers.direct.gov.uk or www.direct.gov.uk/en/Employment.

45 Patent assessor. Before a patent for an invention is granted, the application is examined by an expert to establish whether it is indeed novel and useful and sufficiently different from existing inventions. If you are interested in this career then you will be in good company; Albert Einstein was employed as a patent assessor in Bern, Switzerland (at the time he also published papers on thermodynamics and was working on his general theories). If you consider yourself an expert in a field or would like to know more about careers in intellectual property and patents, then view www.patent.gov.uk and www.ipo.gov.uk.

46 Internal communications officer. Many organizations employ someone to inform staff of change, achievements and developments. These officers will be responsible for writing an internal newsletter or other communiqués notifying staff of the latest news. Find these jobs listed at, for example, www.lgcareers.com and www.opportunities.co.uk.

47 Assistant scientific editor. A background in science is required for this role, which involves commissioning reviews of papers on the latest discoveries submitted for publication and selecting research articles for publication in scientific journals. A good place to look for vacancies is www.newscientistjobs.com.

48 Trend spotter. Someone working as a trend spotter will present reports or presentations on the direction they believe an industry is moving in. Industries like the cosmetic and fashion industry use trend spotters to get their designers and buyers thinking about and discussing what the next big thing might be. Trend spotters also provide reports on web search behaviour, social media monitoring and market data. For further information visit www.trendsspotting.com and www.trendwatching.com.

49 Supply change manager. Organizations that produce tens of millions of items every day, for example manufacturers of big-brand food or toiletries, must ensure that their supply chain stays abreast of every development. The sourcing of ingredients or components and the distribution of the product on this kind of scale take an enormous amount of planning, forecasting and risk analysis. A background in engineering, maths or a physical science translates well to supply chain management. For further information, visit the site of the Council of Supply Change Management Professionals at www.cscmp.org.

50 Technical procurement specialist. When organizations buy computer or telecommunications systems or other specialist equipment, they turn to a procurement specialist in the field to ensure that they obtain a system that is fit for the purpose and offers value for money. You can find procurement jobs at, for example, www.procurementspecialist.com.

Set 4: Impatient for some venture (enterprising)

Take seriously your desire to be your own boss and to start a business. There are an almost unlimited number of possibilities out there, and if you are the sort of person who is full of ideas then it's time you made a shortlist and drew up a business plan for the best of them. If on the other hand you like the idea of starting a new venture but can't decide what it should be, then have a close look at some of the franchising opportunities around. To give you a flavour of the opportunities that exist I have reviewed 20 areas in which franchising is big. However, not all franchises are good investments. I have included below website addresses as a source of ideas only and I do not know if the opportunities listed on those sites are good or bad. Before you sign an agreement to become a franchisee, ask to meet with people who already hold a franchise with the company, search for any bad press and take professional advice from, for example, an accountant or lawyer, or preferably both. Google 'the franchise fair' for dates and venues where you can meet and discuss franchise business ideas with exhibitors.

It is also worth considering new business tax breaks. For information on start-up grants visit www.startups.co.uk or www.smallbusiness. co.uk and www.businesslink.gov.uk.

1   Vending. We have all seen coin-operated machines that dispense products, mostly candies, sugary drinks, snacks and toys. Many of these machines are operated by franchise holders who each operate many tens of vending machines from multiple sites, usually small retailers' premises.
    You start by negotiating with the retailer permission to site your machines and then service them. For further information, see for example www.franchisedirect.com.

2   Internet-based franchises. This area of franchising includes web-hosting and web-advertising businesses. For example, you may provide a service advertising small businesses and sole traders on the internet, helping the owners to become sponsored links on search engines or come up higher in searches. Browse for example www.franchisegator.com.

3   Child-related franchises. This area comprises party providers, cakes and balloon suppliers, supplementary tutoring academies, children's sports clubs, drama clubs, art classes, inflatable amusement rental for parties and public events. See, for example, francise.com for ideas. You can find out about child-related franchises at, for example, www.whichfranchise.com.

4   Advertising franchises. These include packaging suppliers and sign makers, printing T shirts, embroidering logos on items such as baseball caps, and supplying a huge range of promotional gifts from rubber ducks to printed coffee mugs and pens. View openings at, for example, www.franchiseopportunities.com.

5   Automotive franchises. This is one of the biggest areas in franchises and might suit you if you are in a mechanical trade and want to run your own business. It includes car wash and oil change, battery retailing, in-car audio systems, scratch and chip repairs, alarm, immobilize and tracker installation, brake and clutch repairs, tyre changing and home tuning. There are also franchises for motorcycles and bicycles. For automotive franchises see, for example, www.automotivefranchise.com.

6   Travel. If you are interested in travel then there are franchises that allow you to become a cruise ship agent, an event manager organizing business meetings or passes and accommodation for attendees at trade shows for example,

a wedding planner franchise where you organize weddings in faraway exotic locations or a promoter of holidays and hotels on the internet. For information on running a travel agent franchise, view www.explorertravel.co.uk.

7 Cleaning franchise. There are many offers for cleaning franchises and they might well suit the very active person. There are specialist offers in carpet cleaning, dry cleaning of clothes, oven and hob cleaning services as well as general residential or business premises cleaning franchises. There are also franchises where you can operate coin-operated laundries, graffiti-removing services and rubbish removal. You will find cleaning franchises advertised at www.franchisedirect.co.uk.

8 Food franchise. This is the largest of the franchise areas and some very big names in the catering business have been involved, including McDonalds, KFC and Pizza Hut. The food franchise business can start small, with businesses selling for example popcorn, baked potatoes, cookies, hotdogs and pretzels, or it can involve large-scale investment. To buy a franchise to run a big-brand fast-food restaurant will require a major investment of capital and buy you the opportunity to run a multi-million dollar turnover fast-food restaurant or even a number of such operations. Find out more by visiting, for example, www.franchiseexpo.co.uk.

9 Beverages and ices franchise. Coffee franchises are big business. They can be run from the back of a small van or a store with seating for customers. Some franchisees have built large businesses, starting with a single store and reinvesting until they run multiple stores serving thousands of coffees a day. There are many less expensive franchise opportunities to start a beverage or ice franchise providing, for example, ice drinks, ice creams, juices and smoothies. Coffee, smoothie, fruit bar and ice cream franchises are listed at, for example, www.franchisesolutions.com.

10 Senior-care franchises are a growing area. They may well suit someone with a background in nursing. They involve the provision of services ranging from home visits to help with medications, the provision of an emergency contact in the event of an accident or fall, and an assisted taxi service for the less mobile, through to a franchise to run a care home. Franchises in senior care are advertised on www.seniorcarefranchises.net.

11 B2B franchises. B2B stands for business to business and involves providing any of a very wide range of support services to businesses. Businesses use these services so that they can concentrate on their core activities. Examples include billing and debt collection, computer and network maintenance, the procurement of telecommunications services, accounting or book keeping, human resource management and marketing and advertising. If you have experience in any of these fields and have always wanted to be your own boss then investigate further, but be sure to take a long careful look before you commit. You can find advertisements for B2B franchises at www.franchisedirect. co.uk/b2bfranchises.

12 Beauty franchising. This is one of the really big areas and is still growing fast. It might well suit you if you have experience in hair dressing. There have been franchise businesses in the hair and cosmetic industries for many years and some very big high street names have relied on franchises to expand their brand. There are a great many opportunities in hair styling, beauty treatments and therapies and cosmetics, to name but a few. For further information google 'beauty franchises'. Advertisements for beauty franchises can be found at www.selectyourfranchise.com/uk/ franchise-directory/Beauty-Franchise.html.

13 Pets and pet care is a significant area in franchising. If you love animals and would like to be your own boss, then take a careful look at the pet and pet care franchise offers. There are business opportunities in dog grooming, pet hotels, dog walking, pet foods and accessories, pet registration services to help recover an animal if lost, name-tag engraving and for pet insurance agents. Franchises for pet sitting, dog walking and pet boarding and more are advertised at, for example, www.petpals.com, www.barkingmad.uk.com and www.animalsathome.co.uk.

14 Sports-related franchises. If you are accomplished in one or more sports and like the idea of being your own boss, then investigate some of the many sports-related franchises that are available. You can invest in and run five-a-side soccer

leagues, aerobic, dance, fitness and weight-loss classes, big-brand gyms and pro-tennis clubs to name but a few of the many opportunities. You will find advertisements for sports-related franchises at www.franchisesales.co.uk/search/Recreation and www.theukfranchisedirectory.net/showcaselist/sports.

15 Financial services franchises. Franchises are available in the sale of services such as pensions, life insurance, the provision of loans, and services in trading and investments. There are also franchises in pay cheque cashing. You will have to become licensed by the appropriate authorities and the franchiser should provide advice on this. For advertisements for mortgage franchises see, for example, www.startups.co.uk. For financial service franchises generally, see www.smallbusiness.co.uk.

16 Computing franchises. If computers are your thing, then investigate some of the franchising offers in computer services. Find yourself a good franchise and it should mean that you can trade under a known brand and benefit from the support of a larger organization while running your own local show. Franchise ideas for people with a computing or technical background can be found at, for example, www.selectyourfranchise.com.

17 Environmental franchises. This is a relatively new and fast-growing area in franchising. You can get started in energy conservation for business, renewable energy systems for homes, and environmental audits and consultancy services by signing up for a franchise. Environmental franchises are listed at, for example, www.selectyourfranchise.com/uk and www.business-opportunities.net/business/environmental-franchise-uk-green-assess.html.

18 Virtual retailer. The internet offers many opportunities to take your first tentative steps towards a career as an entrepreneur. If retail interests you, then there are countless breaks. More and more people are taking the plunge and shopping online so perhaps now is the time to start in virtual retail. You can cut your teeth by opening virtual shops on sites such as eBay and as you become more experienced venture out to open your own stand-alone stores. You will of course have to find suppliers and make sure that customers

can find you. Who knows what it will lead to (be sure to take the same precautions as those mentioned in career idea 19, entrepreneur). It needs no introduction, but see if you would like to join the tens of thousands of virtual retailers at www.ebay.com and www.ebay.co.uk.

19 Entrepreneur. There is no reason why you should not start a business of your own without the support, collective marketing and brand associated with a franchise. Invest in yourself by ensuring that you have the right skills to run a business, and get some professional advice from the start, so that for example you limit your liabilities (in case your business should not succeed). Be sure to register your business activities with the appropriate authorities as time penalties often apply if you fail to do so. Read all about them at www.entrepreneur.com.

20 Business angel. If you've 'been there and done it' in terms of running your own business, then becoming a business angel might interest you. Business angels both invest in a business and join the board. This way they bring their capital, expertise and experience to help make the venture a success and share in it. View the information at the British Business Angels Association at www.bbaa.org.uk.

21 Find a business angel. If you want to find an investor who will help make your business idea work, then visit for example the UK Business Angel Investment Network at www.angelinvestmentnetwork.co.uk.

22 Buying a business. Visit, for example, www.daltonsbusiness.com to view hundreds of businesses for sale. Before you buy however, be sure to obtain all the right information and take some professional advice.

23 Invest in a business. You can obtain advice on investing in a business at, for example, www.investni.com for businesses in Northern Ireland, www.sdi.co.uk for investing in Scotland and ukinvest.gov.uk for investments in the UK. Many regions of the UK also have organizations to attract investment or relocating businesses.

24 Develop your existing business. If you are already in business, then visit www.investorinpeople.co.uk for advice and services to develop your business and its staff.

25 Ready-made UK companies. You can buy off the shelf a ready-made dormant UK company and start trading almost immediately. Google 'ready-made UK companies' for leads.

Set 5: Evidence and deduction

If you have good laboratory techniques and data analysis skills or are adept in computer database management, then any of the 60 careers outlined below would suit you well. Some but not all require scientific or engineering training to graduate level or above. Great websites include www.jobs.ac.uk, www.environmentaljobs.co.uk and www.newscientistjobs.com.

1 Laboratory technician. This work entails supporting scientists in the delivery of laboratory procedures and maintaining the day-to-day operation of a laboratory. Laboratory technicians undertake laboratory procedures, input data and results and keep equipment clean. Search thousands of science jobs, including laboratory technician positions, at www.jobs.ac.uk/jobs/technical. If you are interested in laboratory work with animals, then browse the Institute of Animal Technology's site at www.iat.org.uk.

2 Scientific statistician. This specialist branch of statistics involves supporting scientists by using mathematical, statistical and computational methods and tools to analyse field data and data arising in the laboratory. You will find scientific statistician vacancies posted at www.jobs.ac.uk.

3 Laboratory manager. Laboratory managers oversee all support staff, including technicians and cleaners, and manage the day-to-day operation of the laboratory. They ensure that consumables are stocked, health and safety procedures are followed, the area is secure and maintenance routines are upheld. They are responsible for financial budgets and ensuring that the laboratory is operated within the laws and regulations that apply. They are the formal point of contact between the scientific staff, support staff and management of the organization or institute that owns or operates the laboratory. Laboratory manager positions are often advertised at www.newscientistjobs.com/jobs.

4 Nuclear inspector. Nuclear or radioactive material is used in many locations, including hospitals, some laboratories, the military, industry and the power generation sector. The nuclear protectorates employ inspectors whose role it is to protect people and society from the hazards of the nuclear industry. For background information on the role of the nuclear inspectorate, see for example www.sellafieldsites.com.

5 Scene-of-crime officer. These specialist officers are employed in police forces to collect evidence from crime scenes. They keep records from the scene, produce written and verbal reports and prepare samples for analysis. They provide evidence in court if required. For information about a day in the life of a scene-of-crime officer see www.surrey.police.uk/careers/day_in_the_life_profile_rosie.asp.

6 Scientific officer. These are specialist civil servants and they work for the government in one of a vast number of specialist scientific advisory or link roles. See for example www.careers@civil-service.gov.uk for details.

7 Food technologist. This work involves advising on the production of processed foods. Food technologists specify the recipe, monitor the quality of ingredients, pilot the mass production of goods and oversee the full production process. You will find further information at the site of the Institute of Food Science and Technology: www.ifst.org.

8 Tactical manager. These specialists oversee the collection of performance information regarding trends and hotspots, and its reporting in the form of intelligence to inform future policy. They might work for example in the Highways Agency helping to improve road safety, or in retail to reduce the incidence of shoplifting. The agency responsible for maintaining and developing the road network of England is found at www.highways.gov.uk.

9 Survey geologist. Work in the field involves carrying out field mapping and collecting core samples and other geological data at sites. Survey geologists produce computer-generated 3-D models and scientific interpretations of collected data, core samples and other geological data. For further information on the role of a survey geologist, see www.earthquakes.bgs.ac.uk and www.geolsoc.org.uk.

10   Biodiversity officer. The post holders are responsible for the writing of a biodiversity policy and strategy and sustainable development policy for an area. Biodiversity officers are usually employed by a local authority or local government. They oversee the implementation of that authority's policy and review it at strategic points during the year. Local authorities all over the UK are employing biodiversity officers; see for example officers in Northern Ireland: www.doeni.gov.uk/niea/biodiversity/local_ biodiversity_action/northern_ireland_local_council_ biodiversity_officers.htm.

11   Marine officer. Marine officers develop marine conservation and education policies for marine educational areas or areas of interest or of special scientific interest. They obtain approval for the policy and work towards its implementation. They undertake reviews and make written and verbal reports on the various projects that make up the policy. You can find out lots more about the role of marine environment officers at, for example, Natural England – Sea change: securing a future for Europe's seas: www.naturalengland.org.uk/ ourwork/marinewww.defra.gov.uk/2010/08/20/protection-uk-seas and www.mcga.gov.uk.

12   Assistant scientific editor. People employed in this role rely on their scientific training and background to select submitted articles and summaries of research findings for publication in scientific journals. They also commission reviews of research finds for publication. It is really important that their knowledge of the field in which they work remains current. For examples of the sort of services scientific editors get involved in, visit www.clarkscientificediting.com, www.ease.org.uk and www.bioedit.co.uk.

13   Research assistant. Someone fully trained in a scientific field can gain employment as a research assistant, providing support to a research team through for example sampling, database management, field data collection, computer modelling or empirical or statistical analysis. You will find a listing of jobs at www.newscientistjobs.com.

14   Research technician. These specialists undertake highly technical laboratory procedures in support of a research team. They collect and report the findings of those procedures and ensure their correct entry for analysis. They provide technical support to the research team on laboratory technique and methods. Positions for research technicians can be found at, for example, www.nature.com/naturejobs.

15 Wetland project officer. If you don't mind if your feet are wet, then why not work at an educational site or site of special scientific interest to maintain and improve the environment and biodiversity. To find out more about this role, google 'wetland project officer'. A good place to start your search might be www.biology4all.com.

16 Developmental software technician. These workers are software specialists who assist in the development and piloting of software tools for use in scientific research. They may help for example to develop data warehousing products for the scientific community. Examples of employers in the field are www.bbconsult.co.uk, www.cirrussoftware.com and www.geeks.ltd.uk.

17 Science communications officer. This is a growing area in science and is a response to the scepticism or mistrust that the general public sometimes show towards the scientific community and its research findings. It is the role of communications officers to communicate the objectives and expected benefits of a research project and help explain the meaning of the research findings to the public at large. Details of organizations that use the services of science communications officer can be found at www.senseaboutscience.org.uk and www.absw.org.uk.

18 Validation technician. Post holders are responsible for the calibration of scientific and medical equipment. They record the results produced by specialist equipment and run trials to check that the instruments are producing results within acceptable tolerances. They certify results and the accuracy of the equipment. Both UK and international jobs are listed at, for example, www.scienceprospects.com.

19 Good distribution practice inspector. This work involves inspecting the supply chain and distribution chain to seek out improvements in terms of security, energy efficiency and reliability. You can find out more about the good manufacturing practice inspection process at www.mhra.gov.uk.

20 Terrestrial officer. These workers are responsible for a site and plan and co-ordinate its management to realize the objectives of the project, which may be ecological or educational. They may work to remove invasive species, or commission other contractors to do so. They may manage woodland or grasslands to enhance biodiversity, ensure its sustainability and to maximize the benefit of the community. You can find this type of employment listed at, for example, www.opportunities.co.uk.

21 Laboratory support technician. People employed in this role process glassware, sterilize equipment and dispose of contaminated material. They receive and record deliveries and monitor and stock consumables. If you are interested in working as a technician in cancer research, then visit for example www.jobs.cancerresearchuk.org.

22 Hazardous materials surveyor. These surveyors work mostly in the building trade, investigate reports and survey hazardous materials in the built environment. They report their findings to the appropriate authorities and are consulted on how best to deal with the material. For ideas visit www.uksurveyors.net.

23 Marine ecological monitoring officer. This work involves undertaking surveys of bodies of water such as rivers, lochs and lakes. Marine ecological monitoring officers collect samples and investigate instances of pollution. They report on stock levels and biodiversity. You can find all sorts of work with animals and marine life at, for example, www.animal-job.co.uk/marine-jobs-uk.

24 Good manufacturing practice inspector. In this role the post holder works to reduce risk of injury, improve the quality of the product, reduce waste and save energy. In pharmaceuticals for example, see www.mhra.gov.uk.

25 Clinical trials co-coordinator. Individuals in this role are senior and experienced scientists or research medics who oversee research applications and active projects to ensure that they adhere to policies and protocols, especially regarding ethics and regulations. They may, for example, oversee a clinical trial involving animals or patients to ensure it is both ethical and legal. You might begin your search for a job in the life sciences at, for example, www.jobsinscience.com.

26 Youth and schools scientific officer. These officers work for a project or institute to raise awareness amongst young people and school children of the objectives of the work of the project or institute. They may for example invite school groups to visit the project, or communicate the work through school projects, websites or open days. You will find a listing of local authority and public sector jobs at www.opportunities.co.uk.

27 Medical statistician. In this branch of statistics you undertake statistical analysis of data from studies. The analysis of medical statistics can lead to important discoveries as to the cause of diseases or factors relevant to them. Statistical analysis for example provided one of the first indications that lung cancer is linked to smoking. A list of the jobs available through a recruitment agency specializing for the science can be seen at www.seltekconsultants.co.uk.

28 Medical officers. These officers oversee clinical trials and medical research and provide technical advice on how a clinical trial should be conducted and what should be inferred from clinical analysis. You might find something of interest at, for example, the Medical Research Centre, Harwell site website, which is found at www.har.mrc.ac.uk.careers.

29 Trial safety manager. This work involves advising medical research teams on the safe operation of clinical trials and the requirements to meet regulations. These specialists are mostly involved in the trial of new drugs or therapies and help ensure that the interests of the volunteer patients are observed and that no unnecessary suffering takes place. They will ensure that any unexpected or adverse effects are correctly reported and may advise that a trial should be stopped or reviewed. Find pharmaceutical and medical clinical study manager jobs from top employers and recruitment agencies at, for example, www.jobsite.co.uk.

30 Science lecturers. Scientific lecturers teach science to undergraduates and undertake peer reviews of the publications of research scientists. They collaborate on

research projects and the publication of the results of that research. For positions as science lecturers, visit www.jobs.ac.uk/jobs and www.education-jobs.co.uk.

31 Water hygiene consultant. In this work post holders help ensure that water supplies are safe by undertaking tests and providing technical advice on water management and the design and maintenance of water supply systems. For an example of water services offered by water hygiene consultants visit, for example, www.commercial-water-services.co.uk.

32 Environmental consultants. These specialists write and advise on policy and compliance with environmental regulations. They design monitoring procedures and management plans to ensure effective environmental management. For background on the work of environmental consultants, visit www.environment-agency.gov.uk/jobs or google, for example, the environmental consultancy SKM Enviros.

33 Data analyst. Post holders are responsible for the management of a scientific database. They ensure the data is secure and accessible to colleagues, and advise on searches and the interpretation of the findings of those searches. You can find out more at www.jobs.ac.uk.

34 Scientific programme officer. This work involves liaising with external partners, compiling financial and technical reports, and representing the project at meetings and events. Career opportunities in the UK medical research council can be found at www.mrc.ac.uk.

35 Science teacher. In this role you would teach science to children in compulsory education and in sixth forms. Science teachers are responsible for inspiring the next generation of scientists and ensuring that all their students have a firm understanding of the fundamentals of science. You will find loads of information at www.tda.gov.uk/get-into-teaching/faqs/becomingateacher, and at the Association of Science Education website at www.ase.org.uk.

36 Support scientists. These scientists work to support the work of research teams. They undertake a wide range of activities, some highly specialized; for example a support scientist may provide quantitative analysis, regulatory compliance audits or administrative support. You might be interested in going to the Nature Jobs Career Expo, and you can find out about this role and more besides at www.nature.com/naturejobs.

37 Bio-analysis technician. These technicians process medical samples by preparing them for analysis and reporting the results of the investigations. In some cases the analysis is in-house, while in other cases the technician must send the sample out to the appropriate laboratory. You can find many scientific jobs listed at www.seltekconsultants.co.uk.

38 Bio-bank technician. In this specialist technician role, post holders are responsible for the storage of biological samples. There are strict regulatory processes regarding the holding of human samples and the technician must operate within those protocols and processes. Once again a great site for all sorts of science jobs is www.newscientistjobs.com.

39 Computer biologist. These life scientists develop web systems to hold, circulate and display data. This might involve sightings of species or their distribution and observed behavioural traits. For vacancies for computer biologists, visit www.thesciencejobs.com.

40 Volunteer co-ordinator. Volunteers are important in many fields of science, and where they are extensively used the project or institute will appoint a co-ordinator to recruit, administer, train and allocate volunteers. For many types of charity jobs and voluntary sector jobs see, for example, www.charityjob.co.uk.

41 Scientific software expert. Science is a major user of software, and scientific software specialists help develop that software, and test and debug existing and new programs. Visit for example www.nbsuk.co.uk.

42 Safety assistant. In this role a worker conducts inspections of laboratories and buildings to help ensure they are safe places to work. They undertake risk assessments, investigate minor accidents or incidents and keep administrative records of those inspections and assessments.

43 Web-based clinical trials analyst. A web-based system offers many advantages as it allows data to be added to the system at disparate locations. Web-based clinical trials analysts will provide web-based systems; for example, they may design and manage a system for tracking samples and collecting laboratory and clinical results. You will find news and jobs for the biotech industry at, for example, www.biospace.com.

44 Science outreach worker. Many scientific projects need to keep a whole host of people informed of progress or developments, including the general public or people living in the vicinity. This task falls to science outreach workers and they achieve it by representing the project at public and peer meetings, collecting and editing information for newsletters and non-technical reports, undertaking visits to clubs, societies and schools, and organizing open days. For insight into the role of a science outreach worker browse www.rsc.org/chemistryworld/Issues/2010/March/ReachingOut.asp.

45 Radiation protection advisor. These individuals work in locations where there is a risk from radiation, providing advice and guidance to workers and ensuring the unit is compliant with regulations. These sort of specialist support jobs are sometimes listed at the MRC careers pages; search at www.mrc.ac.uk.

46 Vegetation surveyor. These workers are usually employed by forestry commissions and national parks to map biodiversity and assess the extent to which ecosystems have changed. For jobs in ecology and biodiversity, start your search at for example www.earthworks-jobs.com.

47 Agronomist. In this profession you would grow experimental crops to identity new high-yield or disease-resistant varieties. Agronomist jobs are advertised at *Farmer's Weekly*: visit www.fwi.co.uk/jobs.

48 Technological development representatives. These workers report the technical advances made by scientific equipment manufacturers. Their reports are submitted to prospective customers who may wish to buy the latest or next generation of equipment. Examples of companies that employ people in technology development include www.linkam.co.uk and www.camsci.co.uk.

49 Medical writers, photographers and artists. Medical schools and institutions employ writers, photographers and artists to record the findings of their research. Writers produce articles and reports for journals and specialist magazines, while photographers and artists may produce images for cataloguing or illustrative purposes. You might start your search by looking at, for example, the Wellcome Trust arts awards at www.wellcome.ac.uk/Funding/Public-engagement.

50 Regulatory manager. Large scientific and medical institutions that are running multiple projects over a number of disciplines must comply with a great many regulations and laws. To manage this they employ a regulatory manager whose role it is to ensure full compliance with the many regulatory frameworks and the timely submission of all necessary reports and submissions. Find regulatory manager jobs (and thousands of other jobs) at www.indeed.co.uk/ Regulatory-Manager-jobs.

51 Industrial incident investigator. These workers are employed by the insurance industry to investigate industrial incidents for which an insurance claim has been made. For information on the national agency responsible for guidance and information on inspections, see www.hse.gov.uk.

52 Biological safety officer. In many laboratories it is necessary to store and use potentially dangerous biological material. This may include, for example, flu virus in a laboratory developing vaccines. In these situations an officer is charged with responsibility to ensure that safety procedures are adequate and properly followed. Why not begin your search by visiting the Oxford Life Science Career Fair: www.sehta.co.uk.

53 Research engineer. Everything manufactured has first been designed by a research engineer who produces the blueprints to show the manufacturer how to make it. Find engineering jobs, including research engineers, at www.jobs.telegraph.co.uk.

54 Fire and explosions investigator. This work involves examining buildings, vehicles and all kinds of material which has suffered a fire or explosion. The investigator seeks to find the likely cause and reports his or her findings to the client, which is usually an insurance company. Find out about training opportunities and companies involved in fire and explosions

investigations at, for example, www.engineering.leeds.ac.uk/
short-courses/fire-engineering/FireExplosionInvestigation or
www.buncefieldinvestigation.gov.uk.

55 Assessment manager. These professionals are responsible
for managing the assessment and accreditation of
laboratories or the assessment and accreditation of
qualifications. In early years education, for example, you can
find out more at www.nationalstrategies.standards.dcsf.gov.
uk/earlyyears. For assessment managers in adult learning
see, for example, www.distance-learning-centre.co.uk.

56 Coastal zone ecosystem modeller. This work provides
information on the best way to manage our coastal
ecosystems, given the multiple uses that include fishing,
tourism and housing. For further information on a career in
ecosystem modelling, see for example the work at
www.pml.ac.uk.

57 Engineering technician. If you graduate from an approved
engineering apprenticeship then you can go on to obtain
professional status as an engineering technician. Go to the
Institute of Engineering and Technology website for
information on approved apprenticeship schemes and
information on the engineering technician qualification.
Visit www.theiet.org.

58 Cargo loss or damage investigator. These specialists examine
reports of damage to or loss of cargoes such as mineral oils
and bulk cargoes such as ores or coal. For information on this
work, see for example www.minton.co.uk.

59 The National Engineering and Construction Recruitment
Exhibition. Every year an exhibition of jobs and
apprenticeships in aerospace, automotive, mechanical,
manufacturing, defence, civil and structural engineering
and construction takes place. For information visit
www.engineeringjobs.co.uk.

60 Undergraduate placements. Many institutes offer
undergraduate placements and sponsorships.
See for example www.sanger.ac.uk.

Set 6: Putting something back

One person can make a difference. In fact, there are so many ways we can make the world a better place. Below are 50 examples, all unpaid, that give a flavour of the variety of opportunities that exist. Voluntary work or internships, either full-time or part-time, bring benefits for volunteers as well as for the communities they serve. Many volunteers are provided with training in skills that will help them in their search for paid work. In industries where applicants far outnumber opportunities, starting as a volunteer can mean you later succeed in your application when many others fail. Voluntary positions exist all over the world as well as in your local community. Volunteers can work a few hours a month, a week or a day, or full-time. The choice is yours. Normally expenses such as travel costs are paid, and often a lunch allowance is provided. Most local authorities have volunteer co-ordinators who can help match you to a voluntary position. The Department of Employment's Jobcentre personal advisors may also help you find voluntary work.

1 Volunteer board member for a youth arts project. Every charitable organization has a management board and a board of trustees, and many are looking for volunteers to serve on their boards. If you have experience from business, administration or finance, or simply lots of common sense, then consider volunteering to serve on the board of a charity active in an area that interests you. For further information visit, for example, www.wigmore-hall.org.uk or www.OperationSmile.org.

2 Teach English in Ecuador or for that matter anywhere that inspires you. Teaching English as a Foreign Language is a huge business and many of the poorer nations rely on volunteers. You will need to train if you are not already qualified, but within a few months of starting you should find yourself on your way to a real adventure. You can find out more from, for example, www.transitionsabroad.com, www.transitionsabroad.com/listings/work and www.teachabroad.com/search/ecuador.

3 Driver for a charity for the elderly. Mobility is a major obstacle to the elderly and a large number of organizations organize volunteer drivers. If you have access to a car and like to drive, then your local authority should have a volunteers'

co-ordinator who will put you in touch with a relevant charity. See for example www.rotary.org.

4   Work at a shelter for homeless children in India. Volunteer positions abroad are available through many organizations. Which opportunities are right for you will depend on the skills you offer, your experience and interest. Examples of projects can be found at www.skcv.com and www.i-indiaonline.com.

5   Translator/interpreter for an inner-city community project. If you speak a minority language then you will always find work helping with translation and acting as an interpreter. This will keep your language skills sharp and allow you to meet people from that linguistic community. You can find information on these sorts of project at www.islingtonvolunteeringassociation. org/contact.php and www.mind.org.uk.

6   Live with a family in Russia and help them learn English. Even if you do not have the qualifications to teach English formally there are many opportunities for you to help and travel. You will find families all over the world willing to provide you with food and lodging in return for teaching English. Find out more at, for example, www.goabroad.com/providers/ geovisions/programs/live-with-a-russian-family-and-teach-them-english and www.serendipity-russia.com/engculture.htm.

7   Minutes writer for a sexual abuse support centre. If there is a charitable activity with which you feel an empathy, then contact them because there may well be some way that you can help. If you have specific skills then your offer may be of considerable value to them. Organizations such as the women's resource centre may be able to put you in touch with a local organization: www.wrc.org.uk. Also worth a view is www.napac.org.uk.

8   Medical volunteer in the Philippines. If you belong to any of the many medical professions, then there are a great many voluntary opportunities available to you. You can choose from projects anywhere in the world. Schemes are described at www.globalmedicforce.org and www.CFHI.org.

9   Listening volunteer. A large number of volunteers give up their time to listen and offer sympathy and sound advice to people suffering a personal crisis. Charities active in this field provide training and support to their volunteers.

For further information see www.volunteerscotland.org.uk and www.samaritans.org.

10 Sea turtle conservation volunteers, Trinidad and Tobago. There are a number of organizations offering the opportunity to work in turtle conservation in the southern Caribbean islands and other parts of the world. Volunteers help with keeping a turtle watch, collecting eggs and incubating them, feeding the young turtles and releasing them into the wild. Find out more at www.seeturtles.org/663/volunteer.

11 Helpline volunteers for a child death charity. Staffing help lines is a major area of voluntary work. If you have personal experience of the area of work of the charity, then you are best qualified to offer such support. Volunteers may also find that it helps them too, in that they feel some small good can come from their traumatic experience. You can find out more at www.childdeathhelpline.org.uk and www.ndcs.org.uk.

12 Volunteer work in an orphanage in Kenya. You don't necessarily need any professional experience of childcare to help in an orphanage. Some of the requests are for people willing to simply spend time with the children and help with daily chores. It's really valuable help all the same and will change lives. You can find out more about such programmes at www.volunteerabroad.com/search/kenya, www.advance-africa.com/Kenya-Volunteer-Orphanages and www.globalvolunteernetwork.org.

13 Guide for a national museum. Many museums, even the very prestigious, use volunteer cultural guides to lead groups, answer the queries of visitors and help ensure they get the most from their visit. Why not contact the volunteer co-ordinator of your favourite museum and find out if you can help. Training will be provided and you will be able to see the back-of-house operations. For further information have a look at the frequently asked questions pages at www.museumsassociation.org.

14 Skills training for young people in the Dominican Republic. A good many organizations provide skills training to young people in developing countries of central America, the Caribbean, Africa and Asia. If you have a craft and you can teach it, then you have the opportunity to start young people

off on a career that they can use for the rest of their working lives. Even if you don't have a craft that you can teach there are still opportunities to teach subjects such as life skills. For further information browse www.crs.org/dominican-republic/projects.

15 Volunteer friend for prisoners and their families. A number of charities provide support to both prisoners and their families by putting them in touch with friends. A friend will listen, correspond and help where they can. It can make a huge difference to the individuals concerned and may help to reduce the likelihood of re-offending on release. There are also organizations that provide support for the victims of crime. You can read more at www.pffs.org.uk/volunteers.

16 Clean up your area campaigners and volunteers. If there is something about where you live that you think could be improved and you have thought 'why doesn't someone do something about it?' then perhaps it's time you took the initiative. You can lead by example, roll up your sleeves and make a start yourself. You may well find that others join you; alternatively, you can recruit others and between you set about the task. Such groups have formed to clear up litter or slow down traffic for example. Find out how you can play an active role in your community by visiting www.csv.org.uk.

17 Special police officer. The police forces in the UK (including the transport police) recruit and use volunteer support police officers. Special constables receive training and uniforms and work alongside a member of the police force at, for example, public events and town centres on a Saturday night. Many use voluntary work as a special to support their application for a position as a police officer. You can find further details at www.policecouldyou.co.uk/specials.

18 Volunteer handyman/woman. If you are a DIY enthusiast there is a constant need for your skills in the homes of the elderly or to help tenants of housing associations. You can find out how to be a volunteer in your community at, for example, www.volunteering.org.uk.

19 Trustee for the management board of a charity. Every charity, large or small, has a board of trustees. It is a responsible position and one to think about carefully before you embark

on it because it may involve you in taking responsibility for the liabilities of the charity if it is not run properly. The charities commission has useful information at www.charity-commission.gov.uk.

20 Sports mentor for youth. If sport is your thing, then there is a great deal of good you can do organizing or getting involved in activities for young people. A number of charities focus on organizing such events for young people believed to be at risk of offending, and they hope that if these young people are encouraged to get involved in sport they are less likely to offend. Find out about this type of voluntary work at www.youthsporttrust.org.

21 Personal finance advisor. Many debt counselling charities recruit volunteer personal finance advisors to counsel their clients on how to best manage debt or negotiate with their creditors. If you have experience in personal finance, then your involvement would be very welcome. There are a number of training programmes available for people who are interested in getting involved but have no direct experience of debt counselling. Visit, for example, the Personal Finance Society at www.thepfs.org.

22 Volunteer law and human rights placements. Societies and pressure groups active in equality and human rights use volunteers to, for example, keep in touch with the families of political prisoners, campaign for appeal hearings or raise public awareness of issues. For more information visit, for example, www.unv.org.

23 Volunteers in animal care. Many charities exist for the care of animals and they use volunteers to, for example, care for rescued stray animals or care for animals that would otherwise be destroyed. Find out more at sites such as www.battersea.org.uk and www.rspca.org.uk.

24 Dog walker for elderly neighbours. Many elderly people living alone greatly enjoy the companionship of a dog but are unable to exercise it sufficiently due to restricted mobility. A neighbour who is happy to walk the dog is doing them a service, and might just stay a little fitter too.

25 Volunteer education advisor. Many developing countries welcome the support of educationalists who are willing to

train teachers in the latest educational theories and practices. Opportunities of this sort are regularly advertised in Southern Africa, isolated island communities in the South Atlantic and the Caribbean. Find out about this sort of experience at www.network4africa.org.

26 Archaeology fieldworker. Volunteers make up a sizable number of the individuals involved in the vast majority of archaeological digs. They work under the direction of the site archaeologist and attend specialist briefings on the discoveries made. You can find out more at, for example, www.archaeologyfieldwork.com.

27 Researcher in the House of Commons. Many backbench Members of Parliament employ voluntary researchers to help with the drafting of questions and analysis of official figures. To see if a position is available, contact your MP.

28 Volunteers in radio and print journalism. These are exceptionally difficult industries to get employed in, and starting as a volunteer is a well-proven way to get started. For projects abroad see www.projects-abroad.co.uk/volunteer-projects. Also visit www.journalism.co.uk.

29 Give business advice to young people. Share your experience in business by helping young people to explore or test a business idea. For further information see, for example, the Prince's Trust at www.princes-trust.org.uk.

30 Fundraiser for a local hospice. A volunteer helping to raise funds for a hospice may help out in a charity shop or help organize a series of fund raising events. Contact your local hospice for information.

31 Provide leadership skills training for young people living in deprived communities. Leadership skills training is about empowering people to help themselves and the communities in which they live. Leadership skills training is provided in many communities judged to be disadvantaged in terms of access to employment or education. See for example www.preset.org.

32 Assembling flat-pack furniture for re-housed families. If you are mobile and handy, then offering to assemble flat-pack furniture for re-housed families is a way in which you can

contribute to your community. Housing associations or local authority housing departments will let you know if they use volunteers for this role. You can browse volunteer opportunities at www.timebank.org.uk. Or you could propose helping with flat-pack furniture at, for example, www.wrvs.org.uk.

33 Overseas volunteer conservation fieldworker. There are many overseas national parks or sites of special scientific interest that rely on volunteers to help with maintenance and management. The work can involve activities such as helping to remove invasive species, building or repairing fences, planting native species, leading groups of visitors and fundraising. Find out more at, for example, www.earthwatch.org.

34 Ranger at a historic site or nature reserve. If you have a favourite place of historic importance or a natural site of which you are particularly fond, then consider becoming a volunteer ranger leading groups of visitors, describing the place to them and answering their queries. You will need to study and become an expert on the location, and most venues offer training to their volunteers. Find out what it's like to work in the UK national parks or how to join as a volunteer at www.nationalparks.gov.uk.

35 Volunteer coastguard. There are charitable organizations that organize volunteer coastguards to provide help in the event of a maritime accident or shipwreck. The volunteer staff watch sites, monitor the radio and patrol inshore in small vessels. The largest of these organizations in the UK and Ireland is the RNLI, which provides all-weather offshore and inshore lifeboats. The UK coastal watch system is operated by the Maritime and Coastguard Agency: www.mcga.gov.uk.

36 Volunteer paramedic. There are a number of charities that provide paramedics and first aid at public events. To become a volunteer and receive first-class training in these life-saving skills, contact for example the St John Ambulance service.

37 Amateur theatre. A great deal of theatre is amateur and everyone involved in these productions is unpaid. Many people in the paid theatre business started their career in amateur companies.

38 Counsellor. A great many counsellors in fields such as marriage guidance are volunteers who give their time freely to help others resolve personal matters. They operate to the same professional standard as a paid counsellor, they often belong to the same professional bodies and attend regular training and case reviews with their peers. Increase your knowledge of what counselling involves and the opportunities available at, for example, www.thecounsellorsguide.co.uk/voluntary-counselling and www.youthlinecounselling.co.uk.

39 Volunteer at the Olympic games. It is not just the athletes who are amateur in the Olympics; representatives of sports governing bodies, judges and invigilators are all volunteers too. For the 2012 games visit www.london2012.com/get-involved/volunteering.

40 Saturday morning soccer team coach. A great army of people help organize and invigilate weekend amateur sporting events for both adults and children. Get along to your local teams and ask how you might help.

41 Local community conservation fieldworker. Educational sites and urban sites of scientific interest use volunteers to help maintain the sites' bio-diversity and sustainability. Your local authority volunteer co-ordinator will have details.

42 Soldier in the Territorial Army. The Territorial Army is staffed by volunteers who train at weekends and evenings and attend longer training events where they exercise alongside the regular army. Members of the Territorial Army go on active service and in times of crisis are called on to help defend the nation. Find out more at www.armyjobs.mod.uk.

43 Volunteer boat watch at a dinghy sailing club. Every dinghy club has a safety boat staffed by volunteers who assist if any of the sailors get into difficulties. Contact your local yacht club or the RYA.

44 Reading coach at a primary school. Many primary schools use volunteers as classroom assistants to help children to learn to read. Reading skills are best developed through one-to-one support and teachers simply do not have sufficient time to provide the required amount of attention to each child when they may have as many as 30 in the class.

Contact your local authority to enquire about voluntary work in schools.

45 Forum moderator. Every internet forum has moderators who check that comments are legal and decent, and administer the site. The larger commercially sponsored or owned forums have paid moderators but the vast majority of specialist forums are run by volunteers. If you are active on any forum, then approach the moderator to see if he or she needs assistance.

46 Representative in local government. Most elected representatives in local government are volunteers in that they freely give up their time to represent the electorate. Google the political party of your choice and click on their 'get involved' page.

47 Adult literacy or numeracy tutor. The formal education system fails many people who leave compulsory education without a sufficient grasp of the basic skills of reading, writing and mathematics. Some of these individuals have the courage to address that failure as adults and will work for many months learning these key skills. Most of the teachers who assist them in this are volunteers. You can e-mail the Basic Skills Agency at enquiries@basic-skills.co.uk.

48 Political party activist. Political activists work as volunteers for the political party they support. They raise funds and canvas for their candidates and call around to help get the voters out at election time. Contact the party of your choice and they will be pleased to gain your support.

49 Mountain rescue or ski patrol. In areas of the world where people practise the leisure pursuits of mountaineering or skiing, there are volunteers who patrol or will go in search of someone lost or injured on the slopes. Visit, for example, www.mountain.rescue.org.uk/contact-us and www.mrc-scotland.org.uk.

50 Blog staff member. Some of the larger and very active blogs are run by a collection of individuals who each post a minimum amount of content each month and share the task of responding to comments and moderating them. Create your own blog or find the top 100 UK blogs and get involved at www.blog.co.uk or www.blogstorm.co.uk/top-100-uk-blogs.

Set 7: The arts, crafts and trades

Your preference for the straightforward and for dealing with real things makes you well suited for any of the following 50 crafts or trades. Consider learning on the job by taking up an apprenticeship. They last between one and four years. There are something like 190 types of apprenticeship offered in the UK, covering virtually every area of industry. You can follow an apprenticeship, advanced apprenticeship (equivalent to two A level passes) or higher apprenticeship. You can find out about them at www.apprenticeships.org.uk and www.direct.gov.uk.

1 Stonemason. Stonemasons build, repair or restore natural stone buildings in, for example, limestone, sandstone and granite. The sawn blocks are cut and shaped in workshops, and some are decorated with designs or figures. The finished blocks are then fixed on site. For further information see, for example, the National Heritage training group at www.nhtg.org.uk.

2 Weavers produce fabrics or carpets on a loom. In Europe hand-made fabrics and carpets are still produced to traditional designs for traditional costumes or for tourists. Weaving is also practised to produce works of art and for clients who want a bespoke product to their own design. See, for example, www.mertonpriory.org and www.axminster-carpets.co.uk.

3 Traditional sign writer. Not everyone wants a sign produced in vinyl; some people prefer one painted by hand. A hand-painted sign suggests quality. Traditional establishments and historic tourist attractions use the services of traditional sign writers. Be inspired by browsing the sites www.petewitneysigns.co.uk and www.waynetanswell-signwriter.co.uk.

4 Conservators and restorers. Fine art, furniture and ceramics may need conserving at some point and the specialists who undertake this work are restorers. They work for museums and libraries (on the conservation of historic books and manuscripts) or are self-employed and undertake restorations on items in private collections. For further information see, for example, www.thebritishmuseum.ac.uk.

5   Fine art copyist. Some fine artists will undertake a commission to produce a copy of another artist's work. Often these are historic pieces, perhaps a painting of an ancestor that another member of the family would also like to own. For further information see the websites of members of the Royal Academy of Art, which can be found in the Royal Academicians section of the website www.royalacademy.org.uk.

6   Thatcher. Some historic buildings and buildings in conservation areas are roofed with a thatch made from reed or wheat straw. A thatcher is someone who makes thatched roofs. The work begins with the removal of the old thatch and the cleaning up of the mess it unavoidably makes. Then, bale after bale of reed are carried up ladders to where thatchers work at laying the new roof. For further information see the National Society of Master Thatcher's website at www.nsmtitd.co.uk.

7   Welder. Welding is used extensively in the automotive industry, agriculture and manufacturing. These days the main types of welding are TIG (tungsten inert gas welding) and MIG (metal inert gas welding). It takes a lot of practice to become competent and years of practice to become really good, but once mastered it can be a rewarding trade. You can begin your research by visiting www.welderwelding.com and www.millerwelds.com.

8   Leather worker. Tanners prepare leather by treating, stretching and shaping animal skins. Other workers fashion the leather into goods such as shoes, bags and saddles. Despite competition from imports, craftspeople can still trade in specialist niches and top-of-the-range hand-made items. Visit, for example, www.leatherworker.net.

9   Dry-stone waller. The craft of building dry-stone walls continues, especially in conservation areas and national parks. You can find out more about both the career and training at the Dry Stone Wall Association website at www.dswa.org.uk.

10 Farrier. A farrier is a specialist blacksmith who shoes horses. See, for example, www.farriertraining.co.uk.

11 Glass blower or glass artist. These are crafts and arts with a fascinating history and a promising future. Glass artists

provide sculptures in glass for architectural settings, glass blowers make beautiful objects for everyday use. Jewellery in glass is very popular. For further information, see for example www.glassart.org.

12 Locksmith. Locksmiths fit locks and assist in emergencies when someone is locked out. There are a number of courses available; see for example www.locksmithcourses.co.uk, www.uklocksmithassociation.co.uk and www.sas-locksandtraining.co.uk.

13 Joiner. Joiners prepare timber and board and make the many fittings used in the construction industry. Entry to the trade is usually through an apprenticeship. Find out about training at www.connexions-direct.com.

14 Roofer. These tradesmen and women construct new roofs, replace old ones or make repairs to roofs, using tiles, metal sheet, thermoplastic products, wood and tar. Some roofers complete formal apprenticeships but this is not always necessary as openings in the profession are usually available to anyone willing to work hard and learn on the job. For a list of employers, visit www.nfrc.co.uk.

15 Blacksmith. Blacksmiths work metal at a forge. These days they make, for example, wrought iron gates and fences, security bars and garden decorations. See for example the website of the Worshipful Company of Blacksmiths and the British Artist Blacksmith Association. Be inspired by browsing www.baba.org.uk.

16 Crane operative. Next time you watch the cranes swinging over a building site delivering the building material at the multiple points where gangs are working, spare a thought for the people operating them. It is a highly skilled and well-paid position. You can find out more about it at, for example, www.towercranetraining.co.uk, www.careers-scotland.org.uk and www.connexions-direct.com.

17 Bookbinder. In this trade you create (by hand) bindings for limited editions or old and rebound titles. Bookbinders are employed in historic libraries, museums and specialist publishers. The binder of historic works must understand the binding technique used when the volume was published and recreate it using appropriate materials and techniques.

Make visiting the site of the Society of Book Binders your next step: www.societyofbookbinders.com.

18   Potter. Potters work in ceramics to produce household items (such as cups, bowls, plates) and works of art. They learn to work clay on a wheel, master the chemistry of glazes and the furnace. Hand-made ceramics remain popular and a potter is often found trading in tourist locations. Be inspired by viewing, for example, www.studiopottery.co.uk.

19   Bricklayer. Bricklaying belongs to the trowel trades or wet trades. Bricklayers build walls or lay floors made from stones. They form the walls by laying the bricks in mortar. There are apprenticeships in bricklaying. You can find out more at www.bricklayer.co.uk, www.careers-scotland.org.uk and www.connexions-direct.com.

20   Steeplejack. In this trade you work at height to maintain or repair buildings such as towers, chimneys and church steeples. Steeplejacks will for example re-point brickwork, paint surfaces, re-tile and affix flashing or weather boards, whatever is required – all at a height or at hard-to-reach locations. You can read about training as a steeplejack at www.slptraininggroup.org.uk.

21   Painters. These workers prepare a surface for painting and apply paint to it. They will apply different specialized paints depending on the type of material and its location. For further information see, for example, the website www.icipaints.co.uk.

22   Decorators. In this trade you will paint a room or wallpaper it; some will master specialist techniques such as marbling, applying gold leaf and reproducing old painted effects. You can find out more at, for example, www.paintingdecoratingassociation.co.uk.

23   Installing and servicing domestic appliances. Washing machines, dishwashers and electric stoves require installing and repairing. This work is undertaken by electricians who choose to specialize in domestic appliances. They are employed by retailers or are self-employed. For information on the sort of training available for this occupation, visit for example www.emagister.co.uk/domestic_appliance_repair_courses and www.apprenticeships.org.uk.

24 General construction operative. The construction industry is varied and a training as a general operative provides the key skills to work in any part of it. It also provides the opportunity to find a specialization that interests you and move into that area. You can find out lots more at www.connexions-direct.com.

25 Lightning conductor engineer. Buildings must be protected against lightning strikes and this work is undertaken by specialist engineers. To find out about this specialization, visit www.steeple-jack.co.uk.

26 Tattooist. Tattooists decorate clients' bodies with permanent designs created by injecting coloured inks just below the skin. You can find out more about the career if you visit for example the Tattoo Club of Great Britain at www.tatoo.co.uk or the Alliance of Professional Tattooists (US) at www.safe-tattoos.com.

27 Colour technologist. Colour technologists produce dyes and pigments for use in industry, or they measure and apply the correct amount of colour additives during a manufacturing process. They achieve this through the application of scientific techniques. To get started, visit www.colourtechnology.org.

28 Dyer. This trade is practised by someone who has learned to apply pigments and dyes in the production of fabrics. Dyers learn their trade through experience rather than a conscious application of scientific techniques. Whereas colour technologists will work to ensure they can produce the same colour repeatedly, a dyer will work to ensure that the finished item is equally beautiful even if slightly different from others. For a listing of artisan dyers, visit www.thefibreholics.co.uk.

29 Papermaker. Industrial paper production relies on workers operating pulping machinery and filter presses. There are artisans who still produce paper by traditional techniques using rags and wood pulp. These craft workers make albums or greeting cards and other high-value paper products. The artisan paper maker is often found in locations frequented by tourists. For example Venice, Italy, has many papermakers. Be inspired by a UK papermaker at www.handmadepaper.co.uk.

30 Set carpenter. In the theatre and film industries, set carpenters build structures used as backdrops or props for the production. These constructions can be substantial, employing a whole team of carpenters. The lead carpenter is usually named in the credits. There is an advanced apprenticeship in set carpentry; see for example www.apprentiships.org.uk.

31 Set painter. The film and theatre industries use painters to finish sets and backdrops. This work is completed by staff employed by the production company or by specialist set-making workshops. The skills of the set painter make the illusion of travel and change of location possible. A set painter may have studied fine art as well as advanced painting and decorating techniques. Be inspired by visiting www.onsetart.co.uk.

32 Printmaker. Traditional printing methods are still practised, and printmakers are employed in the production of, for example, personal stationery such as letterheads and calling cards, invitations and notices. Be enthused by visiting www.valeriesims.co.uk.

33 Etcher. This trade involves engraving or etching metal, glass, wood or other materials for identification or decorative purposes. The work of an etcher includes pantograph engraving and silk screen etching. Etchers can undertake work ranging from a dog's name tag to glass walls etched with a company's logo or design. View the work of a craftsman at www.johnbrunsdon.com.

34 Wooden toy maker. Toys hand-made in wood are popular gifts, and craft workers who produce toys in wood can run a small workshop selling to passing trade in busy tourist locations or supplying specialist retailers. For more information, visit www.robroy-woodentoys.co.uk/index.htm and www.toymakersguild.co.uk.

35 French polisher. In this specialist trade, shellac dissolved in spirit was traditionally used to produce a smooth finish on wood. Nowadays French polishers work with a wide variety of stains, oils and waxes. They work on furniture and household fittings such as doors and panels. See, for example, www.tracyspolishers.co.uk and www.touchwoodpolishing.co.uk.

36 Carpet fitters. People in this trade fit not only carpets but wooden flooring, vinyl and pretty well every type of floor covering. They work in homes, offices, hotels – anywhere where the floor is covered. They have to cut the covering to exact measurements and remove and dispose of old coverings. You can find out about the sort of training available for this work at, for example, www.uk-flooring-academy. co.uk and www.fita.co.uk.

37 Ductwork installer. Ducting is used in a wide number of systems, including communications, networking, heating and ventilation, plumbing and electrical installations. Ductwork installers specialize in the provision of channels and conduits for cables and pipes. In some instances the ductwork that they install is hundreds of miles long, when for example they run ducting along railway lines or under the streets for fibre optic communications. Find out about how to train for this trade at, for example, www.hotcourses.com/uk-courses/ Ductwork-Installation and www.northglasgowcollege.ac.uk.

38 Illustrator of books. Many books, especially technical texts and children's books, include illustrations and these are produced by artists trained in illustration or who simply possess a portfolio of work that wins them commissions. Some illustrators use agents to find commissions but increasingly they can make contact with writers and publishers through web pages and writers' forums. For ideas and information visit, for example, www.ukchildrensbooks.co.uk, www.jackiemorris.co.uk and www.britishscbwi.jimdo.com.

39 Cabinet maker. These workers create furniture and kitchen units, usually as one-offs or in small quantities. They will accept the brief from the customer and agree the design and materials before making the item. Be inspired at, for example, www.dimensionfurniture.co.uk.

40 Plastering. In this craft you produce the finished surface on which paint or paper is applied. Some plasterers go on to specialize in the production and fitting of ornate, decorative plaster details that are attached to walls and ceilings. For courses and information browse www.ukplaster.com, www.constructiontrainingservices.co.uk or www.coursesplus.co.uk/plastering.

41 Glazier. Glass is used extensively in construction, and cutting it and fitting it is the job of glaziers. Some glaziers replace broken windows or install retail display windows. Others specialize in glazing large office buildings under construction. You can find out more at the Worshipful Company of Glaziers' website: www.nhtg.org.uk/careers/occupations.

42 Service and maintenance engineer. These engineers plan and carry out the maintenance of all kinds of machinery and equipment. They are employed in every industrial sector, and service equipment in offices, hospitals, airports, factories, universities and shopping malls. They are employed either by the manufacturer of the equipment, the leaser of it or the organization that owns it. For further information visit www.thecareerengineer.com, www.jobisjob.co.uk/aircraft-maintenance-engineer/jobs and www.justengineers.net.

43 Florist. In this craft you sell flowers and plants and create floral arrangements. Florists provide arrangements for hotel receptions, bouquets for weddings and bunches of flowers as gifts. You can train in floristry at, for example, www.ukschooloffloristry.com.

44 Dressmaker. Dressmakers work freelance from home or a studio and attend fairs, shows and retailers to promote their creations. Many operate in niches such as bridal wear. You can find out more at, for example, www.sewessential.co.uk, www.hotcourses.com/uk-courses/Dressmaking/dressmaking-courses/page.htm and www.weddingframes.co.uk.

45 Model maker. This craft involves creating scale models for the architectural industry or for museums and film production companies. Models are made to scale and may be used to support sales of a prototype or commemorate a famous car, ship or plane. For insight into what this work involves, visit for example www.wallopwoodcrafts.co.uk.

46 Auto parts fitter. This work involves the removal and fitting of parts in the motor trade. It is practical, manual and dirty work. Fitters usually specialize in one area, for example brake systems or transmission. Some fitters become self-employed. Find out more about this career by locating the auto part fitter job profile at www.careersadvice.direct.gov.uk.

47 Heating and ventilating fitter. These fitters install heating and ventilation systems for a very wide range of situations and clients. The system may ventilate a bakery's oven or a blacksmith's forge, deliver clean air to an operating theatre, or provide warm air in an exhibition hall. Fitters are able to fabricate in metal and weld. You can find information about this career at the heating and ventilating fitter profile pages at www.careers-scotland.org.uk.

48 Tool maker. These craftsmen and women set up and operate machining tools such as radial drills, lathes, milling machines, shapers and grinders to produce small numbers of a product. Find out more about this advanced trade by searching for 'toolmaker' at www.careersadvice.direct.gov.uk.

49 Plumber. Whether in a large hotel or residential property, the systems that supply clean hot and cold water, sanitation and hot-water heating are installed, maintained and serviced by plumbers. The Chartered Institute of Plumbers' site is found at www.ciphe.org.uk.

50 Wood carver. If you're looking for something different and are good with wood and can carve figures, then there is a ready market for high-quality figures and puppets. For example, the art of ventriloquism is still very popular and the artist will place an order for a hand-made dummy. Imagine telling people you are a ventriloquist figure maker when asked 'what do you do?' For examples of the highest quality of woodcarving in general, visit the Association of Wood and Stone Carvers' site at www.mastercarvers.co.uk.

Set 8: Sales and retail

Many employers recognize your personality and motivations as ideally suited for a profession in sales. If you have never given this line of business a second thought, then suspend your judgement for a few minutes and review the career breaks that exist in this diverse and dynamic industry.

1 Authors' agent. Fiction writers in particular use agents to find publishers for their work. Agents will consider the work of the writer and decide whether in their opinion it is publishable. Some publishers will only consider manuscripts submitted by agents. Agents take a percentage of the advance and royalties paid to the author if they succeed in selling the work to a publisher. You can find out more at www.literaryagent.co.uk and www.agentsassoc.co.uk.

2 Model. Models market products by being photographed wearing them or by using them, and so persuading people to buy them. Models also promote products at business fairs and public events, and either hand out promotional samples or sell them at the events. Start your search at www.models1.co.uk, www.stormmodels.com or www.bmamodels.com.

3 Rental clerk. Whatever you rent or hire – whether it's a vehicle, item of heavy machinery or specialist tool – a rental clerk handles the transaction. They must check that you are suitable qualified to use the equipment, confirm your ID and secure a deposit. They check that the equipment is serviceable and demonstrate to you how to use it. They must take payment for the rental and issue a receipt and terms of use. Visit the careers pages at organizations such as www.Hertz.com.

4 Counter clerks are the customer contact in establishments such as dry cleaners and repair centres. They present a professional image to visitors, receive the item or items belonging to the customer and issue a receipt for it. They answer queries and take payment. You can find counter clerk jobs at, for example, www.indeed.co.uk. For post office counter vacancies, see your local jobsites or the employment service.

5 Commodity trader. Commodities are the basic ingredients of commerce, such as food items like grain or coffee beans and resources such as oil and copper ore. Commodity traders buy and sell commodities, and even buy and sell future commodities at set prices. They often work for organizations that consume large amounts of a certain commodity; for example an airline will employ a commodity trader to secure supplies of aviation fuel. They are also employed by the producers of the commodity and are used to trade in commodities by private investors. You can find out more at www.commoditytrader.com and www.commoditytrader.net.

6 Business-to-business sales representative. Representatives that operate in the business-to-business (B2B) sector specialize in selling to business. B2B is trade between businesses, for example a manufacturer and wholesaler, or wholesaler and retailer. A good source for B2B sales reps vacancies is www.jobsearch.monster.co.uk/Sales-Business. Look also at www.salesprorecruitment.co.uk.

7 Residential sales representative. This is another way to describe door-to-door selling, which involves a team of sales representatives who usually sell household items by calling at homes. You can find listing of vacancies at, for example, www.thesalesjob.com. For vacancies selling in Spain see, for example, www.timesharestaff.com.

8 In-store demonstrator. Demonstrators promote products in stores or at business fairs. The most common items are cosmetics, kitchen equipment and household goods. In some of the large toyshops, demonstrators provide a carnival-type atmosphere by exhibiting toys to the children and their guardians. Demonstrators are usually paid on commission and a good demonstrator with a good product can make a large number of sales. Google 'in-store demonstrator' for jobsites. See, for example, www.jobisjob.co.uk/west-midlands/store-demonstrator and www.simplyhired.co.uk/a/jobs/list/q-instore+demonstrator.

9 Business development executive. These high-profile representatives generate leads, book and attend business appointments, build relationships with new and existing clients and retain clients through successful account management. For development executive openings browse, for example, www.exec-appointments.com and www.salesnet.ltd.uk. Network through sites such as www.linkedin.com.

10 Financial services sales agent. These agents work for commissions tied to the sale of financial services. Many work online or at call centres, promoting offers to clients and offering advice. Much of the work is done in the evenings and weekends at times convenient to the clients. Check out the regulations at www.fsa.gov.uk.

11 Key account sales representative. These people are responsible for generating, developing and maintaining sales to key customers. They discuss potential sales, prepare quotes and proposals, follow up, negotiate terms and close deals. They participate in trade shows or scientific meetings and other activities relevant to their companies' products and they usually undertake a great deal of travel. You can find these vacancies listed if you search at, for example, www.simplyhired.co.uk and www.randstad.co.uk.

12 Insurance sales agent. Insurance sales agents advise their clients on which insurance policies to buy. They specialize in different types of client – for example business customers or people with particular interests – and arrange the most appropriate cover. Find out how to become an authorized representative at www.fsa.gov.uk and www.biba.org.uk.

13 100 per cent commission sales representative. If you are confident in your abilities and have a strong drive for results combined with strong selling and customer-service skills, then find the right product and this might be for you. 100 per cent commission sales representatives spend all of their time on the sales floor advising customers, providing product knowledge and advice, and closing deals. 100 per cent commission means that 100 per cent of their income from the job comes from commission made on sales. For listings of commission-only sales positions see, for example, www.freelancer.com/projects/by-tag/100-commission-sales-jobs-work-home.html and www.peopleperhour.com/freelance_jobs.

14 Product promoters. These representatives are charged with getting products into retail chains; they build product awareness and future sales by offering samples, organizing competitions, distributing prizes and promoting special offers and discounts. For ideas on business and corporate gifts to use in the promotion industry, see www.merchandisemania.co.uk.

15 Real estate sales agent. Real estate agents calculate the dimensions of a property and advise the client of its market value. They draw up promotional literature and post it on the internet, their display boards or windows, and circulate it to their list of clients. They show the property to prospective buyers and help with the negotiation and contracts. They charge a fee on the value of the sale. Visit the Real Estate Agents Association at www.naea.co.uk.

16 Telesales. Representatives in telesales generate sales leads for the sales representatives or territory sales representatives. They make outbound calls to new and existing clients, promoting the company and the products and seeking to open leads that a sales representative can convert into a sale. They record information gained from calls to build a database of contacts. For telesales vacancies view, for example, www.telesalesvacancies.com, www.1job.co.uk and www.agencycentral.co.uk.

17 Retail salesperson. Retail sales staff help customers in the store to find what they are looking for, demonstrate or describe a product's features and close the deal. Some items can sell themselves – for example food – and stores that sell such items do not need to employ retail sales staff. However items that are more complex or less essential – such as electronics, clothes and sports gear – sell better if a sales assistant is on hand to offer advice. For insight into the current opportunities in the retail industry see, for example, www.brc.org.uk, www.retra.co.uk/ and www.toyretailersassociation.co.uk.

18 Account manager. Post holders liaise between a company and its clients and ensure that clients are fully benefiting from the product or service that the company offers. In this way they seek to retain clients, inform them about the design of the next product and sell it. Many positions for account managers are advertised at www.jobs.telegraph.co.uk.

19 Technical sales representative. These specialists work in engineering, science, research, manufacturing, health and pharmaceuticals – in fact in any industry that uses complex equipment. They represent the manufacturer of a product and are responsible for its marketing and sales to clients. They also report back to the manufacturer on how the product might be modified to better suit the needs of the clients. You can find technical sales jobs at, for example, www.tech-rep.co.uk.

20 Financial advisor. In this role you provide investment advice and help clients with financial planning. Advisors form a view of their clients' financial needs and goals and their attitude towards risk, and then recommend financial products to them. They are paid either a consultancy fee or a commission from sales or both. See who is listed and the services they offer at www.ftadviser.com.

21   Wholesale sales representative. These representatives sell to wholesalers and retail buyers, or to the procurement officers in large organizations. They sell in large volumes at low margins. They represent a manufacturer or a portfolio of complementary products. Find out more at 'ehow' and view vacancies at 'indeed': www.ehow.co.uk/how_2069001_ become-wholesale-sales-representative and www.indeed.co.uk respectively.

22   Trader whose clients are private investors. This kind of trader provides information about the financial markets and buys and sells shares and bonds, for example, on their clients' behalf. The information they provide is in the form of conversations, financial reports and tips. Find out more at, for example, www.independentinvestor.co.uk and www.uk.saxobank.com.

23   Internet salesperson. Even when people buy through the internet they often want assistance or advice, and obtain this by contacting a salesperson either by e-mail or by telephone. Internet salespersons help ensure that the decision to buy is not based solely on price and that customer satisfaction with both the service and purchase is increased. Internet sales jobs are listed at, for example, www.simplysalesjobs.co.uk.

24   Sales staff supervisor. These individuals manage a team of sales representatives. They will control the timekeeping, appearance and conduct of their team, help recruit new members and deal with disciplinary or grievance matters. They will prepare work schedules and assign members of the team to specific tasks. If their team is modest in size, they will continue to carry out sales duties. See jobs at, for example, www.inretail.co.uk/jobs/shopfloor-sales and www.reed.co.uk/Job.

25   Advertising sales agent. Advertising representatives sell advertising space on websites, billboards, television, radio, newspapers and magazines. At one level this is done by responding to queries and by cold-calling businesses. Advertising reps also develop relationships with advertising agencies and the marketing executives in organizations with

big advertising budgets. See, for example,
www.formula-won.co.uk.

26 Investor relationship manager. Investor relations involves the
    communication of business objectives and performance to
    investors, and a relationship manager is responsible for
    ensuring that investors continue to buy into the organization's
    objectives and recognize the progress made by the
    management team in realizing those goals. The work involves
    for example conference calls, meetings and reporting to
    shareholders and stakeholders. Find out more at, for example,
    www.jobs.efinancialcareers.co.uk, www.jobisjob.co.uk/
    london/investor-relations/jobs and www.jobs.guardian.co.uk.

27 Territory representative. A territorial sales representative is
    responsible for a company's existing and new business sales
    within a geographic area. Typically the areas are defined by the
    number of customers and the distance it is possible to travel
    to meetings and so on. Some territories are necessarily large
    and oblige the representative to undertake many hours of
    commuting. For territory representative positions in the food
    industry see, for example, www.jobs.thegrocer.co.uk.

28 Customer-service manager. These managers work to ensure
    that customers' needs are satisfied; they deal with customer
    complaints and process refunds or the exchange of goods.
    They implement a customer-service policy and deal with
    face-to-face, telephone and internet enquiries from
    customers. Search thousands of vacancies, including
    customer-service manager positions, at www.reed.co.uk/job.

29 Travel agent. Despite the growth of internet sales, travel
    agents are still widely used for travel planning and booking
    arrangements. Most school groups, clubs and business
    travellers rely on agents to find the best deal and put
    together a bespoke package. You will find ideas at
    www.gumtree.com and www.jobs.travelweekly.co.uk.

30 Sales assistant. A sales assistant liaises with clients at the
    point of sale. Assistants that work with high-priced goods
    need both to know the product and its features really well
    and to be very personable. Assistants usually have sales
    targets to reach or a collective team target. They may also be
    responsible for replenishing stock, processing payments and

if appropriate arranging delivery dates. For job listings see, for example, www.jobrapido.co.uk and www.londonjobs.co.uk.

31 Sales agent for a satellite broadcaster. If you know your googlebox from a Seesaw and Tvcatchup, then selling media network subscriptions and peripherals might well interest you. Visit for example the careers page at www.sky.com.

32 Imaging and photographic expert to work in retail sales. Retailers who sell photographic equipment need sales assistants with an infectious passion for photography and a command of the latest innovations. For ideas, browse www.specialtyretailexpert.com and www.dixons.co.uk.

33 Gaming store manager. In this role you would oversee every aspect of the retailing of computer games and accessories. The larger retail chains offer graduate programmes. All stores require staff and managers to be dedicated gamers themselves and able to talk the talk with discerning customers. For openings and ideas, visit www.games-workshop.com.

34 Electronics store colleague. These store colleagues are front of technology store customer advisors who have a good command of most things digital. They will refer customers to in-store experts or advise and close a deal themselves. For further information, see for example the careers pages on the website of DSG international, the parent company of Dixons and PC World.

35 Electronics sales consultant. In this role you help customers make the right product choice by providing impartial advice and demonstrating equipment. View what this career involves at, for example, www.dsgiplc.com.

36 Loyalty consultant. In the mobile phone industry, convincing customers not to disconnect from a network by offering incentives to stay is a common sales strategy and undertaken by loyalty consultants. These specialist consultants are paid a basic salary and bonus for each customer they persuade to stay. Search the sites of the big operators, including www.orange.co.uk and www.t-mobile.co.uk.

37 Customer post-sales support advisor. In this position you handle calls and e-mails from customers after the purchase. These queries may concern how to operate equipment or set it up initially, or may report missing items. Post-sales support jobs can be found with a search at, for example, www.indeed.co.uk.

38 High-end account executive. These executives handle the largest accounts. They have the time to build up personal relationships with representatives of the customer, and the authority to negotiate discounts and unique terms. High-end account positions are sometimes advertised at, for example, www.jobs.dailymail.co.uk/jobs.

39 Foreign language telesales. If you are fluent in another major language, then consider combining that skill with selling by working for an international business handling calls from foreign buyers. You can find openings at, for example, www.telesalesjobs.co.uk/jobs.

40 Green sales. Advising on and supplying green products such as solar panels and wind turbines for residential use is a fast-growing business. Search at, for example, www.greenwisebusiness.co.uk and www.environmentjobs.co.uk.

41 Fundraiser for research. Fundraisers work for institutions or projects to raise funds for the continuation of current research or the funding of future projects. Funds are raised both nationally and internationally through applications to governmental, charitable or private sources and through a great many fundraising activities. You can browse fundraising jobs at, for example, www.fundraising.co.uk and www.charityjob.co.uk.

42 Scientific buyer. If you're good at sales you're good at buying too. Many institutions rely on specialists in procurement to purchase scientific or medical equipment. Such support staff work closely with members of research teams, suppliers and manufacturers of the equipment and those responsible for budgets to ensure that the research objectives are realized in as cost effective a way as possible. See positions advertised at www.newscientistjobs.com.

43 Scientific sales. People working in scientific sales sell laboratory services, instruments and products. They have usually received a scientific training themselves, and this means they are better able to explain the value of the product or service. Scientists sometimes move from research into marketing or sales to promote a service or product to their scientific peers. Search for vacancies at, for example, www.allaboutmedicalsales.com and www.seltekconsultants.co.uk.

44 Sports sales. Most sporting goods retailers employ game specialists who are responsible for providing advice to customers in their purchases. This might include, for example, a tennis player advising on which racket to buy or an athlete recommending the most suitable running shoes. You can find leads at www.leisurejobs.com, www.jobs1.co.uk and www.leisurevacancies.co.uk.

45 Luxury and branded goods and products. The big brands are big names and command a high premium. Selling top-branded goods demands professionalism; the goods must be displayed perfectly and the customer expects impeccable service. Search sites such as www.harrodscareers.com, www.heathrow-airport-guide.co.uk/shops and www.bondstreetassociation.com.

46 Business sales and development manager. Every business needs people to develop sales and identify new business leads. These positions allow the post holder a lot of freedom so long as the new leads are identified and business is won. For sales and development managerial roles look at, for example, www.exec-appointments.com.

47 Ticket sales. This work involves assisting customers with ticket purchases for sporting and other events, informing customers of upcoming events and ticket availability, and helping them select an event. It may also involve providing information and additional sales on subjects such as special assistance and parking. For ticket sales in sport see, for example, www.jobs1.co.uk. For ticket sales generally visit www.ticketmaster.co.uk/careers.

48 Retailer of sports clothing. Sports retail is a high-turnover, customer-focused business. You can specialize in selling sporting clothes, footwear and other branded goods. If you have an in-depth knowledge of a sport, then you can work as a sport specialist advising customers on the best purchase. For an idea of the work and what it involves, visit for example www.jjb.com.

49 Advertising sales. Advertisement slots in magazines, newspapers and on TV are sold by advertising representatives. They advise clients on the specifications required of the artwork and copy, and book the slots. Begin your search at, for example, www.mediarecruiter.com and www.mediaweekjobs.co.uk.

50 Medical device sales. This work involves the positioning and selling of specific products and product solutions. Effective representatives in medical device sales will be well versed in the features, functions and benefits of the device and the evidence that led to its validation. They will also be able to explain its cost/value relative to competitors' devices. Start by visiting www.meddevicejobs.com and www.medreps.com.

Set 9: Earn good money

Every one of the following 50 jobs is well paid. Decide which from the list interests you most and you will have taken the first step towards gaining the financial respect you deserve.

1 IT consultant. Information technology is changing fast and many business operations now depend on highly complex IT systems. IT consultants manage projects or find IT solutions to the challenges facing businesses. Many are self-employed and command high day rates. For information about one of the professional networks, visit www.ISACA.org/Professional-Membership.

2 Recruitment consultant. As a recruitment consultant you will either supply temporary staff or fill permanent positions as a 'headhunter'. Both types require a working knowledge of the industry they serve and a willingness to work hard. A successful consultant can earn a very good basic income plus commission. The Association of Executive Recruits' website is a useful source of ideas: www.rec.uk.com.

3 Environmental consultant. These workers help businesses reduce their carbon emissions and introduce energy efficiencies. Their work starts with an audit of the companies' existing energy use and waste management. They then recommend ways in which energy may be saved and waste better managed. Here are the sites of a couple of environmental consultancies that may be of interest: www.swca.com and www.enviros.com.

4 Banker. They may not be the most popular people but they sure know how to command a top salary. Bankers look after our money and provide loans, credit, and payment services such as debit cards and ATM services. Banks may also offer investment and insurance products. Most employees work in sales and administration. The big money begins with the management positions, which are held by experienced banking professionals. Investment banks provide corporations with investment services, including buying, selling and trading securities, and managing financial assets. Continue your investigation into the opportunities in banking by, for example, browsing www.bankofenglandjobs.co.uk and www.bba.org.uk.

5 Pawnbroker. In this profession you provide loans secured against items of value, called forfeits. Pawnbrokers value an item and advance a sum of money against it; if the loan is not repaid the item is sold. Find out more about pawnbrokers and the sort of work they do at, for example, www.herbertbrown.co.uk and www.pickwickpawnbrokers.co.uk.

6 Bailiff. These workers execute warrants for unpaid magistrates' court fines. They do this by visiting people's homes or places of work. They serve notices and collect money, and maintain records. They have to be able to deal with challenging or distressed people at work and often in the early morning, weekends or evenings when people are at home. You can discover more about a career as a bailiff at www.careersadvice.direct.gov.uk/helpwithyourcareer.

7 Therapist. Counselling and therapy is becoming big business. A therapist in the NHS can earn a professional salary equal to that of any other healthcare professional. A therapist in the complementary therapies can earn between £20 and £50 an hour. The best site for therapist jobs in the NHS is www.nhscareers.nhs.uk.

8 Insolvency practitioner. These professionals are authorized to act as trustees or administrators when an individual, company or partnership is insolvent. See the website of the

Insolvency Practitioners Association (IPA) for details.
For jobs and trainee positions, see for example
www.accountingjobs.co.uk.

9 Debt collector. In this job you help businesses and individuals
collect overdue payments for goods or services. Debt
collectors may also help people manage their finances and
establish plans to pay the money they owe. They chase
unpaid accounts, provide credit reports for clients,
organize the repossession of goods and generally work to
settle unpaid bills. You can find out about becoming
a certified enforcement officer with the courts at
www.thesheriffsoffice.com.

10 Corporate auditors. Their role involves working for large
accounting firms as part of a team that is auditing the books
of national and multinational corporations. The work involves
a lot of travel and paper trails testing the accounting systems
of the client. Within a few years auditors can expect to earn
very respectable salaries. You might find it useful to begin
your research into a career in corporate auditing at the
Financial Reporting Council's website at www.frc.org.uk.

11 Supply teacher. When a teacher is on maternity leave or sick,
the school administrator arranges for a supply teacher to
stand in. A supply teacher does not have the benefits of
being paid when the school is closed and so the day rate is
high. Supply teaching suits teachers who want to save up
some money fast to, for example, go travelling.
For information on a career in education and an example of
a supply teacher agency, browse www.tda.gov.uk and
www.teachingpersonnel.com.

12 General managers at premier resorts and hotels. These
individuals run significant and complex operations and are
paid accordingly. They often specialize in specific types of
resort, for example those with golf clubs or casinos; in some
out-of-the-way locations they must also manage power
generation and water desalination. They usually hold
qualifications in hotel and leisure management and will have
worked their way up the corporate ladder for a decade or
more. Discover some of the opportunities this career offers
by viewing www.raffles.com.

13 Process and manufacturing engineers. These are production experts who develop and improve manufacturing processes with the objective of increasing efficiency. They estimate manufacturing costs and may advise on a product to suggest changes so that its manufacturing cost may be reduced. Find out more at, for example, www.manufacturingmag@iee.org.uk.

14 Chief operations officer. These individuals manage all operational functions of a business and are key members of any corporation's management team. They have a very wide remit and are astute at handling detail and managing staff. They are financially aware and work to targets and budgets. They usually rank second among the highest paid people in a corporation, after the CEO. Other highly paid officers in the corporate world are executives responsible for major subsidiaries or running top-earning divisions or sectors. A large part of the pay packet will be linked to performance and paid in the form of bonuses. You might start your search at, for example, www.economist.com.

15 Business development director in healthcare. In this role post holders will launch new products such as pharmaceuticals and surgical devices. They can command a very good salary once they are proven and especially if they are prepared to join a start-up company. You can begin an exploration of this career at, for example, www.bupa.co.uk/healthcareprofessionals.

16 Visiting lecturer. Many teaching staff in colleges and universities are hired on a freelance basis. Visiting lecturers usually work for a handful of institutions and are often specialists in a particular field (that cannot justify a full-time post). They are paid on an hourly rate. Visiting lecturer jobs are posted at, for example, www.jobs.ac.uk.

17 Intellectual property lawyer. In this branch of law you command top earnings because you will be both a lawyer and an expert in a field such as electrical or mechanical engineering, chemical engineering, biotechnology, pharmacology or computer science. Such people are worth their high salaries because their role is to define or defend the intellectual property of their client, for example through patents and licences to ensure that their client's technology

is not stolen or copied without permission. Continue your investigation into this career at, for example, www.ip-institute.org.uk, www.intute.ac.uk and www.qmipri.org/links.

18 Medical science liaison officers. Pharmaceutical companies employ medical science liaison officers to serve as information providers to doctors and healthcare funders. These officers have science or medical backgrounds and are able to discuss new products or regulatory requirements with their companies' clients. You sometimes find science liaison jobs advertised at www.newscientistjobs.com/jobs.

19 Chief executive officer (CEO). These are the top-paid executives in a corporation and this level is where the buck as well as a great many bucks stop. They answer to investors and are responsible for the legal operation of the corporation. They carry a great deal of responsibility, have immense power and are paid accordingly. Their salary is usually made up of an attractive basic plus bonuses and share options. For these positions, a good place to look is www.ft.com/jobsclassified.

20 Staff accountant. These workers are employed to provide analysis, keep financial records as required by regulation, and ensure the rules are complied with. With four years' experience a staff accountant can expect to earn a very reasonable sum; if the employer is located in a major city they might expect to earn considerably more than at one based in a suburb or small town. Find out more at the website of the ACCA: www.accaglobal.com.

21 Financial analyst. These professionals research a business sector or region and make business and industry recommendations. They may for example recommend to buy or sell stock or commodities, and take into consideration current developments in the field. Most start as junior analysts; obviously the big money is with the senior analysts. Lots of analyst jobs are advertised at www.ft.com/jobsclassified.

22 Credit controller. This role involves running a company's credit department and approving or denying credit to customers. A good credit controller avoids bad debt that would otherwise have to be set against hard-won profit.

For this reason an effective credit controller can expect to earn a good salary. You can find credit controller jobs at, for example, www.reed.co.uk/Job.

23 Biomedical product managers. Product managers working for biomedical companies manage a product from concept through execution to its sales strategy. Once they have a successful track record in bringing products from design to sales, then they can command a very reasonable salary and may well find themselves approached by representatives of competitors seeking experienced managers. Find out more about the work of a biomedical product manager at sites such as www.pfizer.co.uk and www.gsk.com.

24 Air traffic controller. These workers help ensure flight safety around airports by controlling the approach and departure of aircraft. It is a highly responsible job that at times involves working unsocial hours and is consequently well paid. Discover more about the work of an air traffic controller at, for example, www.nats.co.uk.

25 Large supermarket manager. Retail might have a reputation for low pay but the manager of a large supermarket is running a multi-million pound business and managing hundreds of staff, and he or she is paid accordingly. Explore this opportunity at, for example, www.tesco-careers.com.

26 Service station manager. Running a busy service station is big business. Prices are changed daily and health and safety, environmental issues, staff management and stock control are major responsibilities. The manager of a busy station can expect a fat paycheque. Begin your research at, for example, www.q8oils.co.uk.

27 Technology developer. These individuals are experts in skills such as software programming. If they also have experience in finance, trading or analysis then they can earn serious money working for a finance or trading house developing software applications. These individuals are experts in, for example, Microsoft's software programming language so why not take a look at https://careers.microsoft.com.

28 Internet advertising account director. Advertising dollars are moving away from print and television to the internet, and account directors with experience from newsprint or

television are making the same move. A place to begin your search is, for example, www.digitalpersonnel.co.uk.

29 Senior real estate agent. Selling houses, commercial property and land has always had it booms and busts, and most commentators expect the good times and the high salaries to return. A senior agent can expect to be involved in the negotiation of the biggest deals and expect a high salary and commission to match. Find out more at the site of the National Association of Estate Agents: www.naea.co.uk.

30 Legal secretaries. Legal secretaries specialize in a particular field of law, and once experienced provide highly valued support to lawyers. Legal secretaries specializing in patent applications, for example, or fluent in a number of languages and specialized in international law are among the highest paid. You can find out about accredited training at www.institutelegalsecretaries.com.

31 Quality assurance analyst. In this work the post holder evaluates new products to verify that they function according to the user requirements. A good many quality assurance analysts work with software and they compare the product against its design spec to establish whether it performs according to the stated aims and guidelines. You can find these positions listed at, for example, www.people4business.com and www.jobs.guardian.co.uk.

32 Doctor of medicine. Medicine pays well but it is a calling and money is not the prime motive of most applicants. However, if your parents support your desire to attend medical school because they want you to fund their retirement, then they should encourage you to specialize to become a heart surgeon because these are the practitioners who earn really big bucks in the private sector. Find out more at, for example, www.nhscareers.nhs.uk/medical. For information on applying to medical school read *How to Get Into Medical School*, published by Kogan Page.

33 Quality engineer. Quality engineers are key staff in many organizations, but the engineers who specialize in lean manufacturing are really hot commodities. In the automotive industry these engineers will bring efficiencies and reduce waste that over time will amount to the saving of millions of dollars. You can find out more at, for example, www.justengineers.net.

34 Project managers in construction. In this work you oversee building works, and when this involves large commercial or civic projects the budget runs into the tens of millions and managers are responsible for a small army of workers and contractors. They may enjoy the title of director of construction and hold professional qualifications in construction or management. They will also bring to the project a decade or two of experience and they can expect to earn a six-figure dollar salary. Explore the websites of companies that employ construction project managers at, for example, www.wates.co.uk, www.skanska.co.uk and www.balfourbeatty.com.

35 A plant manager. These employees are responsible for directing and co-ordinating all manufacturing activities so as to meet operational goals including health and safety, environment, customer service, quality, cost and productivity. The plant might employ anything from 100 workers upwards and the manufacturing process can be, for example, chemical, mechanical or products for the food industry or building trade. Vacancies for a plant manager in the food industry, for example, might be found at www.northernfoods.com/careers.

Positions that pay well above the average

36 Nurses' positions. Nursing has experienced something of a revolution in recent years and these days a nurse can expect to train to graduate level and have the choice of a wide number of specializations. Specialist nurses earn a salary commensurate with their considerable responsibility and expertise. An agency nurse can earn a higher hourly rate than one employed by a health trust. For further information see, for example, www.nhscareers.nhs.uk, or for a US career www.nurse.com.

37 Lead carpenters. These senior tradesmen and women supervise the on-site completion of construction projects as well as undertaking the most technical carpentry work to finish the job. Traditionally the carpenter was the person present at a site from start to finish, from constructing the forms to fitting windows, doors etc. For this reason it is often the carpenter who is made the supervisor. Find careers opportunities at, for example, www.careerjet.co.uk/ carpentry-jobs and www.theconstructionjob.com.

38 Cable supervisor. This work involves overseeing the work of technicians laying or repairing communication cabling on a site. Supervisors monitor the day's work and ensure company policies and procedures are followed. They ensure that safe working practices are adhered to, and report any problems and the progress of the job at the end of the day. Find the cable companies trading in your area at www.cable.co.uk.

39 Chemical production supervisor. These managers oversee production of chemical products. They are responsible for safe working practices in the production area and the protection of the environment. They supervise the adherence to stated processes and procedures and make sure that packaging, paperwork and labelling are correct. For further information and careers, view www.akzonobel.com/careers.

40 Medical facility housekeeping director. Hospital housekeeping jobs involve cleaning wards, changing linen, maintaining hygiene and keeping the assigned area infection free. The housekeeping supervisor is responsible for monitoring the work of housekeepers, while the director of housekeeping is responsible for staff planning and ensuring that the hygiene and infection control standards of the institute are met. A good place to start your search for further information is www.bupa.co.uk/careers.

41 Flight service manager. Flight service managers are responsible for the quality of all in-flight services to passengers. They review and monitor the performance of flight attendants and make sure that they comply with uniform guidelines. They are responsible for ensuring compliance with the aviation regulatory procedures regarding passenger safety. You can find out more at sites such as www.britishairwaysjobs.com.

42 Train/locomotive engineer. Whether they are driving electric, diesel-electric or gas-turbine-electric trains to transport passengers or freight, train drivers need to be able to work alone for long periods and be relied on to adhere to safety procedures without supervision. They must be dependable in terms of timekeeping and must not drink alcohol or take recreational drugs. It is the best paid of the driving jobs (excluding pilot), and most drivers stay in the career once they have qualified. For all careers in the railway, try www.nationalrail.co.uk/contact/careers.

43 Interior aircraft assembler. The better-paid positions in assembly work are in, for example, the aviation industry. Interior aircraft assembly work involves the process of assembling everything for the inside of an aircraft from mechanics to furniture. For all careers in airbus, visit www.airbus.com/cn/careers.

44 Gas or nuclear plant operator. Maintaining sufficient pressures in pipelines to transport, for example, natural gas or coolants to a reactor is a highly responsible job. Consequently, these operators are paid at a rate higher than the majority of operator positions. You can start your search for further information at, for example, www.sellafieldcitoo.com.

45 Payroll supervisor. These workers oversee staff working on a company payroll, ensuring that pay calculations are correct, that government regulations are followed and correct tax codes are applied. You will find loads of accountancy and finance jobs at www.hays.co.uk/accountancy.

46 Production line assembly supervisor. In this position post holders are responsible for achieving productivity, quality, training and safety targets on a production line. See for example www.ford.co.uk/AboutFord/FordCareers.

47 Data control supervisor in a large, centralized data processing operation. Data control supervisors are responsible for supervising access to, and distribution and reproduction of, confidential or commercial data according to the organization's policies and procedures. You can browse data management jobs in the public sector at, for example, www.opportunities.co.uk.

48 Firefighter. This is one of the highest paying positions in manual work. Because it involves working a rota of shifts, many firefighters are able to hold down two jobs. The other is usually in a trade, working self-employed when off duty.

For further information read *How to Pass the UK's National Firefighter Selection Process*, published by Kogan Page.

49 Call-centre manager. These individuals are responsible for the daily running and management of a call centre and the achievement of customer-service targets. They communicate with the centre's business clients, help solve problems when they arise and oversee the recruitment and training of staff. View all kinds of call-centre vacancies at www.call-centre.topjobs.co.uk.

50 Self-employed emergency plumber. The work may involve antisocial hours and be dirty or require working in confined spaces, but a plumber who advertises as someone offering 24-hour emergency call out can charge a substantial hourly rate as well as a call-out charge. Find out more at, for example, www.plumbingcareer.co.uk.

Set 10: Time to play it safe

All 50 of the following careers are here to stay and they all offer the opportunity for you to get on with doing a good job.

1 Genetic counsellor. These counsellors provide information to families and individuals who may be at risk of passing on or are suffering from an inherited condition. For counsellor jobs in the NHS, visit www.nhscareers.nhs.uk.

2 Memorials officer. In the remembrance garden at crematoriums, memorial officers help mourners and arrange for a plaque or flowers to be left as a memorial. For positions, see the website of your local authority; also look for vacancies at sites such as www.policememorial.org.uk.

3 Community safety officer. These officials work for local authorities to help address crime and anti-social behaviour in partnership with the police and other agencies. Seek out your local government community safety team and your police force's website for ideas and possible job leads. See, for example, www.kirklees.gov.uk/community/care-support and www.gmp.police.uk.

4 Medical laboratory technician. These technicians analyse samples and cultures. For example, they cross-match blood for transfusions and check for abnormal cells in blood and body fluids. They use sophisticated equipment. A good starting point if you want to research a career as a medical laboratory technician is www.nhscareers.nhs.uk.

5   Dietician. In this role you would advise people, families and groups on healthy eating and on weight loss. Dieticians promote diet as a preventative measure and as a means to good health. You will find clinical support positions, including dieticians, in the HNS advertised at www.nhscareers.nhs.uk.

6   Paramedic. Post holders respond to medical emergencies in the home, roadside or public places. They make an assessment of the seriousness of the condition and administer the first care. When appropriate they move the casualty to hospital. For most medical careers, including that of paramedic, a good starting point in your research is www.nhscareers.nhs.uk.

7   Neighbourhood watch co-ordinator. In some residential areas residents have formed a group and work together to reduce crime and the fear of crime through the neighbourhood watch scheme. Neighbourhood watch co-ordinators help with the management and administration of these schemes. Find out more about neighbourhood watch schemes at, for example, www.communigate.co.uk/here/hfdsneiwatch/index phtml, www.keynshampeople.co.uk/.../Neighbourhood-Watch-ordinator.../story and www.chiltern.gov.uk.

8   Receptionist. Working as a receptionist involves answering telephones, greeting visitors and providing information about the department in which you work. Receptionists in a medical facility will manage appointments and help with security. You will find lots of receptionist jobs advertised at www.gumtree.com.

9   Health educationalist. This work involves informing people and communities about disease prevention, for example how to avoid sexually transmitted diseases or diseases transmitted through water, poor hygiene or lifestyle. Health educationalist positions are advertised at, for example, www.nhscareers.nhs.uk and www.jobs.ac.uk.

10   Substance abuse counsellor. These counsellors help people with addictions to alcohol, smoking or illegal substances and

help them beat their addiction. Find jobs in, for example, the Wednesday *Guardian*, www.jobs.guardian.co.uk, and details of training at www.lifelonglearning.com.

11 Medical ethics advisor. Individuals in this role are recruited to a panel and help make ethical decisions on subjects such as patient confidentiality, patient involvement in research trials, treatment costs and the withdrawal of treatment.

12 Work with the public utilities. People will always need water, gas and electricity and for this reason the public utilities offer some of the most secure employment available. Water treatment technicians, for example, operate and maintain water treatment equipment, and monitor the storage, piping and transport of safe supplies and the safe removal of contaminated or waste water. They collect samples for quality testing and inspect the facilities for sign of leaks or contamination. Google any of your local public utility providers and visit the careers page on their website.

13 Hydrologists. These workers make recommendations on the location of water extraction plants and supervise drilling in the construction of water boreholes and wells for agriculture. They work for mining companies to ensure that the flooding of underground works is avoided and they calculate the expected flow of water from a location and its purity in terms of contaminants or salinity. It is very important work. Find out more at: http://www.aihydrology.org, the website of the American institute of hydrology, http://www.hydrology.org.uk for information about the British Hydrological Society, and www.appliedhydrology.org, the site of the Association of Hydrologists of India.

14 Power line technician. The construction and maintenance of power transmission lines, structures and equipment is undertaken by power line technicians. They are responsible for assessing the condition of the power line and must be able to work safely, even with energized lines. See, for example, www.nationalgrid.com/uk/Electricity.

15 Wind farm technician. Technicians on wind farms maintain the operation and maintenance of all mechanical and electrical components. They oversee the maintenance of the wind turbines and power transmission lines and sub-stations.

They carry out inspections and report to the site manager. Examples of an organization that employs wind farm technicians and an association of companies in the renewable energy business are found at www.res-group.com and www.bwea.com.

16 Sub-station electrical test technicians. This work involves monitoring and inspecting the electrical equipment found in electrical sub-stations, such as transformers, generators and relays. Electrical test technicians monitor resistance and temperature to predict the failure of a component before the supply is disrupted or damage occurs, and they ensure coolants are topped up. You can view jobs at www.ukengineeringrecruitment.net.

17 High-voltage electricians. In this trade you would maintain, modify and install electrical systems that operate at very high voltages as high as, for example, 15,000 volts. High-voltage electricians must be well versed in safe procedures and dealing with emergencies as well as general maintenance. Again see www.nationalgrid.com/uk/Electricity.

18 Offshore safety engineer. Engineers who specialize in offshore safety undertake hazard assessments and safety inspections of offshore gas and oil installations. Find all kinds of offshore jobs at www.oilcareers.com.

19 Domestic gas engineers. These engineers carry out servicing and breakdown repairs on gas-fired central heating systems, stoves and other appliances in domestic properties and businesses. For further information see, for example, www.britishgasacademy.co.uk.

20 Loft insulation technicians. Technicians in this position visit homes and businesses to install loft insulation and help customers reduce their energy bills. If you have a full UK driving licence, then for a career in loft insulation see www.britishgasjobs.co.uk.

21 Cavity wall insulation technician. These technicians install cavity wall insulation in homes and businesses. You can find out more about the work of cavity wall insulators at, for example, www.markgroup.co.uk.

22 Water hygiene engineers. Water hygiene engineers ensure water storage tanks, cooling towers and water systems are

disinfected. They visit hotels, office blocks and large buildings and clean the water systems. For an example of an organization that employs water engineers, see www.teamsnorth.co.uk/water.

23 Classroom teacher. The demand for qualified educators is on the rise and demand for teachers is likely to remain strong in the near future. Teachers specialize in particular groups and subjects, and work in government or private schools and colleges. There are routes to retrain to become a teacher, and help with the cost of training. For further information, see www.tda.gov.uk; for jobs, see for example www.tes.co.uk.

24 Teachers in adult learning. This specialization in the teaching profession involves teaching for example fine art, computer studies, languages, music, sports and any number of other subjects. People can also retrain to teach key skills to adults returning to education after perhaps failing to complete their compulsory education. These skills include literacy and numeracy. Find out about teaching ESOL, adult literacy, numeracy and lifelong learning at, for example, www.exploreadultlearning.co.uk/teaching-adults-career, www.nrdc.org.uk/projects and www.wea.org.uk.

25 Special needs teacher. Some teachers specialize in teaching students with special needs, which may be educational or physical. Find further details at www.teachernet.gov.uk and www.hotcourses.com/uk.

26 Pre-school teacher. You can choose to train as a teacher of pre-school-age children. Much of the training can be completed in the workplace as you study both childcare and early years education. Find out more at, for example, www.teachers.net.

27 Teacher assistants. These assistants help classroom teachers. Under the guidance of the teacher an assistant will help students learn and, for example, provide one-on-one instruction. To discover more about what is involved in this role, visit www.tda.gov.uk/support/support_staff_roles.

28 Educational administrator. Administrators in education work alongside academic staff and are responsible for all non-academic business, including the maintenance of buildings, financial administration, health and safety and the admission and welfare of students. Examples of jobs include school secretary, college bursar and caretaker. Search at the following sites will provide you with a lot of further information and details of vacancies: www.hays.co.uk/education/schooladministration and www.education-jobs.co.uk.

29 Vocational qualifications assessor. Assessors monitor an individual's progress towards completing qualifications in work-based learning. The assessor visits learners in the workplace and examines the portfolio of evidence that demonstrates their competencies in the vocation. The assessor is responsible for confirming that learners have achieved the standard required and recommending that they should be awarded the qualification. Vocational qualifications exist in a huge number of subject areas and assessors have industry experience as well as experience in the delivery of staff training. Find out more about assessors and about UK and Scottish vocational qualifications by visiting www.direct.gov.uk, www.questscotland.co.uk and www.hotcourses.com/uk.

30 Military careers for civilians. There are a large number of roles for civilians in the military, providing for example specialist skills, security and administration. Civilians who work in military security, for example, work shifts, including nights, check passes and patrol premises. For civilian careers in the UK military, see www.mod.uk.

31 Administrator in military procurement. The military services spend a great deal of money on equipment, supplies and services, and civilian administrators assist in this. The work involves obtaining best quotes against specifications and assisting in the drawing up and signing of contracts. If you like the idea of a civilian career alongside the armed forces, then start your search at https://www.civilianjobs.mod.uk.

32 Manager of projects for the military. The military services use civilians to manage a great many projects, including construction and IT projects. They recruit people from the private sector with appropriate experience and professional qualifications in project management. Career breaks are listed at www.static.wcn.co.uk/company/civilservicejobs/portal.html and https://www.civilianjobs.mod.uk/JobSearch.

33 IT support to military personnel. The services use civilians to provide IT support to military personnel. Staff help to resolve any difficulties that users of a particular IT system have by, for example, handling telephone calls and replying to e-mails, and providing induction training to new users. In aerospace for example, vacancies can be browsed at www.jprecruit.com/aerospace-jobs-uk.

34 Apprenticeships and advanced apprenticeships with the military. These include a great many opportunities for civilians. The apprenticeship generally takes 36 weeks to complete (advanced apprenticeships longer) and on successful completion leads to full-time employment supporting the armed services. Find out more at www.mod.uk/DefenceInternet/Defencefor/Jobseekers/CivilianCareers/SchoolLeaversApprentices and www.welbeck.mod.uk.

35 Civilian engineers supporting the armed services. The armed services employ mechanical, marine, civil and electrical engineers to work alongside servicemen and women. Apprenticeships with the military are available in, for example, mechanical and marine engineering. Explore jobs at www.armyjobs.mod.uk/jobs and www.mod.uk.

36 Civilian tradespeople supporting the armed services. Plumbers and electricians, for example, are employed by the military and apprenticeships are offered in a number of craft areas. As well as viewing opportunities at the MoD website, visit the Territorial Army site at www.tanearyou.org.uk.

37 Civilian technicians supporting the armed services. Technicians in aircraft maintenance, electronics, salvage and marine operations are examples of the many types of technicians employed by the military. Apprenticeships or advanced apprenticeships are offered by the military in some of these areas. Vacancies are advertised at https://static.wcn.co.uk/company/civilservicejobs/portal.html and www.civilianjobs.mod.uk.

38 Dangerous cargo security inspector. In this position you would investigate goods and cargoes carried by air to establish whether they are dangerous. These officials undertake routine inspections, investigate incidents, produce reports and use trend analysis to ensure air safety. Training and regulations connected with the transport of dangerous cargo by road or air can be browsed at www.dgtrain.co.uk/courses/security-of-dangerous-goods and www.dft.gov.uk.

39 Airport passenger screening officer. These people are responsible for screening passengers and airport and aircraft personnel, as well as checking passengers' hand and hold luggage before this is allowed onto flights. The number of people employed in this important role has increased greatly in recent years and the trend is likely to continue as long as the terrorist threat to air travel remains. For details of all sorts of airport jobs, including passenger and luggage screening, search at www.baa.com, www.heathrowairport.com and www.airportjobs.co.uk.

40 Uniformed security officer in retail or banking. If you are service orientated, personable and composed, then this career might well suit you. It involves shift work and weekend working. A background with the armed services or police would ideally qualify you. A source of further information is www.g4s.uk.com/en-gb/Careers.

41 CCTV surveillance officer. The huge increase in the number of closed circuit surveillance systems means that there are many new openings for officers to watch the footage, report breakages and respond to recorded incidents. For many posts you require a CCTV licence, which you can apply for on receiving an offer of employment. Find out about surveillance jobs at www.police-jobs.co.uk/surveillance-officer-jobs.

42 Security patrol officer. These workers conduct external patrols, checking that the gates and entrances of a complex or office block are secure. They work shifts and keep fit by walking an average two miles a shift. To find out more about a career in, for example, mobile patrols visit www.allsecurityltd.co.uk.

43 Retail loss prevention officer. These positions involve preventing and detecting theft by customers or staff. The officers carry out surveillance and investigate incidents. They interview and prepare reports. They also train staff in loss prevention awareness. You might start your search for a career in retail loss at the site of the British Retail Consortium: www.brc.org.uk.

44 Winemaker. The food industry in general provides very secure employment, and perhaps one of the most secure areas within it is winemaking. If you know your Merlot from your Pinot Noir, then why not train to become a winemaker? The New World estates currently offer the most career openings and you might get to live in a truly beautiful location. For more information google 'winemaker school'.

45 Baker. If you retrain as a baker, you will learn to prepare doughs and bake and decorate bakery products. In urban locations you may work in the bakery section of a supermarket, or in a rural or small community setting you might run an independent bakery. For in-store bakery positions contact www.tesco-careers.com.

46 Supermarket butcher. This work involves ordering and rotating stock and displaying it in a presentable condition, and stocking freezer, deli and fresh meat display cases. To find work in a supermarket department, be it the meat department or pharmacy, visit for example www.sainsburys.co.uk/aboutus/recruitment.

47 Food processor occupations. These employ many different types of workers who process raw food products into the finished goods sold by supermarkets, wholesalers and restaurants. They include meat and poultry cutters and fish filleters. While it is a very secure occupation, in that there will always be a need for it, it means hard, repetitive manual work. Find out about food processing opportunities at, for example, www.northernfoods.com/careers.

48 Human resource manager. This is one of the most secure positions in a company. HR managers administer recruitment, training, disciplinary and grievance procedures, staff reviews and redundancies. Find out about developments in HR and view jobs at, for example, www.personneltoday.com.

49 Dispute resolution specialist. These professionals are employed by large businesses to help resolve issues that might otherwise result in costly litigation, strikes or other disruptions. A dispute resolution specialist might be called to assist in a row between employees, suppliers or subcontractors. A good start to finding a career in dispute resolution may be a browse of the information at www.acas.org.uk.

Set 11: Make a leisure pursuit pay

Almost every hobby can be made a career. You might have to re-arrange your home finances to achieve it or return to learning in order to obtain any required professional qualifications, but if that means you can fulfil a lifelong ambition then it seems a very small price to pay. Below are 50 common hobbies and the careers that are based on them. I hope that they prove that it is possible to make a leisure pursuit pay.

1   Cloud watching. Ok, not every hobby can support a career, but you might widen it to all forms of weather and there certainly are careers to be made in atmospheric science and meteorology. Meteorologists say that it was the wonders and mysteries of the atmosphere that persuaded them to take up the science. This interest has led many to a career as a weather presenter on local TV or radio or a storm chaser, or helping to design a weather satellite. Many careers began with a daily weather posting; these days this would be on an internet forum, and before long one thing leads to another and a hobby becomes a career. Find out about a career at the met office. www.metoffice.gov.uk/about-us/jobs.

2   Team sports. Team sports, including soccer, American football, basketball and hockey, are already or are fast becoming internationally big businesses. There are many careers in them, including for example facilities operations, security, communications and administration. If you love team sports then don't be put off by these titles, because if you dig a little bit deeper you can find roles that are often very much a part of the game. Take administration for example: your role might be to administer game distribution rights for TV or internships (volunteers) or local youth teams. Soccer and team sports generally are spreading around the world and with them are career openings. Many team-sport leagues are opening stores to sell branded goods in, for example, China and a retail career in the team sports industry can offer a great deal. Search for ways in which you might get started at www.uksport.gov.uk/jobs.

3   Massage and therapies. Working as a massage therapist can provide a comfortable living and mean that you help people

mentally and physically. A great many massage and therapy schools offer training that leads to professional status. These courses can take a hundred hours or more and require a significant financial investment too, but they can lead to jobs on cruise ships and in holiday resorts, or much nearer to home working part time in the evenings and weekends. For further information see, for example, www.massagetherapyschools.net.

4   DIY. If you are handy and always busy with some home improvement project, then perhaps it's time to turn professional. There is a very reasonable living to be earned assembling flat-pack furniture, house painting and erecting or repairing garden fences. There are hundreds of courses available where you can train in one of the trades and then move on into the industry. Alternatively, consider working as an advisor in one of the large DIY stores where you can help customers with their purchases. Find a career at, for example, www.diy.com/diy/jsp/corporate/content/careers.

5   Swimming is not only a fantastic form of exercise and great way to relax, it can also provide a rewarding career. The opportunities include posts as pool attendants who possess a life-saving qualification, swimming instructors, even baby swimming class instructors. A recent development is guide/ leader on swimming holidays in open water at venues around the world: see for example www.swimtrek.com.

6   Gardening. The possible careers that can grow from a love of gardening are varied and numerous. There are many professions to follow in horticulture and landscape design, from fruit grower to tree surgeon. There are careers as green-keeper and grounds-worker at sporting locations. You can run your own business providing other gardeners with help or providing hanging baskets for businesses. You can work as an advisor at a retail nursery helping people decide which plants to buy. Search hundreds of gardening events that you might be able to follow up on to see if there are any temporary vacancies at www.rhs.org.uk/Shows-Events.

7   Cake decorating. Everyone likes a celebration cake for a wedding, a birthday and at Christmas. Sugar craft of course involves a lot more than just cakes, and many people are successfully self-employed making sugar novelties such as

sugar mice, and baking and decorating gingerbread houses. You can see how it can be done at, for example, www.cakecraftshop.co.uk.

8 Embroidery and needlework are often sold at craft and Christmas fairs. Hand embroidery and needlework such as lacework and cross stitch is highly appreciated, especially older designs or items with local interest. See, for example, www.rotunda.net for examples of 17th-century and earlier needlework patterns.

9 Ceramics. Hand-built and thrown-clay pottery is both practical and beautiful, and provides many with a good living. A lot of potters operate in vacation centres where people have the time to admire their work and they find the inspiration. They sell their work as mementos of a holiday and may offer introduction classes in pottery. For inspiration see www.kinsaleceramics.com.

10 Folktales and mythology. If you have a love for mythology, then why not become a professional storyteller? Storytelling has enjoyed a resurgence in recent years. Storytellers mainly visit schools and libraries and attend children's parties. They bring props, costumes and sound systems, and a good storyteller will transfix their audience. Most paid storytelling is for children but some venues also provide stories for adults. There are storytelling festivals that you can attend to gain ideas and advice. You might start your search for career ideas at www.mysteriousbritain.co.uk.

11 Water sports. If you love kayaking, dinghy or keel-boat sailing, water volleyball, in fact all kinds of water sports, then you will be amazed at how many opportunities there are to make a living doing what you love. Water sports instructors are in big demand to work at holiday centres, resorts, summer camps, sailing or adventure centres or clubs. If you hate winter, then why not work as an instructor in the summer in the Mediterranean and winter in the Caribbean? For inspiration visit www.uksa.co.uk and see details of the water sports instructor programme.

12 Collectables. There is a profession to be made in every sort of collectable, running a stall in flea markets or collectable and antique fairs, and selling to collectors worldwide through

sites such as eBay. You will need to split your time between sourcing stock, selling and researching your finds to ensure you get the price right. See what others are doing at, for example, www.stores.ebay.co.uk.

13 Museums and galleries. The cultural and heritage sector is a big employer with very good prospects because, for example, lottery grants have created a great many new positions. There are opportunities to work as a project manager, events organizer, marketing officer and guide, to mention but a few of the careers possible in this sector. For jobs see, for example, www.museumjob.com.

14 Creative writing. To see your fictional work published by one of the big publishing houses will first require you to find an agent willing to represent you. In non-fiction you may not need an agent. Visit, for example, the forum www.absolutewrite.com and read some of the excellent threads on finding and researching an agent and getting your first book published. Be sure to read the 'beware' board, which identifies some of the pitfalls. You might also consider self-publishing and then marketing your work yourself. Of course there are many other ways to get paid to write, such as journalism, script writing and so on. For an example of a career writer, visit www.linrobinson.com. For more advice on getting started, visit www.writersandartists.co.uk.

15 Driving is a passion and some people are very good at it. You can earn a living driving anything from a golf cart to a truck or caterpillar earth mover. As a career driver you can teach (driving instructor), tour continents (long-distance truck driver) or chauffeur people (bus, coach or taxi driver). On the road a driver is pretty much his or her own boss, and many take this aspect of the work to its logical conclusion and operate on a self-employed basis. To find out about driving a bus, for example, visit www.stagecoachbus.com.

16 Woodwork. Turning, making or carving something in wood makes a fascinating hobby and career. Building kitchen units or bespoke furniture or turning wooden bowls or making toys is rewarding work. You might even consider selling woodworking tools; see an American example of a woodworking tools franchise at www.woodcraft.com.

17 Family history. Many people research their families, and like any form of historical research this demands good techniques and access to source data. Some families employ historians to research on their behalf and require the researcher to travel to interview relatives and search archives. If a search leads to another country, then they employ a researcher from that country to continue the search (in another language or using local censuses or archives). Most genealogy sites have a facility to 'hire an expert' to help with research, and these experts pay to advertise their services on the site. To get started, visit for example www.familyhistory.uk.com and www.familyrecords.gov.

18 Photography This is a competitive industry, and most professional photographers are self-employed and responsible for all aspects of their business, including advertising, equipment maintenance and film processing. While it is competitive, a living can be made as for example a portrait photographer (capturing family scenes or events at schools or weddings) or industrial photographer (photographing goods or merchandise). Some choose to run a photography shop or market their work on photo library sites. To investigate a career in photography and to showcase or sell your work, visit for example www.jessops.com or www.photolibrary.com.

19 Cookery. A talent as a cook can become a career in many ways. Some dream of running their own restaurant or delicatessen. Others will sell their home-made produce through a market stall or lunches round at local businesses. Some provide food for a party or dinner with a home catering service. Be inspired and find training at, for example, www.gordonramsay.com and www.thegablesschoolofcookery.co.uk.

20 Old books. A love for books readily makes a career. These days second-hand books can be sold through sites such as Amazon as well as eBay. Some professionals provide a service finding rare or antique books for collectors or spend their day searching second-hand book shops or the books in charity shops for bargains to sell on at a profit. Some illustrated books are broken up and the illustrations framed and sold. The majority of book lovers work in libraries, and these jobs tend to have either a research or community emphasis. Why not go along to the world famous www.hay-on-wye.co.uk.

21 Drama. Aside from work as an actor, a career in drama can lead you to stage management, arts administration, teaching drama or practising as a drama therapist. To find out how to take part in the work of the National Theatre for example, visit www.nationaltheatre.org.uk/discover.

22 Travel. A love of travel offers many employment opportunities. You can promote or advise on travel destinations, design bespoke holidays or administer travel or vacation websites. Opportunities also exist for specialist guides, local representatives and tour leaders. For inspiration see, for example, the jobs pages on www.wanderlust.co.uk.

23 Languages. A love for and a proficiency in languages creates many career opportunities. Teaching is the obvious choice, along with offering translation or interpretation services. However, language skills are a valuable qualification in every field and if you combine a love of languages with another interest such as hospitality, business, sales or marketing, then the potential for a great career increases enormously. To view listings of language teaching careers or to teach TEFL visit, for example, www.ukjobsnet.com/language-teaching-jobs and www.tefl.com.

24 IT. These days people working in IT may be analysing a business problem and recommending a suitable software solution or engineering software to control equipment, networks or processes. They might equally be working in sales, advising customers on the best purchase, or repairing hardware. Start your search for a career by reading the daily industry news at www.pcr-online.biz.

25 Diving. Careers in leisure diving include working as a scuba diving instructor, underwater photographer, resort and dive-centre business manager, dive-boat captain and diving-equipment repair technician. A number of centres offer training and career placement in these occupations; see for example www.hallsdiving.com in Florida, USA.

26 Politics. You can turn a passion for politics into a career if you become a political researcher or special advisor, or work for a think tank, trade union or political society. Other related careers include fundraiser, lobbyist, speechwriter and of course a paid representative of a constituency. If it's the trade union industry you are interested in, then you can find details of careers at www.tradeunionjobsdirect.co.uk and www.tuc.org.uk.

27 The environment. Someone interested in environmental issues can make a difference and earn a wage. Environmental charities employ communications officers to raise awareness of their charitable objectives, administrators to organize volunteers, and project workers or field workers to address environmental problems or issues, or to improve the immediate environment. Environmental consultants provide services to industry to reduce waste and pollution and make processes more efficient. You will find a free environmental careers service at www.environmentalcareers.org.uk

28 Local history. An interest in the history of your local community is very common and a livelihood can be made from teaching local history at evening classes, speaking at societies and clubs, and writing and marketing a self-published book that is sold locally. It is also possible to apply for small grants to support research in local history. For further information, see for example www.history.org.uk.

29 Fine art. Artists, like any other business, need help in marketing, exhibiting and selling their work. If you find a space, you can organize exhibitions and display works for sale. The gallery owner receives a percentage of the sale price. A dealer of fine art will buy a number of works from an artist and then trade them or sell them through his or her gallery space or website. Buyers will recommend works and buy them on behalf of their clients. There are careers as curators of fine art in museums and galleries, and critics write for newspapers and websites reviewing exhibitions. Find out more at, for example, www.artshub.co.uk.

30 Keeping fit. You can become super-fit and earn a living at the same time by setting up community keep-fit classes for adults. You can work with national charities such as Age Concern and teach keep-fit to older adults, including chair-based exercises. It is not only a career for the young; you can train as a keep-fit instructor at any age. Some train after early retirement. For training to become an instructor, see for example www.keepfit.org.uk or contact your community college.

31 Antiques. If you are a collector, then the logical next step is to become a dealer. Dealers exhibit their stock at fairs and shows and upload their inventory on antique websites such as antiques.co.uk and goantiques.com. Other careers in antiques include personal buyers, who represent collectors and seek out items to add to their collections, and restorers. You can find out more at, for example, www.sothebys.com.

32 Tea drinking is a pastime that billions of people follow and offers the possibility of a number of careers. You can make a career out of teas by selling fine tea blends, teapots and tea sets, or by running a teashop. For inspiration see www.tea.co.uk and www.whittards.co.uk.

33 Papier-mâché. This is a paste made from paper and glue that when dry becomes solid. It is formed into a great many shapes and used to make puppets, statues, balloons (which are filled with sweets and toys) and masks. In some parts of the world papier-mâché is extremely popular and crafting things with it employs a great many people; for example in Ecuador papier-mâché is used to make statues that are burnt during New Year celebrations; in Venice, Italy, the Venetian mask is formed from papier-mâché and decorated and sold to be worn at carnival. Be inspired by browsing, for example, www.venetianmasksshop.com.

34 Music. As someone who appreciates music or as a musician, you have a great many career possibilities. Teaching music and performing music are the biggest fields of employment. With respect to performing, don't only think of popular music but also armed forces' bands, symphony orchestras and religious choirs and orchestras. There are also careers in arts administration, retail music sales, tour management, music reporting, booking agencies, publicist, business manager, lyricist and acoustics (including acoustic architecture). For opportunities in music view, for example, www.rhinegold.co.uk and www.cdbaby.com.

35 Metal detecting. The thrill of finding a historic artefact, old coin or gold ring means that some people are quite addicted to metal detecting. People who practise the hobby research their finds and many become expert in, for example, old coins. Anyone who has practised the hobby for any length of time will realize that there is a lot more to it than just luck.

If the hobby is to be made a profession, then people must rely on knowledge not luck, and they will study where for example old stage-coaching inns or taverns were located and search these sites. They will search a beach that people used historically to visit, establish whether it once had an amusement park or other attraction and focus on this area. They will visit a beach after a storm because the sand would have been shifted and artefacts buried deep down might have been brought closer to the surface where they can be found. Look for a way to turn your hobby into a career by browsing, for example, the following sites: www.treasurehunting.co.uk and www.greenlightpublishing.co.uk

36 Walking. If walking is your vocation, then don't think you are destined to nothing better than carrying a sandwich board advertising a local business. A love of walking can qualify you for many vocations; consider for example a career as a ranger or guide. Even if you live in a city you can earn a living taking people on walks by offering urban tours or ghost hunts. You will need to research your area and establish interesting facts and stories about its past so that you can entertain your clients. Alternatively, become a dog walker and exercise people's pets when they are out at work or are unable to exercise their animals themselves, or become a postal worker sorting and delivering mail. For ideas, have a look at, for example, www.ramblersholidays.co.uk, www.hikingforums.net/forums/ showthread.php?11455_become-a-guide and www.trails. com/how_1666_become-mountain-climbing-guide.

37 Blogging. Some influential bloggers have found themselves offered careers in mainstream media. A popular blog may earn some revenue from advertising or links. Blogging can get you noticed and opportunities may follow. The authors of really quite modest blogs have received offers to write and career breaks in journalism or editorial work. There are a number of careers that serve blogs. For example there are people who administer blog search engines, and trends in blogging are watched carefully by online marketers working for a whole host of companies. For tips on how to make money blogging, visit www.problogger.net.

38 Magic. Bring out the entertainer within you and start offering magic shows as a kids' entertainer or at locations such as homes for the elderly. If you are good enough, then earn a living with close-up magic or street magic, and perform at carnivals and public events all over the world. See for example www.magictricks.com.

39 Board games. If you have heard of games like Yinsh, Dune, Goa, Dragon Quest, Forbidden Island and Race for the Galaxy, then you might well count yourself a board game geek. Board games are a healthy business and the best-known designers have a large following of players and are commissioned by game publishers to come up with the next top games. As in every other form of publishing, it is not easy to get your first game idea published. But that does not mean you should not try, so get yourself and your games to game and toy trade fairs and keep proposing and developing your ideas. Find out about the industry and the latest games, news and reviews at, for example, www.boardgamegeek.com.

40 The countryside. A love for the countryside qualifies you for many occupations. Rangers and wardens are employed all over the nation to share their knowledge with visitors and maintain and conserve sites. Guides offer tours of locations and identify species of plant and animal as they walk with their clients. People are employed to provide countryside and conservation holidays and to provide training in countryside skills. For ideas, visit for example www.btcv.org.uk.

41 Yoga. You can train as a yoga teacher at many locations and begin a career as a teacher, or organize retreats and sell mats, blocks, books, clothes and DVDs. See information on, for example, training to be a yoga teacher in India at www.yogapoint.com.

42 Food critic. Food is a perennial topic in newspapers and magazines, and on radio, TV and the internet. If you know good food when you taste it and have always considered yourself something of an aficionado, then why not give the career of food critic serious consideration? As with all forms of writing, competition for commissions is fierce and to succeed you will need to learn to write well and know how a kitchen and restaurant work. You could start as a freelance food writer. Write a few reviews, get yourself a web page and start marketing to commissioning editors. Better still, get some training in journalism, which together with a knowledge of the food industry should get you off to a good start. See for example the Cardiff school of journalism: www.cardiff.ac.uk. For ideas and to get started, visit www.andyhayler.com, www.thetimes.co.uk/tto/life/food/ and www.journalism.co.uk.

43 Crosswords and word puzzles. If you enjoy word puzzles, then why not turn your hand to writing them? Publishers, newspapers and websites are often seeking new talent. You could get started by writing a few examples and sending them out to the major publishers of word puzzle books. You might find www.writersandartists.co.uk or *The Writers and Artists Yearbook* a useful source of contact details (most libraries stock a copy in the reference section). Here are a few places to look to keep the interest going: www.crossword-compiler.com, www.lovatts.com.au, www.crauswords.com and www.puzzlepublisher.com.

44 Beachcombing. Searching the shoreline for items that have been washed up fires the imagination and is a great excuse to dwell somewhere beautiful. It can also provide a living. It would be illegal to recover items from a wreck without informing the correct authorities but in many locations you are allowed to collect shells, fossils, driftwood, pebbles, discarded or lost fishing floats, old bottles and so on, and these items can be crafted or painted and turned into works of art or household items and sold. See for example www.drbeachcomb.com.

45 Animals Aside from the work available with animals in farming, medical research and veterinary science, there is also employment in sports such as horse racing and jumping, and greyhound racing. Work is available as a groom or you can establish your own pet parlour. Another popular area of work is animal training. Many people breed and sell pedigree dogs and cats as pets, or run a dog hotel where people leave their animals when they go on holiday. Dog handlers work for security companies and the police, and the armed services employ people to work with dogs and horses. You can find out about a career with, for example, the RSPCA at www.rspca.org.uk/in-action/aboutus/careers.

46 Fishing. There are many occupations linked to recreational fishing, and all provide an outdoor working life in idyllic surroundings. Some people make a living supplying bait and tackle. A few individuals are good enough to make a professional living from fishing competition winnings, sponsorship from tackle manufacturers and fees for instruction to newcomers to the sport. In most holiday resorts or coastal towns a number of boats will offer sea fishing trips. Most freshwater fisheries have a gamekeeper responsible for the maintenance of the site and selling licences to fish. Game fishing in tropical locations around the world employs many, and the captains and fish masters of the top boats are celebrities. For inspiration visit www.gamefishingcharters.com.au.

47 Handmade candles and soaps. Working with moulds, fragrances, oils and colours you can create truly beautiful designs of candles and soaps. Many websites sell starter kits and have pages of ideas. For ideas see www.candletech.com and www.candlewic.com for supplies.

48 Sea glass. Glass that has been weathered by the sea is called sea glass and collecting it is a popular hobby. Some people incorporate it into jewellery and create some really beautiful works. Some are able to sell enough to become professional sea glass artists; see for example www.seaglassassociation.org.

49 Hunting. Sustainable hunting and gathering is a legitimate occupation and employs people who have permission to, for example, gather mushrooms, wild fruit and shellfish or hunt deer, rabbit and other game and sell it to specialist wholesalers or directly to restaurants. Find out more at, for example, www.countrysports.co.uk and www.huntinguk.com.

50 Garage sales and car boot sales. Someone's junk is someone else's find of a lifetime. Garage and car boot sales, both real and virtual, are immensely popular and dealers often negotiate a previewing so that they can take the cream of the items on offer. Many of the traders at these events are professionals. They start by selling personal items after a de-clutter and in due course start trading full time. There is money in junk. For a directory of events visit, for example, www.carbootjunction.com and www.yourbooty.co.uk.

51 If you have a whole host of hobbies and interests and can't decide which you would like to make a career of, then why not open a hobby store or webshop? For an example of a website, visit www.hobbies.net.

Set 12: Sports and leisure

The sports industry offers a surprisingly large number of employment opportunities. Reflect on the 50 examples below and see if you can make a career from your interest in sport. A great website is www.uksport.gov.uk, and www.leisurejobs.com is also well worth a visit.

1 Sporting body administrator. Amateur sporting bodies represent a sport nationally, and their administrators are responsible for the administration of the sport on a national level, the growth of the sport at both junior and senior levels, overseeing rules and regulations, legal requirements such as insurance, and liaising with other sporting associations and government bodies. You can find a list of UK sporting bodies at www.allsportsinternational.co.uk/governingbodies.html.

2 Volunteer development officers. A great many sports rely on volunteers and employ officers to develop, retain and motivate them. They oversee training and development programmes, recognition programmes and communications with volunteers. Find employment in the voluntary sector at, for example, www.charityjob.co.uk and www.jobs.guardian.co.uk/job.

3 Community sports trainers work in primary and secondary schools delivering multi-skills and sport-specific coaching both during curriculum time and in after-school clubs. During half term, the coach runs holiday clubs and visits youth and sports clubs and facilities. For further information visit www.uksport.gov.uk/jobs and www.sportsleaders.org.

4 Physical activity officer. The role of these officers is to encourage greater sport and physical activity in a community. This is done through partnership with schools, clubs and venues. Often there are priority groups within the community that the post holder is expected to target. These are usually groups most at risk of the effects of inactivity or those who do not currently use sporting facilities. Examples of the work of physical activity officers are found at, for example, www.pro-activewestlondon.org/jobs and www.sheffield.gov.uk/...activity.

5 Participation officer. Motivating more people to take up a sport or a form of physical exercise is an objective of local and national government. Many local authorities and major sporting clubs employ participation officers to promote sport to the general public by attending schools and public venues. Details of the latest jobs and events can be found at www.uksport.gov.uk.

6 Referee or judge. All sports use adjudicators to oversee the game and record the results. Referees need to be fit and know the rules inside out. They have to make good decisions quickly and show leadership. Sporting associations recruit and register referees or judges and will provide information on how to train to become one. In some parts of the UK there are bursaries available for training as a referee, judge or umpire; see www.sport-kingston.co.uk/sports-officials-bursary-london.htm.

7 Sports PR. There are many careers in sports PR, including accounts director, advertising manager, corporate or marketing communications and media and public relations. For a listing of careers see, for example, www.prweekjobs.co.uk.

8 Sportscaster. The most public person in sports broadcasting is the sportscaster. He or she appears on air and provides the commentary or conducts the interviews and hosts the sports talk shows. In some cases the sportscaster is an ex-player or is joined on air by ex-players who provide comment in support of the sportscaster. Details of TV and radio training courses can be found at www.radioandtelly.co.uk/courses.html and www.london.floodlight.co.uk/london/courses.

9 Sports nutritionist. To become a sports nutritionist requires as a minimum a qualification in nutrition or dietetics and an interest and some experience in the sports nutrition field. To get started, offer to work voluntarily with a local sports team and go on from there. Many positions are part time, so sports nutritionists often also work in other sectors such as clinical or community nutritional work. You will find the website of a nutritionist at www.sportsnutritionvlog.com/uk-sports-nutritionist.

10 Tennis or golf coach for children. Getting the next generation hooked onto sport is a worthy objective. Running children's tennis or golf classes is one way that sporting clubs and associations ensure their future membership. For information see www.sportscoachuk.org.

11 Sports security. As in all security work you will mainly be involved in patrolling the premises to prevent and detect signs of intrusion and ensure the security of doors, windows and gates. You will monitor security systems to ensure they are operational, and answer alarms. You would call emergency services in the event of the discovery of a fire or unauthorized persons. For further information on crowd management and security visit, for example, www.showsec.co.uk.

12 Sports catering. This is primarily events catering and involves the highest standards of event management and catering. You may find yourself looking after 10 people in an executive box or 1,000 guests at a corporate event, or serving hundreds at a fast-food outlet. It will only be a matter of time before you are cooking for some high-prestige sporting personalities. You can find out about work in sports catering at, for example, www.crowngroup.co.uk and www.leisurejobs.com.

13 Soccer coach for children. At weekends, during school holidays and for birthday parties you can work as a children's coach for many sports, but especially soccer. The work is often outside and the children are aged between 2 and 12 years. You must have loads of energy and an infectious enthusiasm for your game. Examples of organizations that employ soccer coaches are www.midlandsoccercoaching.co.uk and www.premiersport.org.

14 Strength and conditioning instructor. Designing and overseeing conditioning programmes for athletes or a national squad is the pinnacle of this career. To get there you may well need to study sports science and then start as a volunteer. Ideally, find a coach with good connections and study under him or her. That way you will build up the right sort of experience and references and will find yourself much more attractive to teams or governing bodies when they recruit. See for example the American National Strength and Conditioning Association at www.nsca-cc.org.

15 Tennis pro. If you are able to play to a really high standard and have great communication skills, then why not work as a tennis pro at a club or holiday resort? The contracts are usually for 12 months, the pay is good and you get to live in some really beautiful locations. Update your CV and google 'tennis pro jobs' for vacancies. Find out about tennis jobs at www.tennisjobs.com.

16 Pool managers are in charge of a pool facility and its various functions. Managing aquatic facilities includes co-ordinating activities at the pools and in the office. All sorts of leisure jobs are listed at www.leisurejobs.com.

17 Golf pro. There are many careers in golf including golf retail, instruction and management where you oversee all operations at a golf facility. For information visit www.pgajobfinder.com.

18 Aquatics instructors teach swimming. They give lessons for children of all ages and adults. They can work at a pool complex or coach at swim camps with either indoor or outdoor facilities. Details of the work, training and qualifications can be browsed at www.sta.co.uk/staff, www.scottishswimming.com and www.londonleisurecollege.co.uk.

19 Personal trainer. This career has become competitive and so you should get a qualification and consider certification in a specialism such as being a personal trainer to people with a medical condition or the elderly. Once qualified you can apply for positions in fitness clubs, corporate gyms, cruise ships or spas, or you can become self-employed or even work as an online personal trainer. Contact your local college of further education, which is very likely to offer fitness instructor training courses. Find out about becoming a trainer at www.nrpt.co.uk.

20 Sports marketing. Information officers act as a liaison between teams and sporting stars and the media. They prepare press releases, photo opportunities and media events. Corporate marketing managers organize advertising, sponsorship, product endorsement and brand licensing.

View the work of a sports marketing agency at, for example, www.fasttrackagency.com and www.perfectmotion.org.

21 Teacher of physical education. Teachers of physical education supervise track and field events, and teach sports, health and exercise. Visit the websites jobs.ac.uk and tes.co.uk, and consider sports and leisure as well as physical education as a possible specialization. Details of training and employment can be viewed at www.education.ed.ac.uk and www.tes.co.uk.

22 Aerobics teacher. Recreational sports and fitness activities are immensely popular, and perhaps aerobics is the most popular of all. The role of the teacher is to motivate and lead a group exercise programme. Fitness and aerobics instructors may work for health or exercise clubs, sports training facilities or gyms. Opportunities to train as an aerobics teacher can be found at, for example, www.discovery.uk.com/ aerobics-instructor-training-course and www.thefitnesseducationacademy.co.uk.

23 Fitness instructor. Here you would help people to improve their health and fitness by leading and organizing fitness classes for groups and individual exercise programmes. Instructors usually specialize and work with one age group or type of exercise. Courses are offered all over the country; browse, for example, www.innervatetraining.com.

24 Physiotherapist. These professionals treat people with sports and other sorts of injuries. They aim to restore a person's movement and will treat people of all ages. For further information visit the Charted Society of Physiotherapy: www.csp.org.uk.

25 Community liaison officer for a league team. Most league teams employ community liaison officers, who are primarily responsible for raising awareness amongst residents about issues that are going on in the club. They promote people's involvement in community projects run by the club, and plan and attend meetings where residents voice any concerns they may have. Find out more at, for example, www.football-league.co.uk.

26 Talent scout. Most scouting positions are awarded to former players. Talent scouts evaluate potential and they travel

constantly to find athletes who in their opinion have the promise to succeed at the top level. To see how it is done in the United States, see for example www.scout.com.

27 Youth team coach. There are many coaching positions besides that of first team coach, including part-time coach, reserve team coach and youth team coach. Getting one of these positions can be a stepping stone to the top (first team) coaching positions or, in the case of the foremost clubs, is viewed as a major achievement in its own right. Workshops and coaching framework information is available at, for example, www.sportscoachuk.org.

28 Sports journalism. You can work as a sports journalist for a local newspaper or for magazines, websites or fan clubs. As a freelance journalist you can specialize in writing pieces on a number of minority sports. You will get to meet sporting stars, their managers and coaches, and of course you will see the games close up on the press bench. To succeed in this career you should first know well a major sport as well as a number of minor games; you should also train in journalism. Find out more about the work and training that leads to it at www.sportsjournalists.co.uk and www.courses.brighton.ac.uk.

29 Events staff co-ordinator. Sporting events require a lot of staff but they take place at venues only weekly or biweekly. This means that a lot of staff are required only a few hours a week. Many venues or clubs employ a full-time co-ordinator to manage the logistics of employing a few hundred staff for one or two events a week. These are usually employment specialists, often with a background in working for a temporary employment agency. An example of an events company that employs co-ordinators can be seen at www.gcgeventpartners.com.

30 Sports broadcasting. Many, many thousands of hours of sporting feed are produced each year. The major sporting channels cover as many as 65 different sports. Sports broadcasting rights earn teams and sports governing bodies large sums, and a great many skilled people are employed in this field. Behind the scenes there are many careers available in sports broadcasting; these include, for example, video camera operators, editors, writers, producers, computer technicians, telecommunications technicians and administrative staff, to name but a few. Find out more at, for example, www.bbctraining.com and www.bbc.co.uk/sportacademy.

31   Press officer. Press officers act as the official media contacts for a team, club or sporting body. They answer journalists' enquiries, write press releases and news articles, monitor press and broadcasts, and hold conferences and briefings. They manage the media in a potential crisis situation and accompany players to publicity events. Find the latest news at www.prweekjobs.co.uk.

32   Fire marshals. At every crowd-pulling sporting event, trained people will be present to assist in the event of a fire or other emergency. Fire marshals attend training courses and undertake pre-game checks. Obtaining a qualification as a fire marshal will help strengthen your application for other jobs in the sports industry. Training as a fire marshal is available at, for example, www.london-fire.gov.uk/FireWardenCourse.

33   Sports agent. A sports agent represents athletes in finding a position on a team or a transfer, and in contract negotiations. They promote their athletes to club owners, managers and coaches. Good agents know their sport intimately and are on first-name terms with the key people in it. You might start in the business by first working for an agent as an assistant. The Association of Professional Sports Agents' site is found at www.apsa.org.uk.

34   Sports management. There are many sorts of managerial positions in sport. The most high profile is the team manager, who is responsible for co-ordinating all the activities of the players, their training, game preparation and morale. Other sorts of managers are involved in ticket sales, sponsorship, advertising and human resources. The team manager will work his or her way through the ranks of coach and assistant managers, and might start out with a degree in sports management. Most other managers will have studied another specialism and may have cut their teeth in other industries before moving across to sport. Find out about training in sports management by viewing, for example, www.uniguru.com/.../uk/.../uk/.../sports-courses.

35 Sports ground staff. Maintaining the field or pitch for games such as golf, cricket, soccer, American football – indeed almost every ball game – is a serious business. Imagine getting the ground ready for an international match or a major league game: ensuring sufficient water is applied so that the ground is not too hard or soft, applying dressings, cutting grass, maintaining machinery, attending to areas of damage or wear. All these tasks fall to the ground staff. Many will hold qualifications in horticulture, landscaping or sports management. Details of what the work involves can be viewed at www.wpcc.org.uk/sport.html or www.sportsmark.net.

36 Instructor. Every sport needs instructors. Skiing, athletics, cycling, martial arts, you name it, someone is a paid instructor in it somewhere. For many sports there are a small army of instructors and every small town upwards will have one. Instructors provide training for newcomers to the sport or help players improve. In the case of children the instruction is usually in small groups, while for adults it is often one-to-one. Many instructors work part-time. For a career at fitness for example, first visit www.fitnessfirst.co.uk/...jobs.

37 Executive box steward. You might first think of airlines and cruises when you think of a career as a steward. A steward attends to the needs of customers wherever they might be, and in the executive boxes at sporting events will attend to the needs of the VIP guests. The steward will meet them at a gate and escort them to their box and provide refreshments and food in the intervals. Stewards will have proficiency in silver service and bar skills. A major provider of staff and catering in staff boxes can be browsed at www.uk.sodexo.com.

38 Bookmaker. An interest in and knowledge of sport and basic mathematics would qualify you for a position in bookmaking. These days betting shops are full of plasma TVs and terminals for placing bets electronically. Many bookmakers start their careers as cashiers and progress to store manager and then the manager of multiple stores. See for example www.abb.uk.com for information about a career in bookmaking.

39 Entries officer. Major sporting events such as the London marathon and the Round the Island race (one of the largest sailing races in the world) involve many thousands of contestants, all of whom must register prior to the event. Registering contestants in events big or small falls to administrators employed by the race organizers or sport governing body. Contact the governing body of your sport or the organizer of your club for opportunities to get involved. In the case of swimming for example, information is found at www.swimming.org/britishswimming.

40 Events management. If you are a natural at planning and super-organized, then consider a career in events management specializing in sporting events. It's a fast-growing industry. See sites such as www.eventsmanagement.com for the next step forward.

41 Sports sponsorship. Sponsors fund athletes and teams to tour, and in return the athletes or teams endorse the sponsors' products. It's an essential aspect of the sporting industry and offers careers such as sports account handlers, who find new sponsors and who ensure revenue targets from sponsorship are realized, and executives who handle the really important client relationships. For further information, see for example www.sportscareerfinder.com.

42 Crowd and queue management. If crowds and queues are properly organized at sporting events, then public safety is assured and customer and staff frustrations are reduced. Security staff and stewards usher the audience to their seats; maintenance workers ensure that the public address system, barriers, fences, gates and emergency exits are serviceable; and health and safety representatives and inspectors oversee emergency drills, check that exits are clear and emergency equipment functioning. For information see www.hse.gov.uk; for careers see, for example, www.healthandsafety-jobs.co.uk.

43 First aider. Every sporting event requires arrangements in place in case an emergency should arise. You can train to become a specialist in sports first aid so that you are qualified to provide pre-hospital assistance to athletes on the field or in the sports hall. See for example www.basem.co.uk. You can also train in first aid in order to assist a member of the audience should they suffer a medical emergency. See for example the website of the UK's leading first aid charity, St John Ambulance: www.sja.org.uk.

44 Fitness manager. Organizations that require personnel to maintain a high level of fitness employ fitness managers. These organizations include, for example, the armed services, fire departments or authorities and police forces. Details of fitness manager jobs and training can be explored at www.leisurejobs.com and www.health-club.co.uk.

45 Corporate entertainment co-ordinator. A lot of big events host corporate entertainment activities. These include VIP lounges and seating in executive boxes with food and beverages. Companies invite employees and customers to these high-profile events in order to reward them and build relationships. Contract caterers and facility managers Compass employ co-ordinators; you can find out more at www.compass-group.co.uk.

46 Sports academies. These are multi-sport training facilities that offer accommodation for students while they train to improve in their chosen game. They also offer weekend and summer programmes. There are a great many careers to follow in an academy. The accommodation needs to be managed, the catering and retail facilities staffed, and admissions and marketing organized. Most importantly, an academy needs coaches, and will usually offer a wide range of internships (volunteer positions) where you can gain really valuable experience teaching your sport or running a summer camp. The American academies are by far the biggest and best. For an impression of what they are about visit www.imgacademies.com.

47 Seasonal sports positions. Many sports are seasonal – some winter, many summer – and this means that a large number of sporting careers are seasonal too. Skiing, snow-boarding and water sports are examples of seasonal sports, and work associated with them is seasonal too. Seasonal work often appeals to students looking for summer vacation jobs. Other people combine seasonal sports careers – one summer, one winter – so that they succeed in finding all-year employment. Some travel between the northern and southern hemispheres, following the summer or winter in order to continue their career uninterrupted. You will find a listing of opportunities at, for example, www.seasonworkers.com.

48 Housekeeping. Every establishment, including sporting clubs and venues, needs a team responsible for cleanliness, maintenance, and monitoring and ordering of consumables. These roles are often called housekeeping. Managers in this area may gain their experience in the hotel industry (a big employer of housekeepers) and then transfer to another sector such as sport. For information on what the roles involve, google 'hospitality + housekeeping careers' and remember to apply what you read to the sport industry. For further information, visit the websites of Sodexo and Compass at www.uk.sodexo.com and www.compass-group.co.uk.

49 Lifeguards. These workers watch over pools at any number of venues, including public pools and pools in private clubs, hotels and resorts. Lifeguards are responsible for overall safety in the pool and pool area, preventing accidents and injuries, and treating injuries with first aid. Strong swimming skills are obviously required. For pool and lifeguard jobs have a look at, for example, www.leisurejobs.com.

50 Sports charities. There are many sports charities and charities linked to specific sports. United through Sports, for example, is a South African charity that seeks to bring communities together through sport. Caddy for a Cure gives golf fans the chance to caddy for world-class players in return for raising money for charity. See for example the charities pages on www.jobs.guardian.co.uk for hundreds of jobs in charities, some of which are sports related.

Set 13: Travel

You love to travel so why not make a career out of it? Skills that will stand you in good stead are languages, first aid, a driving licence, strong organizational skills and a qualification in customer service. To improve your chances of landing a job, spend more time trekking/ travelling; there are not many jobs that can be said for! A great web-site is www.wanderlust.co.uk/jobshop.co.uk. Peruse the following 50 travel-related jobs or jobs that can become a passport for travel.

1 Tour leader. Lead a group of travellers on their holiday, ensuring that they experience the culture and natural beauty of the country and have a fantastic time. See the jobs at www.wanderlust.co.uk.

2 Specialist chef. Many of the world's best hotels recruit specialist chefs, the most internationally mobile of whom include, for example, sushi chefs, chefs de partie and chefs de cuisine. Browse jobs by location at www.caterer.com.

3 Travel consultant. Create and price tailor-made travel itineraries, act as a go-between for the client and local suppliers, arrange and book travel arrangements, accommodation guides and tours. Explore possibilities at, for example, www.travelagentcentral.com and www.travelweekly.co.uk.

4 Security manager. Renowned hotels and resorts must provide a secure environment for their guests and experienced security managers are recruited worldwide. Find out more at, for example, www.counterterrorexpo.com.

5 Bar and club managers. Become responsible for the smooth functioning of a bar or club, and take your pick from a huge array of beachside or city venues worldwide. For information about hospitality jobs listed by locations, visit www.caterer.com.

6 Travel industry marketing assistant. Support the marketing team in the advertising of holidays and tours through general administration and analysis and reporting on marketing activities. You will find loads of marketing assistant jobs listed at www.redgoldfish.co.uk.

7 Sports coach or sports official. Organizing international sporting events both amateur and professional, officiating at these events and coaching teams are jobs that involve extensive overseas travel. Feed your aspirations at www.uksport.gov.uk/jobs.

8 Spa manager. Specialize in this management role and take your pick of locations from tens of thousands of destinations worldwide. Be inspired and browse vacancies at www.spaandleisurejobs.co.uk.

9 Tour operations manager. Manage every aspect of the delivery of tours on location, supervise staff, solve problems,

keep records, respond to change. A good place to start your research is www.wanderlust.co.uk.

10 Super-yacht valet. In the right season you can earn €100 a morning polishing the topsides of super-yachts in the world's most prestigious ports and harbours. You will need to be highly presentable and be wearing an immaculate white shirt, shorts and trainers. Simply approach the deck security officer first thing in the day. Check out Antibes marina at www.worldwidemarinasales.com.

11 Flight attendants. Provide for the safety, security and comfort of air travellers and expect to be away from home one-third of the time. Find out about the work at, for example, www.virgin-atlantic.com/en/au/allaboutus/.../jobprofiles/cabincrew.jsp.

12 Casino workers. If you are good with people and very presentable, then learning to specialize in for example dice, roulette or cards may mean that you find work in major cities and tourist destinations worldwide. Why not head for Las Vegas? You can search for jobs at, for example, www.hardrockhotel.com/info/company-info/employment and www.worldcasinojobs.com/nevada-casinos/las-vegas.

13 Travel sales executive. Sell tours, holidays, accommodation, cruises – almost anything to do with the travel industry. Insist on lots of sales visits to destinations so that you can really promote the product. Browse jobs at, for example, www.jobs.dailymail.co.uk/jobs/sales or www.traveljobsearch.com.

14 Deckhand. Handle mooring lines and water sports equipment, undertake watch keeping and security on a super-yacht. See www.uksa.co.uk/careers for information.

15 Picture researcher. Feed your passion for travel by searching image libraries for suitable pictures to fit a brief. Edit the photos and submit them to travel firms for use in advertising, publicity and shows. Find out more at the Picture Research Association website: www.picture-research.org.uk.

16 Overland tour driver. Drive a specially adapted overland vehicle in Africa, Asia or south America. See for example www.dragoman.com and www.wanderlust.co.uk.

17 School group co-ordinator. Liaise with schools and ensure the smooth delivery of every aspect of group adventures and tours. Read more about work as a group tour co-ordinator and school trips at www.albatrosstravel.com/private-group-tours, www.activ4.com and www.teachernet.gov.uk.

18 Eco-trail leader. Lead expeditions of volunteer conservationists that include a mix of trekking and voluntary work at a local project. You can discover more about this career at www.frontier.ac.uk.

19 Entertainers. Children's entertainers, comedians, magicians, dancers, musicians and singers can find work internationally on cruise ships and at hotel complexes. Find out about working on a cruise ship as an entertainer at, for example, www.cruiseshipentertainment.com/princess.htm.

20 Country specialists. Use your in-depth knowledge and experience of one foreign country or region to design and sell tailor-made trips. Country specialist vacancies are often listed at www.wanderlust.co.uk.

21 Adventure specialists. If you are an accomplished trekker, climber, skier, hiker or naturalist, then turn your passion into a livelihood and organize and lead tailor-made adventures for groups. For international summer camp work, visit www.ccusa.com and www.jobs.usnews.com/a/all-jobs/list/q-Adventure+Specialist.

22 Website and brochure writer. Draw on your travel experience or comprehensive knowledge of a region or continent to write convincing copy for travel company websites or marketing material. For inspiration browse the websites of these writers: www.philcopywriter.co.uk, www.carolinegibson.co.uk and www.juliepenfold.co.uk.

23 Sports professionals and coaches. Sports pros and coaches are employed worldwide at holiday centres and hotel complexes. Whatever your sport, an academy or camp will be looking for staff each summer; see, for example, www.itausa.com.

24 Recreational protection. You can find seasonal work in locations across Europe and the Americas as a lifeguard or ski patrol, overseeing recreational areas such as pools, beaches and ski slopes to provide assistance if called upon. The websites of the Countryside Management Association and Careers-Scotland (search for countryside rangers/warden) might be of interest. Visit www.countrysidemanagement.org.uk or www.careers-scotland.org.uk.

25 Run a bed-and-breakfast establishment. Feed your hunger to experience the world by taking up a role that brings the world to you. Get some ideas by viewing the establishments at www.bestbandb.co.uk.

26 Health and beauty services. Hairdressers, fitness trainers, gym instructors, beauticians, manicurists and masseuses are recruited to work on cruise ships and at many large holiday complexes around the world. Be inspired by the world-class facilities at locations such as the Amrita Spa, Dubai. Find out more at www.raffles.com.

27 Internationally mobile general managers. Hotel groups like the Hilton have something like 2,800 hotels in the world's top locations and they offer a graduate programme in hospitality called the 'elevator', which aims to supply their businesses with the management skills they need. Find out more, for example, at the careers page at www.hilton.co.uk.

28 Air marshal. You will combine travel while protecting passengers and crew on passenger flights. Air marshals are present on many airlines and fly worldwide. While most career opportunities exist in the United States, European and other nations also employ air marshals. America leads the way in this area of employment. It might be useful to see how it is approached there. See the last of these links for training in the United States: www.tsa.gov/lawenforcement/people/fams, www.legal-criminal-justice-schools.com and www.leftseat.com/marshal.htm.

29 International truck driver. Long-distance truck drivers move goods across national boundaries. They move fruit from the south of Europe, wood from the Scandinavian countries, fish from the Atlantic coasts, manufactured goods from northern Italy and Germany. For driving jobs of every description visit www.uk-driving-jobs.co.uk.

30 Silver service. Banqueting and conference providers recruit casual waiting staff for large events throughout the year. Staff trained in silver service techniques are always sought after and it is a skill that has helped fund many world tours.

Box waiters and silver service vacancies are posted at, for example, www.hospitalitystaff.co.uk.

31 High-end retail. On a desert island paradise you won't find a supermarket but you might find a holiday resort and if you do it will have stores selling branded sunglasses and swimwear, even diamonds and gold watches. Get started by visiting www.selfridgescareers.co.uk.

32 Director of construction. If you can manage construction projects then your work will take you all around the world, building government buildings, roads, viaducts, tunnels or airports. You will find this sort of vacancy and many other high managerial posts advertised at, for example, www.jobs.telegraph.co.uk.

33 Teaching overseas. A teaching qualification can be an effective permit to see the world. For example, thousands of teachers from Australia and New Zealand come to see Europe, and fund their travel by working as supply teachers. The opportunity to combine teaching and travel applies to everyone. One of the most popular teaching qualifications for the travel addict is English as a Foreign Language. You can find opportunities for teaching oversees at, for example, www.gumtree.com.

34 Oil and gas exploration. Geoscientists, seismic imagers, sub-surface explorers and petrophysicists are just a few of the jobs that will take you around the world. For training and graduate positions with, for example, BP visit www.graduate-jobs.com/training.../BP_International_graduate-jobs.

35 Logistics. If you work for an international freight firm then you will organize the shipment of goods to destinations all over the world. The work involves tracking items and ensuring the correct paper work and customs declarations are attached. Visit the sites of the big players such as www.tnt.com.

36 Naval surveyor. The work of a marine or naval surveyor involves a great deal of travel to undertake survey work on ships, usually for insurance purposes. Other marine careers that involve travel include officer of the watch.
The Royal Institution of Naval Architects' site is found at www.rina.org.uk/professional.

37 Academia. The world of academia is not all dusty books. Visiting lectures and exchange lectures mean that academics also get to travel to other centres of learning and attend conferences, and so combine study and teaching with travel. Search academic and related positions at www.jobs.ac.uk.

38 Yacht delivery skipper. Recreational sailors use the services of a delivery skipper to return a yacht at the end of a holiday or to deliver a yacht to wherever the owner will join it. Charter companies such as Moorings and Sunsail employ delivery skippers to move their fleets between cruising areas and yacht manufacturers, and brokers use delivery skippers to bring boats to trade shows or deliver them from the factory. One of the big players in the field is www.pydw.co.uk.

39 Playgroup leader. Every holiday resort has a children's club and the personnel who run these activities on liners get to join the cruise. Cruises visit an incredible number of destinations, and as a playgroup worker or leader you could visit locations such as Alaska, the Gulf, the Indian ocean islands and the Caribbean. For a career on a cruise ship visit the career pages at, for example, www.costacruise.com.

40 Diplomatic, Commonwealth or European positions in the Civil Service. Some departments of the Civil Service offer the opportunity to travel and be based abroad. See for example www.europeanfaststream.gov.uk for information.

41 Internal auditor for an international company. International organizations need internal audit departments whose members visit regional and national subsidiaries to undertake appraisals and stocktaking. International financial institutions also employ auditors. Organizations such as the World Bank, Inter-American Development Bank and Bank for International Settlements employ many banking, social policy and economics professionals who are based worldwide in regional offices. Visit the career pages of their websites for examples of job descriptions. See for example www.careers.deloitte.com.

42 Worldwide work in agriculture. Paid work as a farm hand is available in locations worldwide and can involve fruit picking in New Zealand, work on an organic farm in Italy or grape picking in France. The pay is low but accommodation and food is provided. You can find further information about farm work abroad at for example www.transitionsabroad.com.

43 Session musician or street artist. Many artists, including musicians, can fund their travel with their art. There are all sorts of reasons why someone might need to hire a musician, and this applies to a travelling musician as much as to one who stays at home. Street artists who make pavement drawings perform at many of the world's top tourist attractions. The world's carnivals provide the perfect opportunity for artists to perform and earn. See for example www.trinijunglejuice.com for a calendar of carnivals.

44 Charity worker operating internationally. At community, national and regional level, international charities employ staff to deliver programmes, oversee partnerships, and investigate and evaluate projects. See, for example, www.oxfam.org.uk/jobs or www.theglobalfund.org/jobs.

45 Golf cart mechanic. It may not sound much like a career with a licence to travel but there are golf courses all over the world, and where there are golfers there are golf carts and they need to be serviced and maintained. The manufacturers provide some training; otherwise it seems experience is what counts. For further information, try searching the career pages at the golf cart forum, www.buggiesunlimited.com, and www.trumpnationallosangeles.com.

46 Au pair. An au pair lives with a family and helps with childcare and household tasks in return for accommodation and an allowance. Many countries allow foreign nationals to take up employment as an au pair although they are denied the opportunity to take other types of work. For information, see for example www.aupair.com and www.aupairjobs.org.

47 Nursing overseas. The skills and knowledge that a UK or European-educated nurse gains are highly regarded and can open doors to a broad range of opportunities for working abroad. For employment advice view, for example, www.overseasnurse.com.

48 An employee with a United Nations programme. Unicef, UNDP (United Nations Development Programme) and the FAO (the Food and Agricultural Organization of the United Nations) are examples of organizations funded by the United

Nations that recruit internationally for positions at head offices, regional offices and field representatives. Find out more at www.careers.un.org.

49 Summer jobs worldwide. You might like to help run a summer camp in America, organize water sports on a resort in the Mediterranean, or be a galley slave on a charter yacht in the Caribbean. There are thousands of openings for summer work, and who knows what they might lead to? You will find opportunities for summer work at, for example, www.summerjobs.com, www.anyworkanywhere.com, www.backdoorjobs.com and www.jobmonkey.com.

50 Home entertainments and communication technician. Technicians in this area of work are in high demand and they get to travel to customers' second or holiday homes to install, configure, test and repair networking and communications equipment and home entertainment equipment and ensure it is interfaced with all the other existing devices. Find out about an apprenticeship in this field and many others by searching for electrical/electronic engineering apprenticeships at www.apprenticeships.org.uk.

Set 14: Fill your senses

Butterflies can settle in the 50 careers reviewed below. Every one of them will reinforce the reason you chose the work and so will hold your interest for years to come.

1 Herb grower. Herbs – their colour, smell and taste – bombard the senses. They are used in drinks, cooking, around the home, in treatments and cosmetics. They are sold cut, fresh, dried, even frozen or in pots. Growing them commercially does not require a very large space, highly technical expertise or very expensive equipment. It does guarantee, however, involvement in the whole process from sowing to selling. Visit some of the herb gardens around the country for inspiration. Visit www.herbexpert.co.uk for information.

2 Prop maker. If you can create things that look remarkably real using little more than smoke, mirrors, bits of string and duct tape (and a whole host of other stuff obviously) then fabricating props might be your dream career. You can specialize in the production of miniatures for motion pictures or theatrical sets. Be inspired by www.propmaker.co.uk.

3 Vegetable seller. Aren't vegetables just breathtaking? So consider a role that involves the handling, display and selling of seasonal fruit and vegetables such as artichokes, asparagus, endive, squash, snap peas and rhubarb. Aim at the top end of the market and build long-term relationships with your customers, sharing recipe ideas, information about your growers and what's coming into season next. It need not require expensive premises but might involve a stall at a local market or a vegetable round delivering your produce to homes. You might find your dream opportunity at www.uk.businessesforsale.com/uk.

4 Production assistant. If you are looking for a role that is both creative and administrative, then consider becoming a production assistant for film, TV or theatre. These are sought-after positions, but if you are lucky enough to get the opportunity then you will circulate technical scripts and lists and produce schedules, as well as spending time at rehearsals and during shoots and productions. Information about this career and vacancies can be found at www.prospects.ac.uk and www.jobs.guardian.co.uk.

5 Tour manager. A tour manager is the one who keeps everyone happy as well as sorting out tickets, reservations and so on. If the band members want to go and see the sights after the show, it's down to the tour manager to sort that out at short notice. If tempers get frayed, it's the tour manager's job to makes things tranquil once again. Be inspired by browsing www.tourconcepts.com.

6 Micro-brewer. In a micro-brewery, you will be involved in all stages of the brewing process from fermentation to packaging. To become a brewer, you may first need to study chemistry or food science and then apply for a position as a trainee brewer. Australia leads the way in micro-brewing so start your search at, for example, www.probrewer.com and www.microbrewing.com.au.

7 Graphic designer. This profession involves developing the overall 'look' in print and digital media. Using colour, type sets, logos, designs, photos and illustrations, the graphic designer's job is to communicate and make a strong positive impression. Get ideas and inspiration at www.kevadamson.com and www.toastdesign.co.uk.

8 Coffee shop proprietor. Serving a coffee should come with so much more than free WiFi. Source the best beans and roast and grind them on the premises, offer an ambiance that makes people linger and you have the makings of a great coffee shop. Bring your enthusiasm and passion to the venture and as long as the location is right it will be a sure-fire winner. Identify the winning ingredients by browsing, for example, www.independent.co.uk/.../the-50-best-coffee-shops-1903388, www.timeout.com/london/restaurants/features/6361.html and www.guardian.co.uk/travel/2009.

9 Gallerist. An art dealer trades in art but a gallerist represents artists and invests in the marketing and display of their work in return for a percentage of sales. A gallerist owns a gallery and puts on shows. An exhibition may last a matter of a few days or a few weeks. A gallery can be any kind of space and double as a wine bar, canteen, private home or garden. See what's possible at www.thesassongallery.co.uk, www.saatchi-gallery.co.uk/yourgallery and www.londonart.co.uk.

10 Baker. No smell is as captivating as that of a bakery filled with oven-fresh bread, bagels, sourdoughs and flat breads. It is a demanding career and you will need to go back to school to learn the craft. Google 'bakery schools' to get started. You can almost smell the bread at www.moreartisan.co.uk.

11 Animator. Draw on your artistic flair together with a competence with computers to produce moving images. Digital animators work on, for example, computer games, cartoons and public information clips, and produce a series of frames, each one a work of art, which when run create movement. See what's possible at, for example, www.aardman.com.

12 Confectioner. Boiled sweets every colour of the rainbow and favoured with fruit juice, bon bons, bubble gum and butterscotch are examples of traditional sweets made with natural ingredients and once sold in old-style sweet shops. A confectioner prepares the ingredients and shapes and

cooks the sweets and other sugary treats. It's work that calls on your artistic side and requires a love of baking and decorating. You can find out more at, for example, www.miette.co.uk and www.tangerineuk.net.

13 Local talent agent. If you are a people person and love children's parties, storytellers, after-dinner speakers, comedians and musicians, then why not become a local talent agent? The work involves scouting for talent and helping find bookings and auditions for your acts in return for a percentage of the fee. For ideas see, for example, www.curtisbrown.co.uk and www.newfacestalent.co.uk.

14 Cheese seller. You either love it or you don't. The texture, smell and taste makes some people crave it. The hundreds of different cheeses from countries all around the world and from different milks, including the unusual ewe, mare and even camel milk cheeses, means there will always be something new. For information see www.cheese.com.

15 Reader for a literary agent. Authors, especially authors of fiction, rely on literary agents to negotiate contracts, advances and royalties. Agents review hundreds of submissions from aspiring authors, and many employ readers to sift the submissions. To succeed in your application to be a reader, you are very likely to have had a career in publishing and/or success as a writer yourself. To look further into this career visit www.literaryconsultancy.co.uk.

16 Style consultant. Personal appearance counts and looking good opens doors. A good makeover boosts your clients' self-esteem enormously and makes a rewarding career. You need to get to know your clients and help them decide on the look they like. The advice can include dress, as well as makeup and hair style. See what this career involves at www.colourmebeautiful.co.uk.

17 Pastry chef. In a small establishment your morning would start with the number one ingredient, your labour of love, and end with tarts, pies, tatins and vol-au-vents.
Your reward will be the smile on your customers' faces.
Be inspired by browsing www.williamcurley.co.uk.

18 Rose grower. With spring, the rose starts to burst into life and the grower makes plans for the season. You would grow red, long-stemmed roses with an incredible scent in heated greenhouses for Valentine's day, and outside for the rest of the season. Start your investigations at www.classicroses.co.uk and www.garden-roses.co.uk.

19 Advertising storyboard artist. Many advertising agencies use freelance illustrators to illustrate advertising concepts for their clients. You will need a portfolio of your work in order to win commissions, and you will specialize in one area of illustration. You will need to learn to use technical computer programs and learn about the printing process.
Many illustrators begin by taking a foundation course at an art school; see www.ucas.ac.uk for information.

20 Exhibition designer. You will first come up with a concept and sell it to the client, then oversee preparation of the artwork and construction of the exhibit display. The work will involve travel. You will get a good idea of what is involved if you visit the website of www.finessegroup.com.

21 Cameraman/woman. This is a role that is both highly technical and creative. The post holder must operate all associated equipment, including monitors and lighting gear, as well as providing advice and deciding on the best angle for the shot. Most camera operators work their way up in the trade and many have studied photography. Visit the website of cameraman and director of photography Mark Bond for insight: www.markbond.co.uk/cv.htm.

22 Choreographer. Classical ballet, modern, ballroom, a choreographer must be knowledgeable in all forms of dance, music and costumes. Most are former dancers with experience of the theatre and dance companies. For a taste of what is possible, browse the website of www.hugoviera.com.

23 Wholesale florist. Florists buy their flowers from wholesalers, who are constantly looking for novel foliage as well as supplying the usual favourites. A good wholesaler will celebrate the seasons with the arrival of spring, summer and autumn lines. Find out more at, for example, www.trianglenursery.co.uk and www.sunflora.co.uk.

24 Events organizer. There are many types of event, but the person who organizes them typically has to co-ordinate timelines, venues, suppliers and staffing. Organizers must

book a venue and organize security, insurance catering, equipment hire, ticketing and possibly sponsorship. As soon as one event is over they are busy with the next. For further information visit, for example, www.eventworld.co.uk.

25 Set designer. Working from the script and with the producer and director, a set designer must research architectural and soft-furnishing historical styles, present drawings and select props for a production. They must then oversee and co-ordinate the set construction. Take the next step and visit the website of the Society of British Theatre Designers: www.theatredesign.org.uk.

26 Spa therapist. If you have a healing touch and care about the physical and mental well-being of others, then consider graduating from a massage training school where you will become proficient in treatments including waxing, manicure, body wraps and massage techniques and qualified for employment at a therapist at a spa. Indulge in pure tranquillity at, for example, www.spachancerycourt.co.uk.

27 Commissioning editor. Commissioning editors work mostly in the book publishing business, where they are responsible for building their publisher's lists. They do this by presenting book proposals to the weekly or monthly publishing committee, and ensure that successful proposals become manuscripts that are delivered on time and to the agreed specification. You will find jobs advertised at, for example, www.mediauk.com/newspapers/jobs and www.jobs.guardian.co.uk/job.

28 Wine taster. A few experts can earn a living tasting wine but most will be employed as stewards conducting wine tastings. A successful tasting-room guide will educate and entertain the customer while promoting the wines. See www.winejobs.com for opportunities.

29 Party organizer. If you have an eye for detail, are creative and most of all love a party, then this could be the role for you. You might start by working for a party company that offers murder mysteries or lingerie parties and move on to organize corporate parties at top sporting venues. See how you can bring your style to a fast-moving career by visiting, for example, www.henheaven.co.uk.

30 Care home entertainer. Of all the various circuits in the entertainments business, perhaps the care home circuit has the reputation for being the toughest. But can you think of a more laudable career? An act that drew on, for example, contemporary history, the golden age of cinema or the reconstruction of local history would bring a welcome change to the usual offering and would help recover memories. Find out more at, for example, www.carehome.co.uk.

31 Industrial designer. In this career you would work with fabrication engineers and modellers to develop things such as new interior designs for automotive vehicles. You would need a strong senso of form, and graphic and drawing skills honed while completing a design degree at university. Get ideas from sites such as www.sproutdesign.co.uk.

32 Fashion buyer. Buying for the fashion industry involves an incredible number of specializations. You might find yourself in the teen market or the big-and-tall sector. All buyers will enjoy travel and negotiations, and you will work closely with other members of a merchandizing team. You will also have a passion for fashion and be an avid follower of trends. The key to your next career might lie with www.drapersonline.com.

33 Recreational therapist. People who facilitate recreation activities that improve or maintain the physical, mental and emotional well-being of individuals with disabilities or illnesses are called recreational therapists. They use a great many different activities, including art and music, crafts, animals, games and dance. You can find courses at, for example, www.studydiscussions.com/recreation-therapy-courses-in-uk.

34 Teaching citizenship. Non-EU immigrants must now pass a citizenship test before they can become citizens, and many colleges and community centres offer short part-time courses in citizenship. Your students will be drawn from all over the world and you will gain insights into their traditions and cultures as you provide them with access to yours. To make a start in this career visit, for example, www.teachingcitizenship.org.uk, www.citizenshipteacher.co.uk and www.redcross.org.uk/What-we-do/Teaching-resources.

35 Roadside repair technician. If you have mechanical skills and can solve problems, and most of all have a flair for communication, then consider this rewarding career. You would attend roadside breakdowns and if you can't solve the problem arrange for a tow. The job is becoming even more challenging, given that more vehicles are using alternative fuels. This means that you really will not know what to expect until you get there. You will find the career pages of the RAC at www.jobs.rac.co.uk.

36 DJ. A disc jockey is employed to provide music at venues such as private parties, nightclubs and radio stations. You must have a wide knowledge of music and be musical as well as outgoing and creative. Most of all you will need absolutely loads of personality and love to show it. For the complete beginner through to the competent performer, you will find training at, for example, www.djacademy.org.uk.

37 Wool grader. Most agricultural products must be sorted and graded. Everything from oysters to apples. Most of these jobs are carried out in cold agricultural sheds and are highly repetitive, but some grading jobs are different and perhaps the best of them all is the wool grader. Wool graders will assess the strength and quality of the fibres that make up a fleece by look and feel. They may examine them through a microscope but mostly they will rely on separating a tuft of the raw wool between their fingers. They will then grade the wool and classify it in terms of its quality. They can also advise on the mixing of bales to create a blend of wool for processing into yarns. See, for example, http://www.curtiswooldirect.co.uk.

38 Glass moulder or bender. This work involves heating glass to form or mould objects or to repair cherished items. The artisan glass worker makes colourful figures or items such as glass jewellery and Christmas decorations. See what is possible at, for example, www.hounslowglass.co.uk/ and www.beadsashore.com.

39 Midwife. To care for women during labour and birth is to share something very special. It requires, as well as technical skills, a personal and understanding nature and a family-centred approach. Women who move into midwifery from a career other than nursing do so from a very wide range of backgrounds. Find out how to train to be a midwife at www.nhscareers.nhs.uk.

40 Colour consultant. If you have an eye for colour and how it impacts on what we wear and how we decorate our homes, then consider this career. The aim of a colour consultant is to advise clients on the most appropriate colours of clothes, makeup and accessories that are complementary to their hair eye and skin colour. Find out more at www.improvability.co.uk.

41 Cocktail bartender. Can you see yourself mixing an award-winning Manhattan? Bartender schools in America are reporting record numbers of students enrolling to learn the art of cocktail mixing. As well as mixing a mean cocktail, the job requires you to be at ease behind the bar and willing to chat with clients, some of whom may become friends and confidants. Get inspired by the world classic cocktail championship www.ukbg.co.uk/competition results.html.

42 Picture framer. If you are confident in handling colour, contrast and balance, then consider picture framing as a career. To see what is possible, visit www.frameworktroon.co.uk.

43 Recitalist. A recital is normally associated with music but it can just as easily be a reading. It will be a performance in public, often performed solo. Recitalists work for theatres, at tourist venues and public events. For a listing of recitalists, visit for example www.churchmusic.org.uk.

44 Pet photographer. These specialize in producing pictures of pets, and the work means more varied clients than a portrait photographer. A pet photographer will work either at the client's home or at a studio. Get some great ideas from, for example, www.pawspetphotography.co.uk and www.roberthooper.co.uk/pets.htm.

45 Tapas chef. Eating tapas has always been a social event and preparing it an art form that involves bringing traditional ingredients and flavours together in a series of tasty bites. Complementary chefs have taken this art beyond its Spanish origins and draw freely on flavours and ingredients from a great variety of cuisines. See for example the work of chef Andrea Mellon at www.dukrestaurant.co.uk.

46 Perfumeries seller. Smell somehow uniquely triggers our self-consciousness. A smell will conjure a positive image in one person and a strong dislike in another. Finding the right perfume for a client requires insight. You can see how online at the world's most famous department store: www.harrods.com.

47 Nail artist. Creating beautiful nails is fast becoming one of the most popular treatments in beauty therapy. It's spectacular and highly creative. For inspiration, see www.nailsmag.com.

48 Book surgeon. Many writers before they submit their novel to an agent or publisher employ a book doctor or surgeon to undertake a careful read and provide a critique and constructive suggestions. Book surgeons are usually published authors or trained editors who provide an independent service to writers. You can see an example of a company offering this kind of help, as well as proofreading and copy-editing, at www.a-star-editing.co.uk.

49 Landscape architect. In this profession you design and plan outdoor spaces, both hard features such as paths and patios and soft features including all the plants and water features, and garden structures such as decks, gazebos and docks. For information, see the Society of Garden Designers at www.sgd.org.uk.

Set 15: The outdoor type

There really are dream jobs for the outdoor type and you must dare to imagine winning one. It is clear that your spirit is meant to be free and your work should not lock you away from the open spaces that you cherish. There still are wild places but you might have to look abroad to find work in one. One possibility is to work in America's great outdoors. The easiest way for a non-American to work in the United States is to apply for a J-1 temporary work visa. You must be a full-time university student or within six months of graduation to qualify. There are agencies who can advise; for example, visit www.ciee.org for information.

1 Marine ecological monitoring officer. Would you enjoy undertaking investigative surveys of rivers and freshwater lochs and lakes? You might well find yourself up to your armpits in pond water and spend your afternoon counting tadpoles. But if that's the kind of thing you might enjoy, then this might well be the career for you. You can find the latest science jobs at www.newscientistjobs.com.

2 Vermin control officer. Roaches, rats, pigeons – the control of animal pests is necessary in homes, retail establishments, factories, farms, in fact anywhere that humans come into contact with unwelcome animals. Many officers work in an urban setting but they are very much their own boss. You need to be fit and active and happy to crawl into small spaces and lofts and roof spaces. You will need to be competent in handling dangerous chemicals and understand the important of wearing protective clothing.
   For a career with, for example, Rentokil visit their website at www.rentokil.co.uk/careers/index.php

3 Fish hatchery manager. Fish farming is now big business. It was once mainly trout and salmon but now many more species are farmed. Sea fish farms are located in coastal areas and comprise large tanks ashore where the fry are raised and larger tanks or pons, sometimes offshore, where the older fish are grown. The manager is usually provided with accommodation but this may be only a caravan. Find out more about a career in fish farming, fish and shellfish, for example at www.scotland.gov.uk/Topics/marine/Fish-Shellfish and www.fishfarmer-magazine.com.

4 Gardener. You might be employed by local government to maintain the city parks or by a landscaping company, or be self-employed working on private gardens. Irrespective of your employer, jobs will vary with the seasons, and you will spend your days for example tending plants, cutting and pruning, operating mowing or cutting equipment, planting and weeding. You will find a listing of gardening events at www.rhs.org.uk. If you follow up the ones in your area you might find it could lead to a temporary position.

5 Survey geologist. Carry out field mapping, collect core samples and other geological data from sites, and produce computer generated 3-D models and scientific interpretations of the data. You can find out about the sort of

undergraduate training that is available by searching geology degrees at, for example, www.exeter.ac.uk.

6   Agricultural machinery operative. This work will entail operating farm equipment to till, plant, cultivate and harvest crops. The machinery may for example be used to thresh and bale at harvest time. During the winter you may be ploughing and operating a mechanical excavator to maintain drainage ditches. If you are a follower of the organic movement, then you might find the opening you are looking for at www.soilassociation.org/Farmersgrowers/.../ OrganicFarmingmagazine.

7   National Parks information officer. You might have to start in a seasonal position to gain sufficient experience and then start applying for a permanent post. You will spend most of your time outdoors working in conservation, perhaps leading a group of volunteers to clear invasive species, or patrolling and providing information to visitors. Jobs in the National Parks can be viewed at www.nationalparks.gov.uk/jobs.

8   Forestry fire warden. The work entails patrolling and keeping watch, and fighting fires on forestry land, as well as explaining to the public the risk of forest fires and what causes them. Wardens maintain records, submit reports and enforce forest fire laws. To find out what vacancies there are in the UK forestry commission, view www.forestry.gov.uk/vacancies.

9   Cell phone mast erector. The mobile phone network is reaching ever further and mast-erection gangs are responsible for extending the network into the most remote areas of the world. Mast erectors in the Canadian outback have to post a bear watch to ensure their safety while they work. For a listing of wireless jobs and telecommunication networking jobs visit, for example, www.wirelessmobile-jobsboard.com or www.jobsearch.monster.co.uk/Telecommunications-Network.

10 Wholesale horticultural nursery worker. Nursery workers seed, pot on, tend and sell plants and trees. Wholesale nurseries supply plants to retail stores, florists and landscapers. For jobs in horticultural work and agriculture generally, browse www.fwi.co.uk.

11 Underwater explorer. If you think such a job seems too farfetched to be true, then google 'diving with legends' or 'global underwater explorers'. To land such a career you will need to be an experienced diver and probably a graduate in one of the marine sciences. There are exceptions of course, and one would be the work of controlling one of the remote submarines, a job which is usually held by people who are fantastic at computer games.

12 Ranger. The job of ranger covers many different areas such as recreation, heritage, conservation and fire management. Heritage involves both the culture of aboriginal people and the historic heritage of the site and the way it has been changed by humans. To be a ranger in the royal parks, see www.recruitment.royalparks.org.uk

13 Retail nursery worker. Retail nurseries supply plants to the general public. This work involves potting on, tending and selling plants, shrubs and trees. Jobs in garden centres are listed at, for example, www.bloominggoodjobs.com and www.hortweek.com.

14 Shepherd. If you prefer the company of a dog to people, then tending a flock of sheep or goats roaming common land in some part of Europe might just provide a subsistence living. To make a living as a shepherd in the UK you would need to live in a part of the country where there is sufficient common land, and combine the care of your flock with tourist or educational activities. For example you can offer tourists the opportunity to spend a morning walking the flock with you. You might also make and sell sheep or goat milk, yoghurt and cheese. You can read about all things meat at www.meatinfo.co.uk.

15 Water sports instructor. Someone has to hang out at the pool or beach organizing games and providing instruction in how to use wind surfs, sea kayaks and sailing dinghies, and it really could be you. Some instructors work the Mediterranean season, then the Caribbean and back to the Mediterranean. After a few years they are well placed for a management position organizing the other instructors. See for example www.markwarner-recruitment.co.uk.

16 Tree surgeon. Work at heights using harnesses and hoists. They use chainsaws to prune and remove diseased wood.

They also cut down trees. A tree surgeon must establish that the tree he or she is working on does not cross the boundary to another person's land, and if it does permission must be obtained before work can begin. For information see, for example, www.treesurgeonsregister.com.

17 Lawn care technician. This job involves caring for the grass lawns that make up golf courses, parks and playing fields. The technician mows, edges, dresses or mulches, waters and weeds the grass. The work can be really very technical as the lawn may be in use all year round so it may have to be heated from underground, or it may be located somewhere where lawn does not normally grow, in which case the technician may have to monitor saline levels or provide shade to prevent the grass from being scorched. For information, search for ground care and groundsperson at, for example, www.hortweek.com/careers and www.inputyouth.co.uk/jobguides.

18 Inshore fisherman/woman. There is a secret army of licensed fishermen/women operating in inshore waters from small craft and selling their shellfish and white fish direct to the public from the beach, at farmers' markets or through specialist shops and restaurants (for example live fish to Sushi restaurants). This kind of fishing is much more sustainable than the factory ships working offshore. You will need to purchase a commercial licence before you can sell your catch, and be warned it is a hard living that involves many skills and relatively high risks. For information on training and careers, visit www.seafish.org/sea/training.

19 Exotic animal keeper. Zoos, animal sanctuaries and some farms and medical research institutes employ people to tend to animals more normally associated with the savannah of Africa. Poisonous snakes are kept to milk their venom to produce antiserums, primates are used in medical research, crocodiles are farmed for their skin and meat, and many zoos and other tourist attractions display animals such as lions, water buffalo and elephants. For the latest about jobs working with animals, view for example www.animal-job.co.uk.

20 Harvest vacancies. If you are willing to travel, then you will find harvest work throughout the year. It involves harvesting

fruit and vegetables and helping with tasks such as shearing when there is not enough local labour. To take your pick of harvesting jobs, go to www.pickingjobs.com.

21 Environmental educator. This work involves teaching groups of school children, but also family groups, so as to increase awareness of environmental issues, conservation and sustainability. Often the work is based at a nature reserve or park and the educator leads the groups on an excursion, explaining the environmental issues in the context of the reserve. You will find pages of green jobs at, for example, www.greenjobs.co.uk and www.environmentjob.co.uk

22 Biological anthropologist. The science of biology can provide amazing insights into our past. A biological anthropologist examines remains and excavates ancient latrines, burial grounds and waste dumps, and uses his or her scientific training and knowledge to establish, for example, what our ancestors ate and how they lived. For further information about graduate and postgraduate programmes, visit www.bioanth.cam.ac.uk.

23 Driller and derrickman. Both these jobs involve drilling to obtain either soil and rock samples or gas or oil. The driller is in overall charge of the drilling operation and the derrickman is usually his Number 2. You will find more information at, for example, www.oilcareers.com.

24 Motorman and toolpusher. These are workers in the drilling business. They are skilled technicians responsible for key operations on the rig. If you are interested in a career in drilling for the gas or oil industry, then google either for details.

25 Roughneck and roustabout. These are two more job titles in the drilling business and are both general labouring position. They help set up, take down and transport drilling rigs, and undertake cleaning, fetching and carrying, and maintenance duties while the drilling is taking place.

26 Solar system service and installation engineer. This is not some science fiction role where people maintain planets, moons and stars. The work involves the installation and servicing of solar panels and systems for both residential and business applications. For examples of these jobs, see www.greenjobs.co.uk.

27 Game warden. If you like the idea of patrolling reserves or private grounds to prevent poaching or investigate reports of damage to crops and the theft of wildlife, then consider becoming a game warden. The work involves touring by car, boat, horse or even airplane and carrying out inspections to ensure that hunting methods and equipment are lawful. If you find that someone is using illegal methods or fishing or hunting out of season, operating in a restricted area or hunting a protected species, then you must make an arrest, seize equipment and give evidence in court. Find out more at www.countrysports.co.uk.

28 Volcanologist. If you like the idea of living in a tent for months at a time collecting the data needed to predict future eruptions of an active volcano, then this specialist area of geology might well suit you. Another side to the work is to design systems that will harness the power to produce carbon-free electricity. Get started by enrolling in a geology first or master's degree course. For details of a geology course that includes volcanology, visit www.es.lancs.ac.uk/vgrg/newsite/study.html.

29 Water engineer. Designing and building sewer improvement schemes or flood-defence programmes, pumping stations and pipework is work undertaken by water engineers. In more outdoor/hands-on positions the work will involve monitoring flood levels and the maintenance of water and sewerage infrastructure. To search water engineering jobs, view www.workgateways.com/Engineering.Water.Jobs.

30 Horticultural assistant. This work involves maintaining interior and exterior gardens, landscaping and maintaining fish ponds. You will operate equipment such as mowers, trimmers and sprayers. You can find openings in horticulture at www.horticulturejobs.co.uk.

31 Environmental impact assessment officer. Mostly these officers work for local authorities or are self-employed consultants. Whenever there is a planning application for a new development, then an environmental impact assessment must be produced and measures proposed to counter any negative impact the assessment identifies. You can find more by searching at, for example, www.businessgreenjobs.com.

32 Pastoral farm worker (the use of grass pasture for livestock rearing). Move animals. Fertilize pastures to encourage growth and mow to produce winter feed, identify sick animals and treat for parasites. Assist with animal births and with milking. Drive agricultural vehicles. Find out the latest news and vacancies in agriculture at www.fwi.co.uk.

33 Arable farm worker (on land that can be ploughed to grow crops). Operate tractors, tractor-drawn machinery and self-propelled machinery to plough, harrow and fertilize soil, or to plant, cultivate, spray and harvest crops. Identify pests and weeds. Load agricultural products and drive agricultural vehicles. Again the best place for a search of all things agricultural is www.fwi.co.uk.

34 Nature photographer. Photographing nature involves accepting assignments, researching the subject, devising photo story ideas and travelling to sites. However, you can't ask a fish to jump out of the water or a rainbow to appear, so you have to wait and when the moment arrives catch it. You then submit your images or post them onto photo libraries. You might start your career at a photography school or as an assistant. Be inspired by viewing the work at www.uk.naturephotographers.net and www.nature-photography.co.uk.

35 Treasure hunter. There are a number of careers in treasure hunting. One involves selling metal detectors and other treasure-hunting equipment. A second is organizing treasure-hunting holidays. If you are thinking that this is not really treasure hunting, then visit www.shipwreck.net, the website of Odyssey Marine Exploration. They use the latest sonar and mini-submarine technology and extensive historical research to find treasure in shipwrecks, and they have been remarkably successful. Their website has a careers page.

36 Earthquake scientist. Some geophysicists spend most of their time outdoors studying seismic events. The data they collect is used to predict the likelihood of earthquakes and recommend safe locations for structures such as dams or nuclear power stations. You will find loads of information if you search at www.hotcourses.com/uk.../Geology-degree.

37 Astronomer. Astronomers observe celestial and physical phenomena and develop theories to explain them.
In more practical work, they also help develop astronomical instruments and products for navigation, space flight and satellite communications. You can study astronomy by distance learning; for example see www.astronomy.ac.uk.

38 Geologist. These scientists are employed in the field to find oil, metal ores and many other minerals, and this is no doubt the side of geology that will more interest you. They search for rocks that contain important metals and locate geological features that produce oil, natural gas and groundwater.
See, for example, www.geology.com.

39 Outdoors instructor. This career involves training and leading groups in, for example, bushcraft, climbing, canoeing and expeditions. The delegates may be groups of school children, adults on staff training events or students for the Duke of Edinburgh awards. Most events will be residential.
To train as an outdoor instructor, visit for example www.outdoor-instructor-training.co.uk.

40 Small animal breeder. Farming animals such as rabbits, mink and chinchillas for the fur trade or animals such as mice, rats and guinea pigs for animal research is undertaken on smallholdings in outdoor cages. Most breeders own and run the business but some research institutions breed their own animals and employ people to undertake daily husbandry duties. For medical research see, for example, www.criver.com/en-US/.../Pages/UK. For information on a small animal breeders show,
see www.thesmallanimalshow.co.uk.

41 Prospector. These days you are more likely to meet someone with the job title business prospector than someone involved in small-scale mining and prospecting. But if you look you will find people engaged in, for example, small-scale open-cast mining or collecting and selling fossils, and with the price of many ores, minerals and gems at record prices now might be a good time to get started. Prospecting and mining involves hard physical labour and requires the prospector to traverse rough terrain, looking for signs of minerals, fossils, precious metals or mineral specimens. Prospectors must also make claims by posting notices at a site and registering their claim. For anyone interested in exploring for gems, visit for example www.coloradoprospector.com.

42 Exhibition centre crew member. They may not work outside but some of the venues are really big spaces. The work entails helping erect stages, stands and seating, assisting exhibitors with their goods and props, cleaning and maintenance during the event and packing it all up afterwards. For vacancies at the Excel exhibition centre, for example, go to www.excel-careers.com.

43 Archaeologist. Given your preference for working outdoors, you will find the surveying and excavating side of archaeology most appealing. This work involves walking sites, even using aerial photography, and excavating promising sites and recording features and artefacts. If the site is a permanent one, then the work may also involve leading groups of visitors around the site and explaining it to them. For advice on a degree in archaeology visit, for example, www.archaeology.ws/degrees.

44 Alaska fisheries. Alaska is a frontier land where hard work and a willingness to live a rugged lifestyle will bring opportunities. One example is work as a deckhand on an Alaskan fishing boat. But be warned, fishing is a hazardous occupation. Wages are usually based on a share or percentage of the catch; in the case of a new deckhand this may be as low as 1.5 per cent. Crew licences are required and are available to non-residents; visit www.admin.adfg.state.ak.uk/license.

45 Animal technologist. These workers care for laboratory animals used in medical research. Some technologists are involved in experimental work and will be licensed to undertake procedures. Animal technologists spend their day with the animals and they undertake routine cleaning and feeding tasks. See www.iat.org.uk for information.

46 Camping holiday jobs. In Europe and America, tens of thousands of families holiday each year in organized camp sites and there are thousands of seasonal jobs serving this business. Help set up for the season, putting up tents, or be a team leader managing the on-site team, or organize and deliver fun daily activities for adults and children. Visit www.holidaybreakjobs.com/camping for job leads.

47 Amusement parks. You can work as a ticket-taker, performer or ride operator, or in food service. US amusement parks hire many international students on J-1 work visas.
Visit www.corporatedisney.go.com/careers for openings.

48 Ranching. The best site for job leads in the ranch business is www.coolworks.com. On this site you will find seasonal work for staff to drive wagons, prepare cookouts, lead children's events, be a tour guide, even wash dishes.

49 Mountain jobs. If you love the idea of living in a mountain community then MountainJobs.com is the site for you. You will find hundreds of jobs there for the summer and winter seasons as well as permanent positions.
For training and volunteering, visit www.pyb.co.uk and www.bluedome.co.uk.

50 Rigger. This work involves replacing or installing wire supports to hold up structures used in architecture and engineering. It originally involved the rigging of ships to carry sails (and still can). Most riggers learn their trade assisting a professional rigger. You will need a head for heights.
For further ideas of what the work involves, visit www.shop.spencerrigging.co.uk.

Set 16: The chance to make yourself indispensable

There are a great many employers who would be eager to have someone like you on their team. Review the following 50 careers in which your qualities and motivations will help you excel, and decide where to focus your talent and determination. A great website for jobs is www.lgcareers.com.

1 Publicist. People like you make great publicists. The role is about getting positive press coverage for your clients, and you achieve this through contacts in media organizations and presenting the right stories to journalists. Find public relations news and jobs at www.prweek.com.

2 Litigation associate. This role involves helping lawyers prepare cases by investigating facts and collecting information. The Association of Property Litigation website is found here: www.pla.org.uk.

3 Contract negotiator. Could you see yourself negotiating major contracts? You would work closely with lawyers and staff who would be responsible for the delivery of the contract, and you would take the lead on negotiations. In the telecommunications and oil industry, for example, these jobs are advertised in www.telecom.jobs-career-employment.com/ .../Contract-Negotiator and www.oilandgasjobsearch.com respectively.

4 Consumer advocate. As a consumer advocate you would champion the ordinary citizen against unfair, misleading or dishonest practices by businesses. You might organize a help line or website through which people can report sharp practices. You would most likely work for a local authority or consumer protection charity. For inspiration see www.moneysavingexpert.com.

5 Regeneration officer. Most local authorities and some consultancies employ regeneration officers to oversee the physical and social regeneration of an area. This work involves, for example, the redevelopment of a site and the re-training of residents. For local authority and public sector jobs such as a regeneration officer, see www.opportunities.co.uk.

6 Health advocate. This role involves promoting good health and healthy lifestyles to communities. These might be a body of students at a university, a 'hard to reach' group living in a rural area, or a group of citizens at high risk of ill health. The objectives are realized through leaflets, discussions with elders, displays, and visits to community groups and events. A health advocate will try anything to get the message across. Examples of the kind of services a health advocate offers are found at www.seap.org.uk, www.pacehealth.org.uk/ mental_health_advocacy and www.bhf.org.uk/living-with-a-heart...we.../health-advocate.

7 Equal opportunities manager. Many companies take equality and diversity seriously and employ a team of staff to promote equality of opportunity in recruitment, training and employment. A good place to start your search is www.voice-online.co.uk.

8 Fund raiser. Hospitals, educational institutes, political parties and a host of other charitable or not-for-profit organizations employ fund raisers. The individuals or teams market the good works of their organization and seek gifts to help fund the continuation of the work. If you believe that you could raise funds for a charity or non-profit organization, then browse for example www.fundraising.co.uk.

9 Corporate trainer. Staff training is an investment that should serve the objectives of a company. Good corporate trainers know the organizations with which they work and ensure this knowledge informs the process of identifying training needs and deciding on which training to purchase. The corporate trainer then assists with and evaluates the delivery of that training programme. Examples of corporate trainers include www.dalecarnegie.co.uk and www.lct.uk.com.

10 Public relations (PR) officer. This work is about managing the public image of an organization. A PR officer will seek to build a positive image of the organization in order to maintain goodwill and understanding amongst key audiences. See for example the website of the CIPR, the professional body for the UK public relations industry: www.cipr.co.uk.

11 Homeless persons officer. All local governments employ teams to provide temporary accommodation, re-house homeless people and implement strategies designed to prevent homelessness. For vacancies, visit for example the jobs pages at www.opportunities.co.uk. For information, see for example www.housing.org.uk.

12 Foreign Service officer. This highly competitive role is a part of the Civil Service. The Foreign Service represents a country around the world. Its officers interact with governments and representatives from other embassies, and provide advice to their citizens travelling abroad. You will find all types of Civil Service vacancies at www.civilservice.gov.uk/jobs.

13 Campaign manager. A political party, candidate in an election or company running an advertising campaign will employ a campaign manager to devise a winning strategy. Most campaign managers are highly experienced campaign workers and will have started their careers as volunteers before building a reputation sufficiently strong to command a salary. For information about campaign managers, search for example at www.jobs.guardian.co.uk/job.

14 A legislative assistant or special advisor. In government, legislative assistants and special advisors work for elected politicians and help ensure that new laws serve the policy objectives of the government. To view job opportunities at the House of Commons, visit www.parliament.uk/site-information/job-opportunities.

15 Best-value officer. Most local authorities and government departments employ best-value officers to secure operational improvements in terms of economy, efficiency and effectiveness. You can find out more at www.planningofficers.org.uk and www.ogc.gov.uk.

16 Senior events planner. Whether it is a large corporate meeting, trade conference or public show, an events planner will be behind it. These people are highly adept at communication and organization and are involved in an event from conception to finish. A senior planner will be in charge of high-profile, big-budget events. See for example the homepage of www.carolynactonevents.co.uk.

17 Lobbyist. Companies and special interest groups employ lobbyists to represent them to members of government. They also work to ensure that members of government appreciate the effect of proposed legislation on their clients. They may suggest amendments to legislation and seek elected representatives who will propose and back these amendments. To find out more about the lobby industry visit, for example, www.publicaffairslinks.co.uk/index_uk.html and www.lobbyinguk.com.

18 Special interest group officer. These officers act as advisors working to ensure that a group of people who have an interest different from the norm is not forgotten in the delivery of services. An example might be patients with mental health problems. A hospital or health authority will seek to meet the needs of all clients, but may employ a special interest group officer to ensure that their services also meet the needs of groups such as those suffering mental health problems. A special interest group officer will liaise with service providers, attend meetings and provide

expert opinion on how the needs of the group they represent might best be served. A place to look for jobs is, for example, www.jobsincharities.co.uk.

19 Public policy worker. This role involves winning support for a policy idea so that it is adopted as a policy objective and becomes law. Public policy workers build relationships with key individuals in the policy area. They attend meetings and explain and promote the policy they represent. For an example of the kind of work undertaken by policy workers in the fight against global poverty, see www.oxfam.org.uk.

20 Pollster. This work is a type of market research, the aim of which is to determine the extent to which the general public or representatives of a target group are aware of and support a policy idea, candidate or political party. The results of the research may be used to design a campaign in just the same way that a market researcher will work to gather information on customer preferences and buying habits in order to market a new washing powder. You can find out about the work of a leading company at www.ipsos-mori.com.

21 Democratic services officer. Local governments and many corporations seek to operate democratically. This involves working in an open and accountable manner. They employ democratic services officers to propose actions and ways of working that are more democratic. Find all sorts of local authority vacancies at www.opportunities.co.uk.

22 Elections manager. Local authorities are responsible for the registering of the electorate and the organizing of elections. Elections managers are appointed to deliver this responsibility and ensure that all elections, including European, local and national ones, are organized properly and fairly. Google your local authority and visit the careers pages.

23 Broadcast editor and producer. Behind the scenes of TV news and documentaries, a team of editors and producers is responsible for ensuring that information is coherent, factually correct and balanced. Their job is to write and verify as true the content of these programmes for television and radio. You can view jobs at, for example, www.jobs.bbc.co.uk.

24 News reporter and correspondent. News reporters and correspondents are the familiar voices and faces that present the news. News reporters are generalists while correspondents are specialists brought in to discuss the impact of a news story. You can find out about training opportunities at, for example, www.bbctraining.com.

25 Policy researcher. Many pressure groups, political societies and parties employ policy researchers to conduct research and analysis and advise on relevant research findings. They report verbally and prepare briefings, provide expert advice and represent the organization for which they work at meetings. Find out more at the Institute for Public Policy Research website at www.ippr.org.uk.

26 Dean. Many colleges and universities employ a dean as a part, or sometimes the head, of the administrative services. In many cases the dean of students is responsible for overseeing extracurricular activities, student housing and counselling services, and fund raising. For an example, see www.hope.ac.uk/education.

27 Business prospector. This job requires the post holder to sift all new leads and identify which to discard and which represent a good prospect. Then, together with the sales team, the prospector develops the selected relationships and moves the targets towards becoming customers. For jobs in sales lead generation see, for example, www.b2bprospector.co.uk and www.experian.co.uk/business-information/b2b-prospector.

28 Executive coach. The post holder needs to be at ease with senior management and be an adept catalyst for change. Coaches help identify underperformance and strategies to address it, and are able to build teams. Find out more at, for example, www.coachingconsultancy.com and www.execcoach.net.

29 Single-issue campaigner. This role requires someone to take the lead and champion an issue in the press, at public meetings, on committees and in meetings with key players. For an example of what single-issue campaigners do, see the website of www.greenpeace.org.

30 Head of department (in education). This job entails maintaining standards of pupil attainment and monitoring student progress. The post holder is responsible for leading and managing the staff in a curriculum area and planning its

finances and resources. Find out about a career in education at www.deni.gov.uk and www.education.gov.uk.

31 Emergency planning officer. Local authorities appoint emergency planning officers to prepare for a disaster such as a pandemic, terrorist attack or flood, and to co-ordinate the contingency plan for such an emergency. Find out about vacancies as local authority emergency planning officers at, for example, www.lgcareers.com.

32 Motivational speaker. This role is all about getting attention and energizing people to act in order to achieve a specific set of goals. This might be to get people to do something more with their lives, to spread the word or bring attention to a topic and gain people's support to do something about it. Get motivated by visiting, for example, www.ghinsberg.com or www.craigharper.com.au.

33 Conciliation and arbitration officer. A number of government or charitably funded organizations employ conciliation and arbitration specialists to help with employment relations. They do this by providing information and advice, running training courses and helping to resolve disputes between employers and employees. See for example www.acas.org.uk.

34 Leading a team of debt counsellors. The role of debt councillor involves explaining financial information to members of the public, helping them plan and budget, and negotiating on their behalf with creditors. The team leader must ensure that counsellors are providing up-to-date advice and clients are satisfied with the service. For further information visit the web page of, for example, the Consumer Credit Counselling Service: www.cccs.co.uk.

35 Regional co-ordinator of parent coaches. A parent coach is someone who has raised a family and now wants to offer support and encouragement to other families and mothers. The regional co-ordinator plans and oversees the service for an area of the country, ensuring that services respond to demand and quality is maintained. See for example www.nctpregnancyandbabycare.com.

36 Senior youth mentor. This work involves supporting, guiding and being a friend to a young person during or after school hours or at the weekends. A senior mentor leads a team of volunteers, helps recruit and train new mentors, and tries to ensure that mentors keep in touch with their clients for a year or more. You can find out more at, for example, www.mediatrust.org/youth-mentoring and www.mentorfoundation.org/uk/awards.

37 Community leader. This role is about inspiring others to support a cause and helping them to further their understanding of the issues involved. A community leader makes representations to the wider community and is the local spokesperson for a cause. Charities and campaign groups employ community leaders to represent them in a neighbourhood or district. Many local or regional agencies offer training for community leaders; see for example www.londoncitizens.org.uk/pages/training.

38 Chairperson. The chair of a board of directors provides leadership, together with the chief executive, and helps guide and mediate. He or she assists in strategic planning and resolving issues faced by the organization. The chief executive reports to the chair. You can find online learning for people working for a charity at, for example, www.wfac.org.uk/training.

39 Group spokesperson. A spokesperson represents a company and its products and defends it on, for example, the radio or on television. Their personality and their standing in the public eye become closely associated with the company and its products. They become the human face or voice of the company. For the latest news of charities, not-for-profits and NGOs, see for example www.thirdsector.co.uk.

40 Environmental representative. Many companies appoint environmental representatives to help reduce waste and CO_2 emissions, save energy and encourage recycling. The representative suggests ways in which current practices could be changed, and then works to make them happen. This work is done in partnership with both the employer and the employees. Find out more at for example www.unison.org.uk/green.

41 European officer. Charities, educational institutions and local governments employ European officers to secure European funding for projects and co-ordinate the delivery of the European element of those projects. For current vacancies as a European officer look at, for example, www.lgcareers.com.

42 Consultant. Consultants operate in almost every field. They are either self-employed or work for a firm of consultants or accountants who provide consultancy services. They bring extra resources of skill and experience to an organization, and will have a clear brief towards which they are expected to work very hard. They may for example be brought in to prepare a bid or restructuring, or they may undertake strategic analysis. They normally report directly to a senior director or the board of the client. Find out more at the Management Consultancy Association at www.mca.org.uk.

43 Troubleshooter. This role calls for a logical approach and involves finding and curing faults in products or processes. Troubleshooters are recruited in many fields, including construction, IT and network engineering, financial control, and elevator and escalator engineering, to name but a few. In computing for example, see www.computertroubleshooters.co.uk.

44 Single-subject teacher. Teachers of 11–18-year-olds teach a single subject and are responsible for ensuring that pupils acquire a knowledge and understanding of the curriculum for that subject. A good teacher inspires a love for the subject. For example, see the Earth Science Teachers Association: www.esta-uk.net.

45 Personal advisor. This work involves providing individual advice to adults or young people regarding careers, training, work, benefits and life skills. Personal advisors are employed by government departments, local authorities and charities or not-for-profit organizations. For work as a personal advisor with Jobcentre Plus, visit www.jobseekers.direct.gov.uk.

46 Senior contract manager. Every contract, whether it's to build something or provide a service, will have a manager assigned to it. Contracts of a significant value will be allocated to a senior contract manager. The role involves planning, overseeing delivery, budgeting, invoicing, communicating with the client and solving problems if they arise. Find out more at http://www.ncmahq.org/.

47 Private investigator. A private detective or investigator works on a case-by-case basis for lawyers, businesses, government departments or individuals, and will investigate the facts of a matter. The case may involve someone suspected of making false claims for housing or state benefits. It may concern establishing whether someone is in fact unemployed or incapacitated as they claim. The work involves internet searches and other research and surveillance. Find out more and about training as a private investigator at www.ukprivateinvestigators.com and www.ukpin.com/become-detective.html.

48 Theatre producer. The individual who chooses the production, raises funds and puts together the troupe is the producer. It's a job and a half, whether it's a church hall production or a Broadway show. Be inspired by browsing, for example, www.sindenproductions.com.

49 Inward investment officer. Many local authorities employ inward investment officers to attract companies and investment to an area. The work might include, for example, liaising with a supermarket that plans to open a new store in the district that will create hundreds of new jobs. For a career in inward investment, search at the websites of the regions, for example www.sdi.co.uk. Also look for current vacancies at, for example, www.lgcareers.com.

50 Outreach worker. Many charities, housing associations and local authorities employ outreach workers to engage with individuals from hard-to-reach groups and encourage them to make use of the organization's services. Hard-to-reach groups might include unemployed young people who are not in training or education or claiming benefits, women members of an ethnic minority group, or older citizens living alone. You will find outreach worker jobs by searching at, for example, www.charityjob.co.uk/jobs, www.jobs.guardian.co.uk/jobs/charities and www.jobs.thirdsector.co.uk.

Set 17: Compassionate careers

There are many hundreds of careers in mainstream and complementary medicine to choose from. Consider the following 50 ideas.

A really good website for mainstream careers is www.nhscareers.nhs.uk, so for the suggestions below such as midwife, audiologist, operating practitioner and so on, be sure to visit this site. If you are interested in a career in nursing, then be sure to get hold of a copy of *How to Master Nursing Calculations* by Chris Tyreman.

1 Midwife. A midwife cares for women during pregnancy and childbirth. Find out more about the work of midwives at www.independentmidwives.org.uk and www.rcm.org.uk.

2 Audiologist. This role involves assessing patients' hearing and balance. For more information, visit the sites of the British Association of Audiological Physicians, www.baap.org.uk, and the British Society of Hearing Aid Audiologists, www.bshaa.com.

3 Homeopathy practitioner. Under this discipline, practitioners provide remedies following the work of Samuel Hahnemann. For information see www.homeopathy-soh.org.

4 Qigong practitioner. This discipline follows a Chinese system of physical training for health. Find out more at, for example, www.healthqigong.co.uk.

5 Operating practitioner. An operating practitioner assists during surgery. Find out about theatre nursing and operating practitioners at www.afpp.org.uk.

6 Reiki practitioner. This is a Japanese discipline for stress reduction. See for example www.reiki.org.

7 Veterinary technician. This work involves caring for the animals that are brought to a veterinary practice and assisting the vet during surgery and procedures. Why not find out more at the site of Vetnurse: www.vetnurse.co.uk. And check out jobs in handling and caring for animals in the MoD, for example, at www.armyjobs.mod.uk/jobs.

8 Phlebotomist. This profession involves taking blood samples. For further information visit the National Association of Phlebotomists: www.phlebotomy.org.

9 District nurse. These nurses make home visits and support GP surgeries. Most of their patients are elderly, or have recently left hospital or have a terminal illness. For more

information, visit the site of the Community District Nursing Association: www.cdna-online.org.uk.

10 Orthopaedic technician. This work involves applying plaster casts or measuring and fitting braces and splints. The Association of Orthopaedic Practitioners' website is a good source of further information: www.aot-uk.com.

11 Cytogeneticist. This work involves the diagnosis of genetic diseases. Find out about training and latest developments at the Association for Clinical Cytogenetics: www.cytogenetics.org.uk.

12 Ward manager. The person in this post is responsible for the effective running of a hospital ward. Why not get along to the next hospital and healthcare exhibition: www.hospitalmanagement.net/exhibitions.

13 Dialysis technician. Many people who suffer from diabetes must regularly undergo dialysis. A dialysis technician carries out the treatment. The Association of Renal Technologists' website is found at www.artery.org.uk.

14 Genetic counsellor. The geneticist identifies genetic abnormalities and the genetic counsellor helps patients and families understand and come to terms with their condition. You can find out more about this at www.agnc.org.uk.

15 Histocompatibility scientist or technician. This work involves matching patients to donors. A good place to start your research might be the site of the British Society for Histocompatibility at www.bshi.org.uk.

16 Learning disability nurse. The role of these nurses is to help people lead as independent and full a life as possible. Find out more at www.aboutlearningdisabilities.co.uk.

17 Ambulance care assistant. These workers transport non-emergency patients to and from hospital. Search and you will find more information at, for example, www.careersadvice.direct.gov.uk.

18 Perfusionist. The job title of the technicians who operate the heart/lung machine during surgery is perfusionist. Find out more through the Society of Clinical Perfusion at www.sopgbi.org.

19 High-intensity therapist. High-intensity therapists work with people who suffer depression and anxiety. You can find out more at www.iapt.nhs.uk.

20 Acupuncture/acupressure practitioner. Acupuncturists relieve pain and treat conditions using needles and by applying pressure to points on the body. For information see www.acupuncture.org.uk.

21 Chiropractitioner. Practitioners treat injuries and posture problems. For information see www.gcc-uk.org.

22 Herbal medicine practitioner. These specialists use natural herbs as remedies and supplements. You can find out more at the National Institute of Medical Herbalists and the Register of Chinese Herbal Medicine: www.nimh.org.uk and www.rchm.co.uk.

23 Aroma therapist. These practitioners use botanical oils to treat ailments. For information, visit www.aromatherapycouncil.co.uk.

24 Donor carer. The person who supports donors when they donate blood is called a donor carer. For more information on donor support visit www.uktransplant.org.uk.

25 Radiographer. Radiographers and their assistants undertake diagnostic imaging and cancer treatments. To begin your search for more information, visit the website of the Society of Radiographers at www.sor.org.

26 Light therapist. Light therapy is used to treat conditions such as seasonal affective disorder and depression. For further information visit, for example, www.sadbox.co.uk or www.lumie.com.

27 Alexander Technique practitioner. This discipline teaches awareness and bodily co-ordination. You can find out more about the Alexander Technique and training to become a practitioner at, for example, www.stat.org.uk or www.alexanderteacher.co.uk.

28 Magnetic therapist. Magnetic therapies are used for pain relief and to treat arthritis. Read more about this therapy at, for example, www.magnetictherapyuk.co.uk or www.magnetichealthcare.com.

29 Prosthetic technician. These technicians measure and fit artificial limbs. See for example the information on the site of the US Prosthetic Association at www.anaplastology.org/education-training.

30 Meditation practitioner. There are many traditions in meditation and they offer cures through the emptying of the mind and channelling of thoughts. To link into a network of teachers, visit the British Meditation Society at www.britishmeditationsociety.org.

31 Reflexology practitioner. These treatments involve applying pressure to the hands and feet to stimulate wellness. You can find out how to learn to be a practitioner at, for example, www.learnreflexology.com.

32 Respiratory technician. These workers diagnose disorders such as asthma. Find out more at, for example, the Association for Respiratory Technology at www.artp.org.uk.

33 Natural hormone replacement practitioner. This treatment is used to help with menopause and osteoporosis. For further information visit, for example, www.bioidenticalhormonesociety.com.

34 Osteopath. An osteopath treats illness through the musculoskeletal system. See for example www.osteopathy.org.uk.

35 Chinese medicine. Practitioners of Chinese traditional and herbal medicine follow a discipline that pre-dates mainstream medicine by many centuries. For information see, for example, www.atcm.co.uk.

36 Oxygen/ozone therapy practitioner. This therapy is used to treat conditions such as depression and to detoxify patients. For further information visit, for example, www.ozonetherapy.co.uk.

37 Neonatal nurse. These nurses care for newborn babies. You will find the Association of Neonatal Nurses' website at www.nna.org.uk.

38 Embryologist. These specialists help patients who suffer from infertility. Start your search for further information at www.britishfertilitysociety.org.uk.

39 Cardiac physiologist. These are specialists who fit devices such as pacemakers. Visit the website of the Society for Cardiological Science for more information: www.scst.org.uk.

40 Children's nurse. A nurse can specialize in the care of sick children and the support of their families. The Association of British Paediatric Nurses' website is found at www.abpn.org.uk.

41 Technical instructor. These workers install support devices in the homes of patients and give advice on how to use them. You might start your search for further information at the site of the college of occupational therapists: www.cot.co.uk.

42 Intensive care technologist. The technicians who attend to patients in critical or intensive care are called intensive care technologists. For information on what is involved in delivering critical care, visit www.criticalcaretech.org.uk.

43 School nurse. These nurses visit the schools in a district and help with the promotion of healthy living and child protection. Find out more at www.school-nursing.co.uk.

44 Therapy assistant. Therapists in many disciplines use assistants to carry out some aspects of the treatment. For speech and language therapy, for example, see www.rcslt.org.

45 Cyto-screener. These specialists examine samples for signs of cancer. Find out more at, for example, www.clinicalcytology.co.uk.

46 Mental health nurse. This specialist nurse cares for people who suffer mental illness. He or she visits them in the community and treats them when they attend clinics or are receiving treatment in specialist units. See for example the blog Mental Nurse: www.mentalnurse.org.

47 Adult nurse. Nurses can specialize in a great many areas but their first experience of the profession is in hospitals, nursing sick adults back to health. To find out how to become a nurse, visit www.rcn.org.uk.

48 Assistant anaesthetist. These technicians work under the direction of an anaesthetist and administer anaesthetics to patients and monitor them during surgery. The Association of Anaesthetists' website is found at www.aagbi.org.

49 Immunologist. This role involves the treatment of conditions of the immune system. The British Society for Immunology's site is found at www.immunology.org.

50 Cardiographer. This role involves operating the equipment that monitors the hearts of patients. Find out more at the British Cardiovascular Society site: www.bcs.com.

Set 18: A profession

Get started on establishing yourself in one of the following 50 suggested professions, and in due course you will be able to take pride in the fact that you are a respected authority in your area. Consider previewing the profession of your choice with an internship or work placement. Be sure to track down your chosen profession's professional association and join it. Give serious consideration to taking out professional liability insurance.

1 Educator. If you are an adapt communicator, have an infectious interest in one or more subjects and can handle a great many different situations confidently, then give proper consideration to the possibility of joining this profession, especially if you also obtained a high score in Set 6 or 13. You need not always have a professional qualification in order to teach; for example, teaching English as a Foreign Language or being a tutor in adult learning does not necessarily require a qualification in education. It is possible to begin teaching in these roles while studying part time for, for example, a higher education or further education qualification. See for example www.dcsf.gov.uk or www.natecla.org.uk.

2 Shipbroker. A shipbroker matches ships to cargoes and negotiates fees and collection and delivery dates. It's a worldwide business and involves working across different time zones. For information, see for example www.balticexchange.com and view the website of the professional body representing shipbrokers: www.thisisics.co.uk.

3 Archivist. If you also scored well in Set 2, then a career as an archivist might be worthy of consideration. Governments, universities, hospitals, libraries, institutions and individuals generate or are the custodians of a great many documents, letters, photos, newspaper cuttings and, increasingly, computer-generated records. The archivist preserves, indexes and promotes the information contained in these archives. See for example the Society of Archivists' site at www.archives.org.uk.

4 Auctioneer. If you can capture an audience's attention, excite and entertain them, this might be your perfect role. First you would help value the goods and agree a reserve price. Next display the items for viewing and then begin the sale. These days auctioneers work as much online as in cold, damp auction houses, but the excitement builds just the same until the hammer falls and the highest bid wins. The National Association of Valuers and Auctioneers' website is found at www.nava.org.uk.

5 Pharmacist. Pharmacists dispense medical drugs in hospitals and in the community (from a shop on the high street for example). If you also obtained a high score in Sets 1 and 17, then it might be worth investigating this profession further by visiting for example the website of the Royal Pharmaceutical Society at www.Rpsgb.org.uk. Information on the professional qualification that you must obtain to practise as a pharmacist can be obtained there.

6 Actuary. Actuaries use their exemplary numerical skills to assess risks and model the future in order to inform business decisions. Qualifying in the profession is a demanding process but might be of interest to readers who also scored highly in Sets 1 and 9. Visit www.actuaries.org.uk for further information.

7 Town planner. Town planners help shape our public urban environment by overseeing and controlling the use of buildings, land and roads. They work for local and central government and for environmental, architectural and regeneration consultancies. A career in planning may well be of interest to someone who also scored well in Sets 6 and 14. Find out more from, for example, www.lgcareers.com.

8 Curator. Curators plan and oversee collections and their exhibition. You can be a curator for almost any sort of collection, from the more traditional works of art to a

collection of motor cars, films, photo images, music, geological samples or fossils. The career might well be of interest to people who also scored highly in Sets 1 and 2. For information, see the website of the Museums Association: www.museumsassociation.org.

9 Police officer. A police officer seeks to prevent and solve crime, protect the public and preserve public order and private property. If you scored highly in Sets 10 and 19 then take seriously the possibility of a career in the police force. You can find out more about the recruitment process and discover if you have the aptitude for the force by reading the Kogan Page title *How to Pass the Police Initial Recruitment Process*. Visit for example www.met.police.uk.

10 Healthcare manager. Individuals in this role form part of the management team in hospitals, nursing homes or clinics. They develop and implement policies and manage the business, its finance and human relations. To find out more about this career, why not visit the US Association of Healthcare Office Management at www.pahcom.com.

11 Interpreter. Many government departments and agencies require interpreters to help communicate with clients who do not speak English. Interpreters also work at conferences or in industry, in which case it helps if they also understand the technical issues of an area such as engineering or law. For more information visit, for example, www.apciinterpreters.org.uk and www.aiic.net.

12 Publisher. This person manages the selection, production, marketing and distribution of the books put out by a publishing house. In really large publishing houses there will be a publisher for each division or genre. The term 'book' these days includes e-books. For a guide to the publishing industry visit, for example, the UK Publishers Association at www.publishers.org.uk.

13 University administrator. Workers employed as university administrators co-ordinate campus activities, admissions, finance, academic staff recruitment and management, in fact everything other than the delivery of teaching and research. You can start your search for more information at the website of the Association of University Administrators: www.aua.ac.uk.

14 Underwriter. This profession is about estimating risk for insurance purposes and calculating the price of insurance premiums. See for example the International Underwriting Association's website: www.iua.co.uk.

15 Headmaster or headmistress. The head is a role model for both students and staff, as well as the chief executive of an educational establishment and personnel director and director of finance. For further information visit the websites of, for example, the Headmasters and Headmistresses' Conference and the Society of Headmasters and Headmistresses: www.hmc.org.uk and www.isyb.co.uk.

16 Aircraft pilot. You do not need a degree to go to flight school and become a pilot responsible for flying commercial aircraft. See www.pea.com, for example, for the kind of offer made by a flight school (in this case in Florida, USA). To find out more about this profession, visit for example the Aircraft Owners and Pilots Association's website at www.aopa.com.

17 Lawyer. Training for law may well suit you, especially if you also scored highly in Set 14 (Debate and current affairs) as your quickness of thought, wit, charm and humour, and love of an exchange of views will serve you well in this profession. For an indication of whether or not you have the abilities to succeed in law, google LSAT (which stands for Law School Attainment Test, the test you must pass to gain a place in many American law schools) and practise on some of the free material available. The Law Society website can be found at www.lawsociety.org.uk.

18 Barrister. Barristers are self-employed and, as with law, the profession suits quick-witted people who enjoy an exchange of views. Those in the profession who work with a jury must be good communicators, and so this profession may well suit those who also scored high in Set 8. The profession also provides opportunities where the emphasis is on written submissions and the presentation of a case to other barristers and judges, and these roles may well suit someone who realized a high score in Set 1. You can find out more at the bar council's website at www.barcouncil.org.uk.

19 Stockbroker. To practise as a Stockbroker you must be registered with the Financial Services Authority (FSA) and then you are licensed to buy and sell shares and securities for a fee or commission. Start your search for further information at, for example, the Association of Private Client Investment Managers and Stockbrokers, at www.apcims.co.uk.

20 HR director. Human resources (HR) is about the management of the staff making up an organization. The HR director leads in the compliance with labour law, communication with staff, and management of the organizational structure, pay bands and recruitment. He or she will also play a major role in the management of change, which may involve redundancies, relocation, training or expansion. For training courses, news and vacancies see, for example, www.cipd.co.uk.

21 Probation officer. This occupation involves working with offenders to ensure the safety of the public and reduce the likelihood of reoffending. Probation officers work with two groups of offenders: those who have not received a custodial sentence but are sentenced to community service, curfews and suspended sentences; and those released from prison on probation or licence. For information on the Trade Association for Probation Workers and Court Staff, see www.napo.org.uk.

22 Architect. After at least seven years of study, a student of architecture can take the professional practice exams and register with the Royal Institute of British Architects. For information visit their website at www.architecture.com.

23 Medical facility administrator. Hospitals and organizations have a lead administrator and assistants who specialize in the daily decision making. They might be the administrator for particular departments such as nursing or technology. For information, see for example the Association of Medical Secretaries and Practice Administrators' website at www.amspar.com.

24 Radio/television journalist. Broadcast journalism is highly competitive and served by a number of specialist degree and postgraduate courses and traineeships. For inspiration see, for example, the BBC Journalism Trainee Scheme at www.bbc.co.uk/jobs/jts.

25 Quantity surveyor. This profession provides estimates and manages costs in construction projects. For information see, for example, the website of the Consultant Quantity Surveyors Association at www.cqsa.co.uk.

26 Policy analyst. Foreign, medical, environmental and security policy are just a few of the areas where specialist policy analysts work. A policy analysis evaluates policies against the stated goals and helps explain them to the general public. It will also identify which of competing policies will best fulfil the objectives and undertake cost–benefit evaluations. You can find professionals who work in the field of policy analysis at Linkedin: visit, for example, Zahid Torres-Rahman at www.uk.linkedin.com.

27 Professions in the British Army. To find out about a career as an officer or soldier in the British Army, visit www.army.mod.uk.

28 Notary public. A notary deals with non-contentious legal matters, primarily involving the witnessing of signatures for the registration of land, wills and so on. In the UK, currently a notary must be a qualified solicitor. For information visit www.thenotariessociety.org.uk.

29 Print media journalist. Magazine, newspaper and website journalists seek out and write news items. They research on the internet and exchange e-mails with people involved in the story or those who are experts in the subject. They also attend courts and council meetings, and interview people by phone. Find out more at, for example, the website of the National Union of Journalists: www.nuj.org.uk.

30 Trading standards officer. These professionals advise consumers on issues around buying, selling or hiring. Trading standards officers work for local government, investigating complaints and prosecuting unscrupulous traders. For further information see the Trading Standards Institute at www.tradingstandards.gov.uk.

31 MBA. Many people building a career in business study to become a master in business administration (MBA). Many MBA programmes base admission on the GMAT score and require work experience. For further information, visit www.mbaworld.com. To prepare for the GMAT, use *How To Pass the GMAT*, published by Kogan Page.

32 Headhunter. A headhunter is a recruitment consultant who places senior staff into permanent positions for a fee, usually based on a percentage of the annual salary. A good headhunter knows an industry well and has an extensive network of contacts. They are commissioned by an employer to seek out and approach staff with particular experience and find out what would attract them to change jobs. See the website of the Recruitment and Employment Confederation at www.rec.uk.com.

33 Translator. Translators work with text and translate it from one language to another. The growth of the internet has lead to a marked increase in the need for translation of web pages as well as documents, marketing material and manuals. Find out more at the websites of the Association of Translation Companies and the Institute of Translation and Interpretation at www.atc.org.uk and www.iti.org.uk.

34 Doctor of medicine. To qualify as a doctor you must complete a course of study recognized by the General Medical Council. Following completion of a degree in medicine, you then complete a foundation programme and choose a specialization. UK medical schools require applicants to take either the UKCAT or BMAT; to prepare for these tests use the Kogan Page titles *How to Master the UKCAT* and *How to Master the BMAT*. See any of the other careers in Set 17 also. Visit the website of the British Medical Association at www.bma.org.uk.

35 Structural engineer. This profession involves the design of load-bearing components for architectural structures. For information, see the website of the UK Institute of Structural Engineers at www.istructe.org.

36 Veterinary surgeon. A vet must train for five years at a veterinary school. Once qualified, most either join a private practice or work for the government. The Royal College of Veterinary Surgeons' site is found at www.rcvs.org.uk.

37 Chartered accountant. Most companies must appoint an accountant to audit their books and prepare a stator report. For information see the Institute of Chartered Accountants' website at www.icaew.com.

38 Management accountant. A management accountant is responsible for cost management, performance measures, strategic planning and internal controls (rather than statutory financial audits and reports). For information see the Charted Institute of Management Accountants' website: http://www.cimaglobal.com/.

39 Civil engineer. As an independent civil engineer you would advise on the construction of bridges, tunnels, roads, harbours, airport runways and a host of other projects. For further information, visit the website of the Institute of Civil Engineers at www.ice.org.uk.

40 Mechanical engineer. Mechanical engineers build or design things. They specialize in one area, which may be anything from refrigeration to power plants or electric motors. Find out more at, for example, the website of the Institution of Mechanical Engineers at www.imech.org.

41 Planning agent. These specialists help people make planning applications for new buildings or extensions to existing buildings. They advise on what is likely to be acceptable, complete planning applications and collate all the necessary supporting paperwork. They will also oversee an appeal if an application is rejected. Many planning agents have previously worked in a local government planning department. Start your search for information at, for example, www.rtpi.org.uk.

42 Pathologists and forensic pathologists. Pathologists do laboratory tests to diagnose disease, while a forensic pathologist determines the cause of death. The Pathological Society is found at www.pathsoc.org.

43 Management consultant. These specialists bring expertise, experience, specialist skills and extra hands to a business problem or opportunity. They advise the managerial team on structure, strategy or operations, and seek to improve the business's efficiency and profitability. You can browse the information of the Management Consultancy Association at www.mca.org.uk.

44 Loss adjuster. Loss adjusters are independent investigators of the facts surrounding an insurance claim. They may inspect the damage, interview witnesses with a view to establishing the facts, and establish whether the claim is valid and should be paid. Visit for example the Chartered Institute of Loss Adjusters' website at www.cila.co.uk.

45 Registrar. These individuals are officers responsible for the recording of births, deaths and marriages. Every district in England and Wales has a registrars' office whose staff maintain the statutory records. For career opportunities visit, for example, www.lgcareers.com.

46 Patent agent. When individuals or companies want to patent intellectual property or register a trademark, they may turn to a patent agent to obtain advice on how best to make their application. Agents may also advise on what action to take when a patent has been infringed. For further information visit the National Association of Patent Practitioners' website at www.napp.org.

47 Health visitor. This role involves visiting patients' homes or places of residence to oversee the administration of medication, change dressings, collect samples and check that the patients are as well as can be expected. Health visitors care for the elderly, people with a terminal illness, newly born babies, or people who live alone and have just been released from hospital after surgery. Start your research at, for example, the Community Practitioners and Health Visitors Association at www.unitetheunion.org/cphva.

48 Dentist. To practise as a dentist you must successfully complete a five-year course at a recognized dental school. The work is technical and includes preventative work as well as surgery. For information visit www.bda.org.uk, the site of the British Dental Association.

49 Tax advisor. An independent tax advisor provides assistance and advice to individuals and companies on all kinds of tax – corporate, income, death duty, value added – and all kinds of allowable expenses and allowances that can be legally set off against tax due. Many tax advisors have previously worked for the Inland Revenue as tax inspectors. For further information, visit the website of the National Association of Tax Consultants at www.natctax.org.

50 Company director. A company director is responsible for the success of the company and its legal operation in terms of health and safety and equality of opportunity. The directors

must ensure the business remains solvent and in most
cases they must ensure an annual audit is conducted and
all necessary returns are submitted and taxes are paid.
For information see, for example, the Institute of Directors'
website at www.iod.com.

6

MAKE YOUR DREAM CAREER A REALITY

You have reflected on the listing of careers. Chewed them over, highlighted the ones that most appeal, then checked again to see if you have overlooked something you might never have thought of before. Now you have a shortlist of dream careers. You have no more need to ask yourself 'what shall I do?' All that is left is to find a path that will make one of your dreams a reality. It need not be a long path; in fact you can complete it in as few as 12 short steps.

Step 1. Explore

You obviously want to know as much as possible about the careers on your list, so start your research. Start with any links offered in Chapter 5 and then use Google or one of the other search engines to find more. There are billions of web pages out there and the knowledge you need to make your dream a reality is almost certainly part of that enormous quantity of information. The question is: how can you find it? In most cases a basic web search will do. A Google search is case insensitive and punctuation is ignored, so describe what you are looking for using as few descriptive words as possible, type them in the search box and click on 'Search'. Most of the time you will find what you are looking for. Incidentally, it is always worth having a look at the list of related searches lower down on the page. To undertake a more focused search and reduce the number of false hits, try putting a + sign between your descriptive words. Then the search engine will only link to pages that have all those words (rather than all the pages that have any of the terms). Repeat the exercise using different descriptive words. Take as an example the career 'book surgeon or book doctor': someone who provides independent book editing services.

Example

Google 'book surgeon' and you get lists of books on surgery. If you Google 'book editor + book doctor'. You get the sites of people who describe themselves as book doctors and offer independent editing services and manuscript reading and advice. If you search 'book editor' you get pages that provide primary functions and activities, job descriptions, skills required and salaries for the profession of editor. At the bottom of that page you will find links to related searches including book editor jobs and book editor salaries. If you search 'book editor + job description', high on the ranking are some very good sites such as www.prospects.ac.uk and www.careers.stateuniversity.com

---

Step 2. Get a taste for your chosen careers

It will not be long before you have a good amount of information about the careers on your shortlist. Next, set about trying things out for real, especially anything on your list that you have hardly given a thought to before. Do this by searching for and attending open days at institutions or taster courses offered in the evening or weekends. Seek to visit organizations that offer employment in your local area and study the careers page of any trade or professional association. If there is nothing available in your area or at the time of year, e-mail those organizations for advice. Study the websites of organizations that offer services in the subject, contact them and ask if they have open days, when and how they recruit and if you can visit. Go to a library and browse any textbooks used to teach the subject at college or university. Use every personal contact you have to find people who work in your careers and ask if you can call them to discuss their work. Before you speak to someone or make a visit, jot down a few questions you would like answered.

Step 3. Shorten your list

If a clear winner hasn't emerged, start to reduce your list of careers by dismissing any positions that you consider risky or impractical. Be sure your decision is informed and based on the findings of your research. Before rejecting the idea, investigate any related careers and decide whether they avoid your objection.

Example

A profession such as architect requires seven years of training and many people feel that they cannot afford to commit so much time and cost to their next career. But a closer look shows that some years of the training are based in the workplace and are paid. It is also possible to undertake some or all of the training part time. There are similar positions that require less training: for example, town planner, landscape architect, interior designer and architectural technologist.

You might reject careers from your list because they lack sufficient security or the salary is inadequate. You may decide you do not want to pursue a career because there are too many other people applying and you do not want to face so much competition. Your reasons of course are your own. If you end up deciding that all your careers have some disadvantage or other, don't be disheartened. You might conclude that no career is perfect, and despite a few imperfections one of your careers may still represent your best hope for happiness at work. Realize that you are learning about yourself and discovering what is really important to you. If needs be, go back to Chapter 5 and reconsider some careers in the light of what you have realized is key. For example, if money really matters then reconsider the list in Set 9. If you now realize that security is important, then review the careers in Set 10.

Try using an assessment tool such as SOWT (strengths, opportunities, weaknesses, threats). It's been around for a long time but is still a very useful way to make things clearer and make comparisons. Use it by listing first each career's strengths and opportunities and then its weaknesses and threats. An example might look as follows:

Example: Laboratory technician (this work entails supporting scientists in the delivery of laboratory procedures).

Strengths/Opportunities

1 Be involved in the very latest scientific research.

2 Develop and maintain strong laboratory techniques.

3 Work as part of a team.

4 Study on day release and obtain technical and managerial skills and qualifications.

5 Access clear career progression to laboratory management positions.

Weaknesses/Threats

1 Levels of pay are on the low side of average.

2 Work involves carrying out repetitive procedures.

3 In some laboratories a detrimental divide exists between research and support staff.

Step 4. Choose one career

Now settle on a shortlist of one – or at least a career you will initially commit to and seek employment in (you can always turn back to a second choice at a later stage). You should commit to one choice because you have got to commit yourself 100 per cent if you are to maximize your chance of success. To illustrate why it requires 100 per cent commitment, take for example a CV or speculative letter. Either of these documents, if written in a way to make you look suitable for a number of opportunities, risks failing to make you look suitable for any. To maximize your chance of success you must look and sound the part. Focusing on one career means that you can give a very clear message and present yourself as the ideal candidate whose work history, experience and skills are described as perfect for your chosen career.

Step 5. Get really familiar with it

Review your research on your chosen career, revisit the sites, expand your search and drill deeper for information. Be sure you have information on all of the following: personal specification, job descriptions, companies, employment agencies and jobsites that employ people in that role or list jobs in the career, and if applicable the professional or trade associations that serve these careers. If your chosen career involves self-employment or starting a business, then set about writing a business plan and don't forget to use Brian Finch's *How to Write a Business Plan*, published by Kogan Page.

Make sure that you have spent a day or two as a volunteer helping out at places of work that employ people in your chosen career or offer the service you plan to provide. Remember to undertake a number of visits to organizations that work in the field and hold conversations with people in the role. It is a fact that many voluntary positions turn into an offer of employment, so set out to make a good impression. Be sure to ask if you can use your supervisor in the voluntary position as a referee, as this may well ensure your CV stands out from the crowd.

If you have accomplished all this, then you can take comfort from knowing that you have a really good feel for the job and this will undoubtedly help confirm that it is indeed the job for you. It will also mean that you understand exactly what the role involves, and so you can present yourself as ideal for it. Lastly, going to such trouble to be informed about the role can't help but impress your future employer.

Step 6. Take a good, careful look at yourself

Your research should allow you to identify the qualities that would make an ideal candidate for your chosen career. List them and build a picture of what this ideal candidate would look like in terms of qualities, experience, skills and qualifications. You can often find this information in the personal specification for a position, which lists the essential and desirable qualities. Now in as objective a way as possible, compare yourself to this ideal candidate. Examine each quality, area of experience, skill and qualification and ask yourself if you possess it? You will have many of the qualities but take care to identify any gaps.

Step 7. Fill any gaps

To succeed in your dream you will need to demonstrate all the qualities, experience, skills and qualifications essential for the position. You do this by identifying things you have done that show you possess those qualities. There is no need to exaggerate your past or invent things. Lots of everyday, ordinary experiences will serve to illustrate that you possess the qualities for the job. You can refer to any sphere of your life, so don't limit what you have to say by referring only to work, school or college. Be sure to include references to any voluntary work or involvement in your community if appropriate. It is best not to use the same example to answer all the questions. If you refer to only one part of your life, you risk giving the impression that it is the only thing you have done. If you reiterate the same experience to illustrate a number of qualities, the employer may conclude that you are repeating yourself and not making a new point. If you simply do not have some experience, skills or qualities, then identify courses or voluntary work or internships that will provide you with them.

Step 8. Present yourself in the best possible light

Get rid of your current CV. You wrote it at a time when you did not know what you wanted to do, so it is only suitable for the job you are currently in or did last, or is very general and something you used to apply for a variety of positions. Now you know what you want to do, so set about writing a highly specific CV that presents your experience, knowledge and training as highly relevant to the personal specification of your dream career. Everything you write must demonstrate your suitability for the position. You must describe your past in a way that demonstrates that you have the merits essential for the role. Be sure to read Jenny Rogers' *Great Answers to Tough CV Problems*, published by Kogan Page.

Example: Firefighter

This job requires a lifetime commitment to maintaining your knowledge, fitness and skills, being able to see a difficult job through to the end, effective communication, integrity, teamwork and being able to deal sympathetically with people who are emotional and distressed. The employer will be looking for evidence that you demonstrate these qualities. To present yourself as a strong candidate for the role, you need to present your past in terms of each of these qualities.

Step 9. Register and upload

Register on jobsites. Upload your CV, use the job search tools and complete a personal page on the sites. Register on the career pages of companies that employ people in your chosen career. Attend recruitment fairs and register with employment agencies and head-hunters who deal with your desired position. A company that says it currently has no vacancies may post some tomorrow, so revisit the sites if needs be on a daily basis and be sure to check your inbox daily for notifications of suitable jobs.

There are literary thousands of websites listing jobs. View the big general sites such as www.monster.com, www.snagajob.com and www.gumtree.com. Find the specialist sites that serve careers of the sort you are seeking. Register on the government site www.jobseekers.direct.gov.uk, where you can search and apply for jobs training, voluntary work and childcare.

Step 10. Don't be put off by any psychometric hassle

Prepare for any psychometric assessments. Employers use psychometrics to assess candidates at every stage of a recruitment process. They do this online early in a campaign, or later on with paper or pen or at a computer terminal at a testing centre. Early on in a process they may ask you to complete a questionnaire about your interests, later they may ask you to take a short test of your competencies and later still they may require you to attend an assessment centre and take part in a series of assessments. These may include personality questionnaires, tests of your numerical or verbal reasoning, spatial reasoning, group exercises, presentations, written exercises and many more. The organization should direct you to a description of the assessment or a website of its publisher. The Kogan Page testing list includes titles essential for a winning programme of review at every level of psychometrics. Visit www.koganpage.com and view for example *Ultimate Psychometric Tests (1,000 Practice Questions at the Intermediate Level), How to Pass Graduate Psychometric Tests 4th edition, How to Pass Advance Numeracy Tests 2nd edition, How to Pass Advance Verbal Reasoning Tests 2nd edition, How to Pass Diagrammatic Reasoning Tests* and *How to Pass Data Interpretation Tests* to name but a few.

Step 11. Show them just how good you really are

When you get an interview, attend looking and sounding the part. To get good at interviews, like most other things, you have to practise. Start by reviewing what you wrote on your application form, because some of the questions you are asked may be based on it. Get a good rounded background on the company with whom you have the interview. You may not be expected to answer questions on this but it will help you realize the context of the questions and you will be better able to target your answers. Now start rehearsing your answers to the most likely interview questions. The aim of this practice is not so that you can recite prepared answers. An interview is a conversation, not an oral presentation. You practise your answers so that you have done some of the thinking beforehand and, despite the fact that you are suffering nervousness, you will be better able to call to mind examples and occasions when you have demonstrated the quality they have asked you about. Prepare answers to questions such as 'Tell us about an occasion when you have seen a difficult task through to a successful end' or 'When have you worked with others to resolve a problem?' Practise the answers to possible follow-up questions too; for example, a question about dealing with a difficult task might be followed up with the question 'How might you have done things better?' For over 200 practice interview questions and model answers, get hold of a copy of Martin Yate's *Great Answers to Tough Interview Questions*, published by Kogan Page.

Step 12. Explore every possible avenue

If you can't find the job of your dreams, then consider making one! This is not as crazy a suggestion as it might seem. If you can't find someone to employ you to do what you want, then consider self-employment or starting a business or partnership. To help decide whether starting a business is right for you and access pages of advice, visit www.businesslink.gov.uk

So how did you get on?

The central idea of this book is that the world of work has changed, so to find a new career you need to test your aptitude for it. If it succeeded, then the self-administered questionnaire should have provided insight into your motivations and abilities, and the index of careers allowed you to identify encouraging, unexpected, thought-provoking 'new to you' career ideas. You should now have a shortlist of dream careers and insight into the new world of work and the opportunities it presents. All that is left to do is follow the advice on how to find out more and set about making one of those careers a reality.

If you know of a career that should be listed in this book, if you have a story to tell and would like to star in the next edition as a case study, or if you would like to tell me how the book helped, then do please e-mail me at help@mikebryon.com.

The sharpest minds need the finest advice. **Kogan Page** creates success.

www.koganpage.com